IIASA PROCEEDINGS SERIES

Volume 13

Logistics and Benefits of Using Mathematical Models of Hydrologic and Water Resource Systems

IIASA PROCEEDINGS SERIES

LOGISTICS AND BENEFITS OF USING MATHEMATICAL MODELS OF HYDROLOGIC AND WATER RESOURCE SYSTEMS

Selected Papers with Summary of Discussions from the International
Symposium on Logistics and Benefits of Using Mathematical
Models of Hydrologic and Water Resource Systems,
Pisa, Italy, 24–26 October 1978

Convened by
the International Institute for Applied Systems Analysis
and cosponsored by
the World Meteorological Organization and the IBM Scientific Center (Pisa)

A.J. ASKEW, F. GRECO, and J. KINDLER
Editors

PERGAMON PRESS

OXFORD · NEW YORK · TORONTO · SYDNEY · PARIS · FRANKFURT

U.K.	Pergamon Press Ltd., Headington Hill Hall, Oxford OX3 0BW, England
U.S.A.	Pergamon Press Inc., Maxwell House, Fairview Park, Elmsford, New York 10523, U.S.A.
CANADA	Pergamon Press Canada Ltd., Suite 104, 150 Consumers Rd., Willowdale, Ontario M2J 1P9, Canada
AUSTRALIA	Pergamon Press (Aust.) Pty. Ltd., P.O. Box 544, Potts Point, N.S.W. 2011, Australia
FRANCE	Pergamon Press SARL, 24 rue des Ecoles, 75240 Paris, Cedex 05, France
FEDERAL REPUBLIC OF GERMANY	Pergamon Press GmbH, 6242 Kronberg-Taunus, Hammerweg 6, Federal Republic of Germany

First edition 1981

British Library Cataloguing in Publication Data

International Symposium on Logistics and Benefits
of Using Mathematical Models of Hydrologic
and Water Resource Systems (1978: Pisa)
Logistics and benefits of using mathematical
models of hydrologic and water resource systems.
-(IIASA proceedings series; v.13)
1. Water resources development-Planning
Mathematical models-Congresses
I. Title II. Askew, A. J. III. Greco, F.
IV. Kindler, J. V. International Institute for
Applied Systems Analysis
VI. World Meteorological Organization
VII. IBM Scientific Centre (Pisa)
333.91'00 724   TC409

ISBN 0-08-025662-7

Printed in Great Britain by A. Wheaton & Co. Ltd., Exeter

PREFACE

Recently, mathematical models have been widely used for
the simulation, analysis, and control of hydrologic and water
resource systems. Although water resource models have been
in use for several years, most conferences held to discuss
them have described only their basic structure and mathematical formulations. Experience about the operational aspects
and logistics of these models is seldom exchanged. Thus the
International Institute for Applied Systems Analysis (IIASA),
the World Meteorological Organization (WMO), and the IBM
Scientific Center in Pisa decided to cooperate in the organization of the International Symposium on Logistics and Benefits of Using Mathematical Models of Hydrologic and Water
Resource Systems.

The purpose of the Symposium was to stimulate a fruit-
ful exchange of ideas, knowledge, and experiences about hydrologic and water resource models. The emphasis was on model identification and use, with attention being given to
questions of logistics, such as computer requirements and
support staff, data needs, and the cost-benefit of models in
practical work. The Symposium, which was convened by IIASA
and cosponsored by WMO and the IBM Scientific Center in Pisa,
was held in the Cassa di Risparmio in Pisa, Italy, from 24
to 26 October 1978. Some 80 participants and authors from
15 countries presented a total of 34 papers, 14 of which are
included in these Proceedings. Unfortunately, it was not
possible to include all the papers presented at Pisa in this
volume. Some of the papers have been published in the *Hydrological Sciences Bulletin* of the International Association
of Hydrological Sciences.

The papers were reviewed by rapporteurs, among them
Professor J.C.I. Dooge, President of the International Association of Hydrological Sciences (IAHS). The presentations
stimulated lively discussions on a wide range of topics, including model structures and verification, hydrologic models

for on-line simulation, and the role of computer hardware in water resource modeling.

At the time of the Symposium, WMO was considering the development of a Hydrological Operational Multipurpose Subprogramme (HOMS) as part of its activities in hydrological and water resources. The concept of HOMS has since been approved by the Eighth WMO Congress, which was held in 1979, and the first phase of the Subprogramme will be implemented during the 1980-1983 period. HOMS provides a means for the international transfer of technology used in operational hydrology and for an exchange of information and views among those involved in developing and applying this technology. The introduction of catchment models as an important component of HOMS is expected to act as a catalyst for the international exchange of such models and as a means for increasing the models' transferability and applicability.

The discussions and conclusions of this Symposium will provide a valuable basis for WMO's work on HOMS. Similarly, the future work of IIASA and the IBM Scientific Center in Pisa will draw on the information exchanged at the meeting. But, the value of the Symposium extends far beyond the work of the sponsors to that of the international hydrological community at large. It is for this reason that these Proceedings have been assembled and published. The editors and all concerned with the Symposium hope this publication will be of interest and value to those engaged in developing and applying mathematical models of hydrologic and water resource systems.

The editors wish to thank all those involved in making the Symposium a success. Special thanks are extended to Denise Promper for her smooth and skillful preparatory work in organizing the Symposium.

A.J. ASKEW
F. GRECO
J. KINDLER

CONTENTS

GENERAL REPORT ON MODEL STRUCTURE AND CLASSIFICATION

J.C.I. Dooge

1. INTRODUCTION

The objective of this Symposium is to discuss the implementation and use of mathematical models in hydrology and water resources development. The past 15 years have seen a proliferation of mathematical models in this area and the growth of an immense literature in which such models are recommended, partially described, but hardly ever evaluated. The practitioner faced with the need to solve a human problem without delay is like an unfortunate traveler lost in a jungle. Before his eyes is a riot of growth reflecting a variety of scale, color, and type and his ears are assailed by a cacophany which in many cases can be interpreted as "my model solves all problems". If only a fraction of the research that has gone into the development of new models had been devoted to the objective evaluation of models and the objective matching of type of model to type of problem, the whole subject area would be in a healthier condition. If the aims of the organizers of this Symposium are achieved, at least a small path will have been cleared through the present jungle. The purpose of this general report is to provide a background to the presentation and discussion of the Symposium papers.

One possible methodology for obtaining as objective a choice as possible between mathematical models is shown in Figure 1 (Dooge 1977) and this can serve as a general framework for the present discussion. Thus section 2 of this report is devoted to defining the problem, section 3 to discussing the different classes and types of models available, and section 4 to fitting the model chosen to the problem. The two remaining sections deal with one possible classification of the Symposium papers.

2

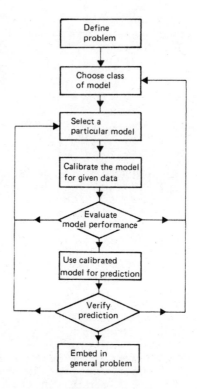

FIGURE 1   A possible methodology for selecting a mathematical
model.

2.   DEFINING THE PROBLEM

It is conventional wisdom that unambiguous and adequate
definition of the problem is essential to its successful
solution.   However, like much conventional wisdom, this wise
advice is frequently ignored in practice.   One prerequisite
toward an adequate definition of any modeling problem is to
be clear about the nature of the prototype system that the
model is intended to represent.   In hydrology and water resources we are concerned at different times with systems and
models whose scope varies from conditions at a point, through
conditions on a small experimental plot or a hillside component of a subcatchment, to a major river catchment of regional or continental scale.   In some cases we may only be
concerned with the physical elements of the hydrological
cycle, whereas in others we are concerned with water quality
and ecological factors, and in some we are concerned with
the water-related problems of an entire socioeconomic system.
In many cases, we are concerned with a hierarchy of models,
either nested one within the other or more loosely linked
together.   Consequently, it is essential to be clear in regard to the boundaries of the system which we are attempting

to model at any one particular time and also to be clear about the variables whose fluxes cross that boundary and whose storages and fluxes within that boundary are of immediate interest.

Another prerequisite for the proper definition of a modeling problem is the objective of the model. The struggle of man to master his environment through knowledge has been described as involving four phases: observation, understanding, prediction, and control. Mathematical models are used in water resources engineering today in relation to all four of these phases. Because the process is iterative rather than sequential, models based on known data frequently give rise to new data requirements and the most efficient way of providing these new data may itself be the subject of mathematical modeling (Matalas and Langbein 1971). Mathematical models play a key role in the formulation of our understanding of natural processes. Thus Shanin (1972) states:

> The basic *function* of theoretical models, which explains their extraordinary significance in contemporary scholarship, is their use as the major bridge between the language of theory and that of empirically corrected data, between the general and unique, between the subject and the object.

The third phase of prediction (without reference to time of occurrence) or forecasting (within a specific time reference) characterizes the main objective of most of the models of catchment behavior presented at this and similar symposia. Mathematical models of water resource systems are, on the other hand, concerned largely with the fourth phase of design and control.

All models are selective and simplify reality in different ways. Each model reflects some but not all the properties of the prototype. Hence the choice of an effective and economic model frequently involves, either implicitly or explicitly, a designation of those properties of the prototype that are considered relevant to the problem.

A further prerequisite for the adequate definition of a modeling problem is clear understanding of the nature of the input data available in the prototype and of the output data required from the model. In the case of hierarchies of models, part of the input to the model under consideration may be the output from another model and the output from the present model may be part of the input to a third model. In such cases the relationship between the models must be carefully considered, and in many cases it is advantageous to study the behavior of a simplified global model before choosing a structure or a solution technique for the individual models.

3. TYPES OF MODELS AVAILABLE

It is not the purpose of this general report to catalog
the various types of catchment models which appear so abun-
dantly in the hydrological literature. The variety of models can be best appreciated by reference to review papers
and proceedings of similar symposia. In this connection one
might mention the proceedings of three symposia organized by
the International Commission on Water Resource Systems at
Warsaw (IAHS 1971), Bratislava (IAHS 1975), and Baden (IAHS
1978); the 1974 Workshop on Mathematical Models for Surface
Water Hydrology held also at the IBM Scientific Center in
Pisa (Ciriani *et al*. 1977); the symposia on open channel flow
held at Fort Collins (Mahmood *et al*. 1975) and Newcastle-
upon-Tyne (BHRA 1976); review papers on stochastic models by
Clarke (1973), Svanidze (1975), and Lawrence and Kottegoda
(1977); review papers on subsurface flow by Freeze (1972,
1978); the collected work on the systems approach to water
management edited by Biswas (1976); the work by Fleming
(1975) describing the structure of 19 conceptual models of
total catchment response which have been fairly widely used;
and the report of the intercomparison study of 10 models of
total catchment response from several different countries
(WMO 1975).

The choice of a mathematical model is governed largely
by the factors discussed in the last section: the structure
of the prototype system, the objective of the modeling, and
the nature of the input and output data. Mathematical models in hydrology and water resources can be grouped for classification in a number of ways. For the purpose of this report, a primary division has been made into (1) models of
catchment behavior that simulate the hydrologic storages and
fluxes relevant to various parts of the hydrological cycle
and in various elements of a catchment area, and (2) models
simulating the hydraulic and economic performance of complex
water resource systems. This primary division seems justified by the clear demarcation between (1) models of catchment
behavior that are concerned solely with relationships between
hydrologic variables, and (2) prescriptive models of water
resource systems that are concerned with decision making.
Such a division is based essentially on the nature of the
objective of the modeling process involved in each case.
It is hard to visualize cases in which it would not be a
simple matter to decide which category of problem is involved.

Once we attempt any further classification of catchment
models or of water resource models, serious difficulties
arise. One usual division of catchment models is into deterministic, stochastic, and probabilistic catchment models in
which the categories may be considered to correspond respectively to the sum of (a) deterministic input data, (b) random
input data, and (c) no input data as such. This classification has the disadvantage that it isolates from one another
deterministic and stochastic methods that frequently are
based on identical mathematical assumptions which cannot be

recognized in the resulting models because two sets of jargon are used to describe them. An alternative classification is to divide catchment models into (a) blackbox models, (b) regression models, (c) simple conceptual models, and (d) models based on the equations of continuum mechanics. Such a procedure is tantamount to classifying models on the basis of the connection between input and output as being assumed to be (a) simple causality of unknown form, (b) statistical correspondence, (c) simplified physical theory, or (d) more complex physical theory developed in order to promote the understanding of the phenomena involved. Catchment models can also be classified according to whether they are (a) linear or nonlinear, (b) time-invariant (i.e., stationary) or time-variant (i.e., nonstationary), (c) lumped (i.e., space-invariant) or distributed (i.e., space-variant), (d) short-memory or long-memory. The question of classification is returned to in section 5 below.

The whole discussion of mathematical models in hydrology would be greatly simplified if a common nomenclature were adopted or at least if the correspondence between different sets of nomenclature were recognized. For example, the only essential difference between the first order ARIMA (1,0,1) model used by O'Connell (1971) to model the Hurst phenomenon in stochastic time and the Muskingum method introduced by McCarthy (1939) in flood routing is that the input in the former case is Gaussian white noise while the input in the latter case is the known (or assumed) flow at the upstream end of the reach. More generally, choosing an ARMA model is equivalent to assuming that the system function (i.e., the Laplace transformation of the impulse response) is a rational function; and that the number of moving average terms is identical to the degree of the polynomial in the numerator of the system function and that the number of autoregressive tons is identical to the degree of the denominator. The outputs from the two model systems when taken continuously are governed by the same differential equation, and when sampled are governed by the same differential equation.

To assume in blackbox analysis that the system behavior can be adequately represented by the first term of a convolution type Volterra series (i.e., the use of the impulse response for identification) is equivalent to making the assumption that the system is governed by a linear ordinary differential equation with constant coefficients. Recognition of such correspondences enables us to recognize equivalent models and to transfer techniques and sometimes results from one class of model to another.

Model simulation of the more complex water resource systems can also be classified in a number of different ways. One obvious basis for classification is the structure of the system itself, i.e., whether we are dealing with a single reservoir, a chain of reservoirs, or a complex water resource system involving diversions and pumpings as well as storages, and so on. Such models can also obviously be

classified on the basis of whether the schemes are single-
purpose or multipurpose. The nature of the input data,
whether single-site or multisite and whether deterministic
or stochastic, provides another element in classifications.
In the case where the operation of the system is described
by a transition matrix, this matrix may be deterministic,
stochastic, or uncertain, and the nature of the model and
the techniques used in it will vary accordingly. It is clear
that in the case of multipurpose objectives the mathematical
model will include a procedure for the reduction (either explicitly or implicitly) of the multiple purposes to a single
objective function and also a methodology for the optimization of this objective function. The methodology used (direct search, unconstrained optimization, constrained optimization, linear programming, quadratic programming, dynamic
programming, simulation, etc.) offers another basis for classification.

All of the variations mentioned above are essential
parts of the description of the particular model and can play
a larger or smaller role in the classification of systems
models depending on the purpose of the classification.

In the analysis of complex water resource systems, it
is frequently useful to formulate an overall model in terms
of a hierarchy of related models. Sometimes a lower-order
model would be completely embedded in or nested in a higher-
order model but at other times the separate lower-order models would be linked in various ways. In this approach the
boundary of the lower-order model is established and certain
assumptions made about its exterior environment, which is
equivalent to the remainder of the model as well as the external environment of the latter. By making plausible assumptions about the boundary conditions of the lower-order
model it is frequently possible to reduce the range of choice
considerably and to proceed to another part of the total model. In many applications this procedure involves an iteration among the lower-order models. Shamir (1970) has outlined the type of nested models used in the national water
planning of Israel.

4. FITTING THE MODEL TO THE PROBLEM

This section is concerned with choosing and fitting an
appropriate model for a given real problem. The huge range
of choice will be narrowed somewhat by the definition of the
problem. If we are concerned with the prediction of catchment response rather than the control of a reservoir system,
our range of choice includes behavioral models and excludes
prescriptive models. If there are no rainfall data, the use
of the unit hydrograph method or of a conceptual model of
catchment response is clearly ruled out. Even after all this
elimination, there is still a wide range of choice in the
case where only records of streamflow are available. The
choice may well be directed by the nature of the problem.

If we are interested only in extreme events of rare occurrence, we might wish to neglect the time dependence between events and hence to use a probabilistic model. If, however, we wish to take minor floods into account, a stochastic model which allows for such persistence is indicated.

Even after choosing the class of model, there is still a good deal of freedom in choosing a particular model from that class and in choosing the structure of the particular model. Basing this choice on prototype data is referred to as model identification. This should be done by selecting a given model (or range of models), fitting the model (or models) to the data in some prescribed way, and evaluating the extent to which the prototype data are simulated by the model. Preliminary examination of the data can give some guidance in narrowing the choice of model. In the case of probabilistic models, the plotting on a diagram showing the relationship between the coefficient of skew and the coefficient of variation (or on a Pearson shape-factor diagram) for one or more sites in a region should give a preliminary indication of whether the regional data are likely to be best fitted by a log-normal distribution, a Pearson type III distribution, or a Gumbel distribution. Similarly, in the case of an ARMA model, examination of the autocorrelation and partial correlation functions of a time-series (Box and Jenkins 1970) should reveal when a purely moving average (i.e., short-memory) or autoregressive (i.e., long-memory) model is appropriate or when it is necessary to use a mixed ARMA model. In the case of catchment elements and components such as surface runoff or the response of groundwater to recharge, the use of a shape-factor diagram based on the dimensionless moments (Nash 1960, Dooge 1973) should be of use as an indicator. In the case of conceptual models of total catchment response no such approach is presently available. This could be remedied if a procedure was available to detect from an input-output set whether a threshold existed in the system and the approximate size of the threshold. If this could be done, the threshold could be removed from the system and the two parts of the input-output record used separately to give some idea of the nature of the two subsystems of the total catchment system.

None of the above procedures proves as objective and reliable in practice as theory would indicate. Part of the difficulty is undoubtedly due to the presence of errors of measurement in the data and to the sampling problems arising from the length of the data record. However, even with long records of very reliable data the approach assumes that the models tested are adequate to represent the prototype. This may not be so. There is scope for research on relating the simple models used in applied hydrology to assumptions about the hydrologic processes. Thus, in the case of probabilistic models, we have the suggestion by Kalinin (1962) that the power transformation of the gamma distribution in the Kritskii-Menkel (1950) model for streamflow represents the nonlinear relationship between runoff and rainfall and that the gamma distribution of monthly or annual flows can be considered as arising from an alternation of wet and dry periods. Becker (1966) and Diskin (1970) have discussed the relationship between regression models and conceptual models. Many authors have discussed the question of "reasonable" parameter values in regression models and conceptual models. However, a great deal of work remains to be done in this area and to be incorporated into the procedure for model selection.

Even when the model type has been chosen there remains the important question of the degree of complexity of the model. Two alternatives are possible: (a) to start with a simple model and move to a more complex one if the model fails to simulate the prototype behavior or (b) to start with a complex model and omit certain components if they appear to make little difference to the performance of the model. The present reviewer has a strong preference for (a), both from the point of view of the principle of parsimony and because the limited information content in the data should not be spread over the many parameters.

The optimization of model parameters on the basis of given data sets is a study area in itself. Given enough parameters, it is possible to fit any set of data, but the parameter values may well be without any real meaning. On the other hand, *a priori* values of parameters, based on laboratory or field measurements, may be unsuitable for use in models because a parameter may represent in the model several features of prototype behavior besides the one that was the basis of the measurement. The need to obtain realistic values of the parameters is particularly important when the model parameters from different systems are to be used as the basis of correlation with catchment characteristics or change of land use. Moment matching, maximum likelihood estimation, Bayesian estimation, unconstrained and constrained least-squares estimation, and direct search techniques are among the methods that have been used to estimate the parameters of models in hydrology and water resource systems. These optimization methods use a variety of objective functions based on some measure of the output from the model. The values of the parameters are frequently sensitive to the objective criterion chosen and to the particular output used in the objective function. Despite much research in recent years, no clear knowledge has developed in this area.

If models or variants of a given model are to be compared, it is necessary to have an objective evaluation of the model or a given version of it. In some cases, techniques are available from standard statistical procedures. Thus in the case of a probabilistic model of a time-series of events assumed to be independent, the Kolmogorov-Smirnov test can be used in the usual way as the basis of whether a model should be accepted or not. Similarly in regression models in hydrology and water resources, the standard analysis of variance can be applied. In the case of stochastic models of dependent time-series the adequacy of the

deterministic part of the model can be measured by the extent
to which the cross-correlation between the input and the output is reduced by subtracting from the measured output the
predicted output from the deterministic part of the model.
The residual output obtained in this way can then be tested
for autocorrelation and a stochastic model fitted whose efficiency can be judged by the degree to which this autocorrelation in the residuals is removed. The properties of the final
residual output, which should approximate Gaussian noise, can
then be determined. The general model, with its triple components of (a) deterministic operation on the known input,
(b) stochastic modeling of the persistence in the residual,
and (c) element of white noise, can be used as a prediction
model. In the case of models of total catchment response,
the question of model evaluation is even more difficult.
This subject has been reviewed in a number of papers, notably
by Nash and Sutcliffe (1970) and by Pilgrim (1975). A good
deal of work still remains to be done on the objective comparison of such models.

5. METHOD OF CLASSIFICATION

   The purpose of this section is to establish a basis for
the description of the papers submitted for this Symposium
in the light of the general principles discussed in the previous sections. A complete classification of the mathematical models used in hydrology and water resources would be a
formidable task. If the classification were to be based on
a multifacet approach, then the vector necessary to describe
any particular model completely would be very large indeed.
If a hierarchical system of classification were used, then
all the difficulties of deciding the basis of the different
levels of hierarchy would be very great. Just as there is
no hydrologic model or water resource model that will solve
all problems, so too there is no method for the classification of such models that will be satisfactory for all purposes. Accordingly, the discussion will be confined to the
description of a classification which is put forward as being
suitable for the purpose of describing within a defined context the papers of this Symposium.

   The proposed classification is not a classification of
mathematical models but rather a classification of the papers
of this Symposium. The classification is based on a list of
10 items which could be considered important in the description of papers on mathematical models in hydrology or water
resources. A list of descriptions is then established for
each item and, for convenience, a symbol is assigned to each
descriptor. The papers are then classified according to
these descriptors and the result presented in tabular form.

   The following is suggested as a suitable list of headings under which mathematical models in hydrology and water
resources could be described:

    (1)   Extent of the model
    (2)   Objective of modeling
    (3)   Hydrologic processes and water uses involved
    (4)   Nature of prototype data
    (5)   Class of model
    (6)   Type of model
    (7)   Algorithms used in solution
    (8)   Computational requirements
    (9)   Method of model evaluation
 (10)   Results of application of model

It will be noted that a hierarchical element is introduced into the classification system in items (5) and (6) but that only two levels of hierarchy are involved. This was thought adequate for the present purpose but might well be varied if the method of classification is adapted for purposes other than that of this report. Only headings (1) to (6) are considered in connection with the tabulation of the Symposium papers since the later headings are the concern of the other general reporters.

The extent of the model, item (1), is concerned with the way in which the boundary of the prototype system which is to be modeled has been drawn. It is proposed that the models in the Symposium papers be classed under this heading according to the following list of descriptors and symbols:

- Conditions at a point (P)
- The state of catchment element (E)
- Water balance of a complete catchment (C)
- Performance of a water resource system (WRS)
- Behavior of a socioeconomic system (SEC)

Some of the above categories are very broad and could readily be subdivided, but the list is thought appropriate for the purpose of comparing the papers under review. The objective of modeling, item (2), has already been discussed in section 2, and the following listing is suggested:

- Observation of prototype system (O)
- Understanding of prototype behavior (U)
- Forecasting of prototype output (F)
- Prediction of prototype output (P)
- Control of prototype system (C)
- Design of prototype system (D)

In the above list the distinction is made between the forecasting (either deterministic or stochastic) of the value of the output at some definite future time and the prediction (either deterministic or stochastic) of the value of the output at some frequency in some future period. The distinction is also made between the control of a system which involves the optimization of its performance for a given system structure and the design of a system which may involve altering the structure of the system or of the timing of its development in order to optimize the given objective. The latter

distinction corresponds to the distinction in economics between short-term and long-term planning.

The need to distinguish between understanding reality
and making useful predictions is important. Kuhn (1957) in
his book *The Copernican Revolution* writes:

> Judged on purely practical grounds, Copernicus'
> new planetary system was a failure; it was neither
> more accurate nor significantly simpler than its
> Ptolemaic predecessors...to astronomers the initial
> choice between Copernicus' system and Ptolemy's
> system could only be a matter of taste.

The question of taste and fondness for the familiar affect
the choice of hydrologic models as well as astronomic systems.

The third basis for model classification listed above
is that which distinguishes between the various hydrologic
processes in a catchment area and between the various uses
of water in a water resource system. While a complete classification would seek to apply both sets of descriptors to
both types of model, it is sufficient for tabulation purposes
to make the above division. Catchment models can be classified in accordance with their concern with the following
variables:

- Precipitation (P)
- Evapotranspiration (ET)
- Catchment runoff (RO)
- Channel flow (CF)
- Overland flow (OF)
- Groundwater flow (GW)
- Physical water quality (WQP)
- Chemical water quality (WQC)
- Biological water quality (WQB)

Many catchment models will involve more than one of the above
hydrologic variables (HV).

In the case of water resource models, the corresponding
classification is in respect to the type of water use for
which the system is designed. The following list of water
uses would appear appropriate in the present context:

- Water supply—domestic, industrial, agricultural—
  (WS)
- Pollution control, including waste water disposal
  (PC)
- Hydropower development (HP)
- Irrigation (IR)
- Drainage of agricultural and urban areas (D)
- Flood control (FC)
- Inland navigation (N)
- Recreational use (R)

As in the case of catchment models, many mathematical models
of water resource systems will be considered with more than
one of the above water uses and will be classified as multipurpose (MP).

The three factors discussed above (the extent of the
model, the hydrologic processes and water uses involved, and
the objective of the modeling) will, when considered in conjunction, narrow considerably the range of choice of a model.
However, this choice will also depend on the nature of the
data available in regard to the prototype which is also an
essential part of the definition of the modeling problem.
The following is one listing of the various types of information that may or may not be available in respect of the
prototype and that may or may not be used in developing the
model structure and determining appropriate values for the
parameters:

- The natural topography of the catchment (T)
- Geotechnical information on soils and bedrock (G)
- Records for meteorologic variables (MV)
- Records for hydrologic variables (HV)
- Records for water quality variables (WQV)
- Regional information for adjacent catchments (RI)
- Data and projections of water use (WU)
- Capacity of hydraulic installations (HI)
- Data relevant to project costs and benefits (CB)
- Information on global economic and social
  impacts (ESI)

As mentioned above, all of this information may not be
required in certain problems, and even when it is required,
it may not be available in reliable quantitative form. The
first six headings listed above are of key importance in the
case of models of catchment behavior, and the last four are
more important in the case of large-scale complex water resource systems. It must be appreciated that each of the
above headings covers a wide area. Thus, the listing of hydrologic variables (HV) covers all of the variables mentioned
under section 3 above. Also a heading such as biological
water quality can in turn cover a very large number of variables and parameters in the case of models with a substantial
ecological component. Similarly, under the heading of global
economic information are included such factors as national
environmental objectives and all information in relation to
the effects of a project of the size contemplated on the economy of the country.

It has already been stressed that the division of the
model into classes and subclasses under (5) and (6) is of
necessity arbitrary. Accordingly, the divisions discussed
below are even more specifically affected by the context of
the Symposium papers than the factors described above. For
convenience, behavioral models of catchment behavior and prescriptive models of water resource systems have been dealt

with separately. Since catchment models are concerned with
the manner in which hydrologic inputs are converted to hydrologic outputs, the primary classification of this case has
been based on the extent to which physical theory has been
used in the basic model structure. On this basis we can distinguish between:

- Models based on blackbox analysis (BB)
- Regression models (RM)
- Lumped conceptual models (LCM)
- Distributed conceptual models (DCM)
- Models based on physical equations (PE)

The boundaries between some of these categories (e.g., blackbox and regression, lumped and distributed conceptual models)
are not sharp, and in some cases, the final classification
contains a degree of subjectivity.

The further subdivision is made for the purpose of the
present general review on the basis of whether the model
structure is linear (L) or nonlinear (NL) and time-invariant
(TI) or time-variant (TV) and also on the basis of whether
the input (and consequently the output) is deterministic (D),
stochastic (S), or a combination of both (D-S).

The choice of the primary basis for the classification
of mathematical models of water resource systems is difficult.
One possibility is to base the classification on the nature
of the objective function, that is,

- The hydraulic performance of the system (H)
- Ecological factors and parameters (E)
- The benefits and costs of the individual project (BC)
- The global economic and social impacts (ESI)

In the case of the latter two types of objective function,
the problem formulation will differ greatly for a subsistence
economy, a market economy, and a fully planned economy.

Another possibility is to classify on the basis of the
type of decision involved into:

- Decision making under conditions of assumed certainty
  (C)
- Decision making under risk (R)
- Decision making under uncertainty (U)

These criteria have the disadvantage that they are not highly
discriminatory in practice since most models at present are
based on decision making under conditions of risk.

A second level of classification can appropriately be
based on the type of methodology used to compare alternative
strategies and might consist of:

- Analytical methods (*A*)
- Mathematical programming (*LP*,*NLP*)
- Dynamic programming (*DP*)
- Simulation methods (*SIM*)
- Game theory (*GT*)

Each of the above categories can be further divided in a number of ways.

6.   CLASSIFICATION OF SYMPOSIUM PAPERS

The models in the 34 papers presented at this Symposium have been divided into models of catchment behavior (summarized in Table 1) and decision models for water resource systems (summarized in Table 2). The paper by Eichert is included in both tables.

The 24 papers in Table 1 are divided as follows:

- 4 papers on catchment elements (*E*)
- 18 papers on total catchment behavior (*C*)
- 2 papers on both types of model (*E*,*C*)

The individual assignments are given in column 2 of Table 1. The papers dealing with catchment elements relate to:

- 1 paper on evapotranspiration (*ET*)
- 1 paper on groundwater (*GW*)
- 3 papers on channel flow (*CF*)

as indicated in column 3. The papers dealing with total catchment response are classified as follows:

- 16 papers on the total catchment runoff (*RO*)
- 1 paper on several hydrologic variables (*HV*)
- 1 paper on physical water quality (*WQP*)
- 2 papers on various models

Again, the individual listings are given in column 3 of Table 1.

The importance of understanding clearly the objective of the model has been stressed above. The papers in Table 1 may be divided into:

- 2 papers on observation (*O*)
- 1 paper on understanding and forecasting (*U*,*F*)
- 17 papers on forecasting (*F*)
- 1 paper on forecasting and control (*F*,*C*)
- 1 paper on prediction (*P*)
- 1 paper on design and control (*D*,*C*)

One paper is not classified because it gives different objectives for different models.

TABLE 1 Descriptive models of catchment behavior.

Authors	Extent of model	Hydrologic process	Object of modeling	Nature of data	Class of model	Type of model
Abbott *et al.*	*C*	*HV*	*F*	*T,G,MV,HV*	*DCM*	*NL*
Anselmo *et al.*	*C*	*RO*	*F*	*HV*	*LCM*	*S*
Askew	*C*	*RO*	*F*	*MV,HV,WU*	various	
Baniukiewicz	*C*	*RO*	*F*	*MV,HV*	*LCM*	*NL*
Bergström	*C*	*RO*	*F*	*MV,HV*	*DCM*	*NL*
Bobiński *et al.*	*C*	*RO*	*F*	*MV,HV*	*LCM*	*NL*
	E	*CF*	*F*	*HV*	*BB*	*NL*
Buchtele	*C*	*RO*	*F*	*HV*	*R,LCM*	
Eichert	*E,C*	various	various	*HV*	various	
Hall *et al.*	*C*	*RO*	*F*	*HV*	various	
Handel *et al.*	*E*	*CF*	*F*	*HV*	*R,PE*	*NL*
Ishizaki	*C*	*RO*	*F*	*HV*	*DCM*	*NL*
Jaworski	*E*	*ET*	*U,F*	*MV*	*PE*	*NL*
Lambert	*C*	*RO*	*F,C*	*MV,HV*	*DCM*	
Liddament *et al.*	*E*	*GW*	*D,C*	*HV,WU*	*PE*	
Manley	*C*	*RO*	*F*	*MV,HV*	*DCM*	*NL*
Matondo *et al.*	*C*	*WQP*	*F*	*HV*	*R*	*L*
Nemec *et al.*	*C*	*RO*	*F*	*MV,HV*	*DCM*	
Ostrowski	*C*	*RO*	*F*	*HV*	*LCM*	*L*
Romonov	*E*	*CF*	*F*	*HV*	*PE*	
Rumiantsev	*C*	*RO*	*O*	*MV,HV*		
Sugawara	*C*	*RO*	*F*	*HV*	*LCM*	*NL*
Svanidze *et al.*	*C*	*RO*	*P*	*HV*	*LCM*	*S*
Volpi *et al.*	*C*	various	*O*		*R*	
Wingard	*C*	*RO*	*F*	*MV,HV*	various	

On the basis of the nature of the model input, the papers can be divided into:

- 1 paper involving meteorologic variables (*MV*)
- 11 papers involving hydrologic variables (*HV*)
- 8 papers involving meteorologic and hydrologic variables (*MV,HV*)
- 1 paper involving topography (*T*), geometric information (*G*), meteorologic (*MV*) and hydrologic variables (*HV*)
- 1 paper involving meteorologic variables (*MV*), hydrologic variables (*HV*), and water uses (*WU*)
- 1 paper involving hydrologic variables and water uses (*HV,WU*)

Of course, the above division is only approximate.

In regard to class of model as listed in column 6 of Table 1, we have:

- 1 paper on blackbox analysis (*BB*)
- 4 papers on regression analysis (*R*)
- 7 papers on lumped conceptual models (*LCM*)
- 6 papers on distributed conceptual models (*DCM*)
- 4 papers on physical equations (*PE*)
- 1 paper on regression and physical equations (*R,PE*)
- 4 papers on various types of models

Again, the division is approximate. For example, it is difficult to determine whether a conceptual model is lumped or distributed from a brief description.

The 11 papers wholly or largely concerned with water resource systems are summarized in Table 2. The scope of the papers is as follows:

- 8 papers on water resource systems (*WRS*)
- 3 papers on socioeconomic systems (*SEC*)

The 11 papers include the following types of system:

- 1 paper on single-reservoir systems (*SR*)
- 6 papers on multireservoir systems (*MR*)
- 3 papers on distribution systems (*DS*)

as indicated in column 3 of Table 2. The water uses involved in the models described by the papers break down as follows:

- 2 papers on water supply (*WS*)
- 1 paper on irrigation (*IR*)
- 7 papers on multipurpose systems (*MP*)
- 1 paper on various water uses

The objective of the modeling (column 5 of Table 2) divides as follows:

TABLE 2   Decision models of water resource systems.

Authors	Extent of model	Type of system	Water uses involved	Object of modeling	Type of objective function	Type of methodology
Ambrosino *et al.*	WRS	SR	MP	C	H	NLP
de Graan *et al.*	WRS	DS	MP	C,D	H,E	SIM
Eichert	WRS	various	various	various	various	various
Fabi *et al.*	WRS	MR	MP	C,D	BC	SIM,LP
Kaczmarek *et al.*	WRS	MR	MP	C	BC	NLP
Nelson *et al.*	SEC	DS	IR	D	BC	SIM
Pearson *et al.*	WRS	MR	MP	C,D	H	SIM
Reid	SEC	DS	WS	D	BC,ESI	SIM
Sexton	WRS	MR	WS	C,D	H	SIM
Sigvaldason	WRS	MR	MP	C,D	H	NLP
Wright	SEC	MR	MP	C	P,BC,ESI	GT

- 3 papers on control (C)
- 2 papers on design (D)
- 5 papers on control and design (C,D)
- 1 paper on various objectives

and classification on the basis of the type of objective function gives:

- 4 papers on hydraulic objectives (H)
- 3 papers on benefit and cost objectives (BC)
- 3 papers on two or three objectives
- 1 paper on various objectives

as shown in column 6 of Table 2.

The final classification on the basis of the methodology of solution gives:

- 6 papers on simulation (SIM)
- 1 paper on linear programming (LP)
- 3 papers on nonlinear programming (NLP)
- 1 paper on game theory (GT)
- 1 paper on various methods of optimization

which is again an approximate division.

Though the above classification may be in error in some instances, it should give a rough idea of the types of models dealt with in the papers submitted to this Symposium. If these models are a representative sample of the world population of models, certain features can be discerned. The most common model of catchment behavior would appear to be a conceptual model that converts an input of certain hydrologic variables to an output of total catchment runoff and is used for forecasting purposes. The most common decision model of a water resource system would appear to be a model of a multi-reservoir system with multiple water uses which is solved by a simulation in order to optimize the control or design of the system. Perhaps we should take these two types of model and study them closely in order to establish a standard against which other models can be evaluated. Whatever we do, if we continue to produce more models that are inadequately evaluated, neither the interests of science nor of technology will be well served and scarce resources of money and manpower will be squandered.

REFERENCES

Becker, A. (1966) On the structure of coaxial rainfall-runoff relations. IAHS Bulletin 11(2):121-130.

Biswas, A.K., ed. (1976) Systems Approach to Water Management. New York: McGraw-Hill.

Box, G.E.P., and G.M. Jenkins (1970) Time Series Analysis
    Forecasting and Control. San Francisco: Holden-Day.

British Hydromechanics Research Association (1976) Unsteady
    Flow in Open Channels, Proceedings of Newcastle-upon-
    Tyne Symposium. Cranfield, England: BHRA.

Ciriani, T.A., U. Maione, and J.R. Wallis (1977) Mathematical
    Models for Surface Water Hydrology. New York: Wiley.

Clarke, R.T. (1973) Mathematical Models in Hydrology. Irri-
    gation and Drainage paper No. 19. Rome: Food and Agri-
    culture Organization.

Diskin, M.H. (1970) Definition and uses of the linear regres-
    sion model. Water Resources Research 6:1668-1673.

Dooge, J.C.I. (1973) Linear Theory of Hydrologic Systems.
    ARS Technical Bulletin No. 1468. Washington, D.C.: U.S.
    Department of Agriculture.

Dooge, J.C.I. (1977) Problems and methods of rainfall-runoff
    modelling. Chapter 6, pages 71-108, Mathematical Models
    for Surface Water Hydrology, edited by T.A. Ciriani, U.
    Maione, and J.R. Wallis. New York: Wiley.

Fleming, G. (1975) Computer Simulation Techniques in Hydrol-
    ogy. New York: Elsevier.

Freeze, R.A. (1972) Role of subsurface flow in generating
    surface runoff, 1. Base flow contributions to channel
    flow. Water Resources Research 8(3):601-623.

Freeze, R.A. (1978) Mathematical models of hillslope hydrol-
    ogy. Chapter 6, pages 177-225, Hillslope Hydrology,
    edited by M.J. Kirkby. New York: Wiley.

International Association for Hydrological Sciences (1971)
    Mathematical Models in Hydrology, Proceedings of Warsaw
    Symposium, 3 volumes. IAHS Publications Nos. 100, 101,
    and 102. Paris: UNESCO/IAHS.

International Association of Hydrological Sciences (1975)
    Application of Mathematical Models in Hydrology and
    Water Resources, Proceedings of Bratislavia Symposium.
    IAHS Publication No. 115. Washington, D.C. Late papers
    and general reports published in Hydrological Sciences
    Bulletin 21(1).

International Association of Hydrological Sciences (1978)
    Mathematical Models of Water Quality, Proceedings of
    Baden Symposium. IAHS Publication No. 125. Washington,
    D.C.

Kalinin, G.P. (1962) O teoretitcheskom obespetchenii krivyh
    raspredelenia stoka. Meteorologia i Gidrologia, No. 6
    (in Russian).

Kritskii, S.N., and M.F. Menkel (1950) Hydrologitcheskie os-
    novy retchnoj hydrotekhniki. Moscow: USSR Academy of
    Sciences Publishing House (in Russian).

Kuhn, T.S. (1957) The Copernican Revolution. Cambridge,
    Massachusetts: Harvard University Press.

Lawrence, A.J., and N.T. Kottegoda (1977) Stochastic model-
    ling of riverflow time series. Journal of the Royal
    Statistical Society, Series A, 140, Part 1:1-4.

Mahmood, K., V. Yevyevich, and W.A. Miller (1975) Unsteady
    Flow in Open Channels, Vols. 1-3. Water Resources Pub-
    lication. Fort Collins, Colorado.

Matalas, N.C., and W. Langbein (1971) Models and data. Pages
    121-126, Mathematical Models in Geophysics, Proceedings
    of Moscow Symposium. IAHS Publications No. 116. Wash-
    ington, D.C.

McCarthy, G.T. (1939) The Unit Hydrograph and Flood Routing.
    Paper presented at the Conference of North Atlantic
    Division of the U.S. Corps of Engineers. Providence,
    Rhode Island.

Nash, J.E. (1960) A unit hydrograph study with particular
    reference to British catchments. Proceedings of the
    Institution of Civil Engineers (London) 17:249-282.

Nash, J.E., and J.V. Sutcliffe (1970) River flow forecasting
    through conceptual models, Part 1—A discussion of prin-
    ciples. Journal of Hydrology 10:282-290.

O'Connell, P.E. (1971) A simple stochastic modeling of
    Hurst's law. Pages 169-187, Vol. 1, Proceedings of
    Warsaw Symposium. IAHS Publication No. 100. Paris:
    UNESCO/IAHS.

Pilgrim, D.H. (1975) Model evaluation, testing and parameter
    estimation in hydrology. Chapter 16, pages 305-333,
    Prediction in Catchment Hydrology, Proceedings of Na-
    tional Symposium on Hydrology. Canberra: Australian
    Academy of Science.

Shamir, U. (1970) A hierarchy of models for optimizing the
    operation of water systems. Pages 284-301, The Water
    Environment and Human Needs, edited by A.T. Ippen.
    Cambridge, Massachusetts: Ralph M. Parsons Laboratory
    for Water Resources and Hydrodynamics, MIT.

Shanin, T. (1972) Models and thought. Pages 1-22, The Rules
    of the Game: Cross Disciplinary Essays on Models in
    Scholarly Thought, edited by T. Shanin. London: Tavi-
    stock Publications.

Svanidze, F.G. (1975) Mathematical models of streamflow for
    water management calculations. Pages 17-24, Vol. 5,
    Proceedings of IWRA New Delhi Conference on Water for
    Human Needs. New Delhi: Indian Committee for IWRA
    Central Board of Irrigation and Power.

World Meteorological Organization (WMO) (1975) Operational
    Hydrology Report No. 7. Intercomparison of Conceptual
    Models Used in Operational Hydrological Forecasting.
    WMO Report No. 429. Geneva.

DEVELOPMENT OF A COMPUTER-BASED FLOOD FORECASTING SYSTEM
FOR AUSTRALIA

A.J. Hall and J.F. Elliott

1. INTRODUCTION

Operational flood forecasting in Australia is the responsibility of the Bureau of Meteorology, a national meteorological service which is part of the Commonwealth Government Department of Science. Flood forecasting is carried
out in the more flood-prone eastern states—Queensland, New
South Wales, Victoria, and Tasmania—by the Bureau's Regional
Forecast Centres located in the capital cities of each state.
Currently there are up to 32 river basins within each of the
larger states for which qualitative flood warnings are provided. Quantitative flood forecasts are made in up to 25
river basins in one state. Where required, quantitative estimates of flood height are given using mathematical models
for up to 10 forecast points within a basin.

As part of a planned automation process and an improvement in meteorological forecasting services a network of
mini-computer systems, termed the Automated Regional Operations System (AROS), is being proposed for installation in
each of the main Regional Forecast Centres. The main function of these computers will be to handle the large amount
of data required for the Bureau's weather forecasting services. The computers will be required to present these data
and the numerical weather prediction output from a larger
central computer to the forecaster and will enable the texts
of forecasts to be made up directly on the computer for automatic dissemination. Flood forecasting will be a special
application of these computers, enabling the same speedy and
automatic collection of operational data, the use of a range
of mathematical modeling procedures, and direct warning and
forecast composition and dissemination. Several of the component subsystems of AROS will be common to both weather and
flood forecasting, e.g., data collection and forecast message
composition and dissemination.

This paper outlines the considerations necessary in properly specifying the hardware requirements. It also outlines the design of the combination of computer programs and data files to match the computer-based system to the operational requirement. Details such as the raw data quantities and the treatment of these data within the system will be discussed. The system is being designed to operate over a wide range of catchments and to cater to forecasting systems of varying levels of instrumentation and hydrologic sophistication. The importance, therefore, of flexibility within the design, particularly in the structure of the hydrologic modeling component, will be emphasized.

2. GENERAL DESCRIPTION OF THE EXISTING MANUAL SYSTEM

Four phases can be identified in the current flood warning organization: routine assessment, flood precautionary, flood alert, and flood forecasting.

(i) *Routine assessment phase:* this covers the receipt and logging of daily rainfall and river height reports, computation of average catchment rainfall and catchment moisture indices (CMIs) to allow initial loss (IL) estimates to be made for all catchments, and the receipt and logging of any special heavy rainfall or flood warning river height reports. This information is summarized for the duty forecaster and used in conjunction with 24- and 48-hour quantitative precipitation forecasts (QPFs) to determine the necessity of entering a flood precautionary phase. Daily bulletins of river height readings and rainfall are also prepared.

(ii) *Flood precautionary phase:* the issue of confidential advice to local authorities; a brief modeling study to assess the sensitivity of the catchment to possible rain amounts (QPF) may be required.

(iii) *Flood alert phase:* the issue of initial flood alert warnings to the public in a qualitative form. This requires additional rainfall readings at 1-, 3-, and 6-hour intervals as appropriate for each catchment and general flood modeling studies to further assess the possible degree of flooding (minor, moderate, or major). Concise summaries of rainfalls and river heights are presented as they are received, and the plotting of observed and forecast hydrographs and flood stage profiles will be necessary in order to decide what action should be taken in the future.

(iv) *Flood forecasting phase:* this involves full-scale modeling with a combination of observed and forecast rainfalls to determine forecasts of future river height for issue as quantitative flood warnings to the public. Incoming data (at 1-, 3-, and 6-hour intervals) are logged and presented as tables and maps for the forecaster's assessment.

Following cancellation of the forecasting phase, model "carryover" values are stored and the data which were collected, received, and generated during the flood are archived.

3. GENERAL DESCRIPTION OF THE OPERATIONAL SYSTEM

The overall AROS is intended to perform operational functions on a regional scale coordinated with the centralized national-scale activities of the Bureau. It will provide modern technological support for operation of the weather service and assistance in improving the grade of the service. More specifically AROS will provide the following:

- An interface with the Bureau's central Melbourne Computer Message Switching Service (CMSS) to ultimately handle all state message switching functions by telex

- An automated data collection system of cooperative observer data handled by telephone, thereby eliminating expensive manual forwarding of data via telegram and the ensuing delays

- Computer-assisted composition of forecast and warning messages and automatic dissemination of these by telex and the CMSS, thereby eliminating the very labor intensive retyping and dissemination of these warnings by telex

- Automated chart plotting and general forecast data display for preparations of weather bulletins and alerts

- Local objective weather forecasting aids

- Local administrative assistance

- Flood forecasting operations and development

- Local user-developed applications processing

The AROS Flood Forecasting Sub-system (AFFS) is designed around the organization described in the previous section and will endeavor to automate many of the operations included in order to increase the efficiency and effectiveness of the flood forecasting service. The AFFS will mesh with other subsystems of AROS and components of the overall system such as data banks and message formulation and dissemination will be shared.

The eventual product of the flood forecasting organization is the flood forecast message. In order to formulate the appropriate message the system has to present to the forecaster a range of maps, tables, graphs, etc., representing both the observed data and the results of any modeling exercises, upon which the forecaster must base the forecast decision. The proposed operational system is composed of a number of computer programs and disc files arranged to suit

the operational requirements described. The general organization of these components is given in Figure 1 and the function of each is described below.

Data Input—RAWFILE—is that portion of the total information received into AROS that is relevant to AFFS. It includes all data that are processed through other AROS subsystems and data that are keyed in manually. Details of the
types and quantities of data are given in section 4.

Data Edit—DATEDIT—performs quality monitoring of the
incoming data, adjusting where necessary (e.g., filling in
missing rainfalls using correlations with adjacent stations,
interpolating to produce regular time period data); organizing the incoming data into suitable files for use by the
remainder of AFFS; converting stage heights to discharge
where required; and providing a hard copy record of all incoming data.

Working Data File—BASFILE—contains all the real-time
working data required for operational use. The type of data
collected and the time interval will depend upon which of the
various phases is in operation. Sufficient capacity is required for all catchments and data stored for each event,
i.e., 5-10 days of 3- to 6-hour intervals for small to medium
catchments and up to 2-3 months of daily data for some of the
long, slow flowing inland rivers. The contents of BASFILE
will be periodically archived onto a permanent storage area.

Data Presentation—DATDISP and MAPPER—prepares all
tabulations, listings, plots, and catchment map representations of data.

Areal Averaging—AVERAGE—calculates areal averages of
BASFILE data where required, e.g., daily rainfall, rainfall
at 1-, 3-, or 6-hour intervals, temperature, and evaporation,
which are held on AVFILE. These averages serve two main purposes: assessment of catchment conditions during routine
phases and input to hydrologic models used in preparing quantitative forecasts. It is considered necessary to separate
the averaging function into a separate module because the
intermittent arrival of observations will mean that averaging
has to be performed as a background operation either as complete sets of observations become available or after a preset
interval.

Routine Catchment Assessment—DATSUM—prepares a summary
of information required to assess the current status of
catchments (moisture index, initial loss potential, etc.) and
the likely consequences of any expected rainfall. A tabulation is prepared containing for each catchment the average
catchment rainfall for the past 2-5 days, the Catchment Moisture Index (CMI), estimate of the Initial Loss (IL), current
stage heights/discharge, forecast discharge for the next few
days (up to a peak) based on a standard range of forecast

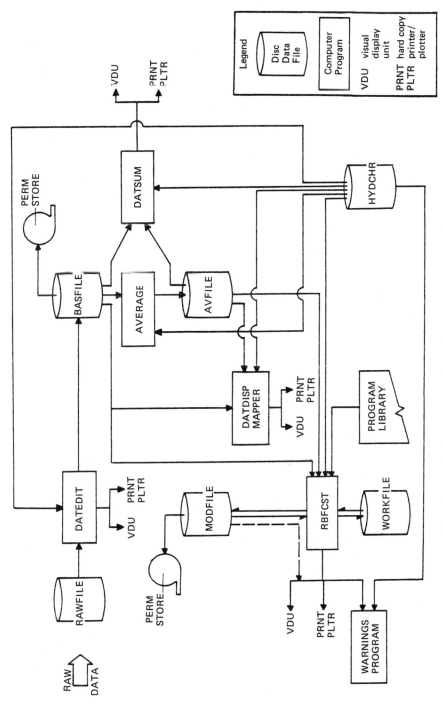

FIGURE 1 General description of the operational system.

rainfall, and an estimate of the amount of rain required to produce a critical threshold flood magnitude. To produce these last two items DATSUM will contain some simplified form of a continuous moisture accounting model, e.g., the Sacramento model (Burnash *et al*. 1973).

River Forecast—RBFCST—controls the detailed hydrologic modeling required for preparing a forecast for a catchment. Because of the wide range of catchments to be handled by the system, the hydrologic modeling component will need to be flexible. As well as having to model catchments of different climatic regimes, the range of real-time observation availability results in forecasting systems that range from complex models with a high degree of catchment subdivision, through lumped unitgraph-empirical loss models, to simple graphical-nomogram type techniques. While the first two groups of models can be generalized in programming structure, the latter type require a unique program for each system. Where possible the modeling will be achieved by arranging a number of generalized modules of each of the separate processes of catchment modeling to suit each particular catchment. It is intended that ultimately RBFCST be used to interpret a control vector defining the combination and arrangement of modules for each catchment and to operate the model so defined.

Modeling Data File—MODFILE—contains all the data used and generated by the operational forecast program RBFCST. These include all forecast hydrographs produced at each interval during the forecasting (and adjustments to these), hyetographs for each subcatchment including forecast rainfall, and values of model parameters such as IL and loss rate that vary between events.

Work Data File—WORKFILE—is used as a temporary disc storage area as required for RBFCST operations.

Permanent Catchment Data File—HYDCHR—contains all permanent characteristics of each catchment used in the transformation of the basic data and operation of models, e.g., rating tables, storage-discharge tables for flood routing, critical or key heights, subcatchment areas, river lengths, areal rainfall station weights, IL-CMI, and loss rate-duration tables (or equations), model parameters, average annual evaporation cycle, profiles of past flood events for comparison, and forecast and warning composition, details of catchment, maps, boundaries, and station locations.

In summary the AFFS will consist of the following computer programs: DATEDIT, AVERAGE, DATSUM, DATDISP, MAPPER, RBFCST, and the following data files: RAWFILE, BASFILE, AVFILE, HYDCHR, MODFILE, WORKFILE.

4. SUBSYSTEM INPUTS

4.1 Data Types and Purpose

The data required for forecast preparation in each
catchment will depend upon the degree of sophistication of
the forecasting model and would include the following.

River stage—height and trend of the river at a particular station at a defined time. Readings are taken at daily
intervals and during flood periods at regular (normally 3-
to 6-hour) intervals.

Outflow rates and storage levels—discharges from hydropower stations or from outlet works of dams are given in the
form of flow rate. Storage levels of reservoirs are given
as a stage height.

Point rainfall—depth of rainfall at a station. It is
normally measured at 0900 hours but during flood periods more
frequently (at 3- to 6-hour intervals).

Station temperature—daily maximum and minimum temperature used for making estimates of point evaporation (evapotranspiration).

Quantitative Precipitation Forecast (QPF)—forecast of
the amount of rainfall over a given area for a prescribed
period into the future, normally 24-48 hours for routine
assessment but during flood periods there is a requirement
for more accurate shorter-term forecasts for the next 2-4
time intervals (usually 6-12 hours).

Heavy rainfall reports—reports from prescribed stations
designed to alert the forecaster that heavy rain (greater
than 25-50 mm) has fallen since the last regular 0900 hours
report, and hence that there is a possibility of flooding.

The use of radar for measuring areal rainfall has been
under development in the Bureau for some time and will eventually be an integral part of AFFS. Similarly, satellite
observations of such parameters as soil moisture and areal
rainfall over large areas have potential use in flood forecasting and future developments within AFFS will need to
accommodate these.

4.2 Data Source and Transmission Mode

Data are provided from synoptic stations, daily tele-
graphic rainfall stations (mainly at 0900 hours), cooperative
rainfall and river height flood observers, "Telemarks" (telephone interrogated encoders), remote sensors, and automatic
stations. They are transmitted using one or more of the following methods: telegram, telex, phoned in by the observer,
by radio from the observer, Bureau telephones the observer

(including Telemark), radio telemetry from a remote sensor,
and land-line telemetry from a remote sensor.

4.3 *Data Volumes*

Estimates of the maximum volumes of data likely to be
handled in the most active Regional Forecast Centre are given
in Table 1 for the routine and flood warning phases. The response of a catchment to storm rainfall is very much dependent on the antecedent conditions, both of catchment wetness
and of recent river trends. For this reason it is necessary
to retain a period of the immediate past data to assist in
the preparation of the forecast. For most of the shorter,
steeper coastal catchments a retention period of 3-5 days
will be adequate. However, for the longer, westward flowing
inland rivers, data must be retained for periods from 1 week
up to 1-2 months.

4.4 *Error Checking*

Data errors can arise during any one of the following
stages: measurement, transmission, or recording. Measurement errors are due to malfunction of measuring equipment or
observer error, or both. Checks for consistency with previously reported values, comparisons with a likely maximum and
minimum value, and testing for continuously constant values
will help detect these. Transmission errors arise between
the time the observer reads the gage, records the observation,
and transmits the tabulation of the data by the Bureau. Common errors include juxtaposition of figures, embedded blanks
(between figures), decimal points misplaced, message in in-
correct format, and data not received in chronological order.
Recording errors will occur between receipt of the data message at the Forecast Centre and placement of the data into
AROS. Data received via telegram or telex are to be interfaced directly into the computer and will only be subject
to possible measurement and transmission errors. Data
received over the telephone, however, will be manually
keyed-in and will be subject to operator errors.

Ultimately AFFS will involve computer-controlled direct
interrogation of all automatic stations. This will eliminate
some of these errors and facilitate improved quality control
of observational data.

5. SUBSYSTEM OUTPUTS

Within the total AROS framework the subsystem outputs
can be considered either internal (generated and used only
within the AFFS) or external (generated by the AFFS for
use in other AROS subsystems). The internal output encom-
passes a range of maps, graphs, tables, etc., by which the
input data and hydrologic model results are displayed and

TABLE 1 Summary of data inputs.

Data item	Routine		Maximum operational	
	Number of observations received per day	Number of observations needed to be held by system in real-time	Number of observations received per day	Number of observations needed to be held by system in real-time
River stage	84	1,160	1,280	13,000
Outflow rates and storage levels	39	470	320	3,200
Point rainfall	250	500	2,080	10,400
Station temperature[a]	70	140	70	140

[a]Not used at present; estimate only.

presented to the forecaster. The main external output is the flood forecast message and the daily river height bulletin.

During the flood precautionary, alert, and forecasting phases, a request to observers for more frequent reporting schedules would originate from AFFS and be transmitted by another AROS subsystem.

Internal outputs would include graphical hydrograph displays and tabulations showing observed and predicted hydrographs based on both observed and forecast rainfall; catchment maps showing rainfall station locations and progressive totals, river stations, missing data, subcatchment boundaries, isohyets, etc.; tabulations of station rainfalls; and a catchment condition summary and historical river height profiles.

During the transfer of data from RAWFILE to BASFILE using DATEDIT, a hard copy of all data is made automatically as a backup to data held on BASFILE. Similarly, for legal and other reasons, a hard copy of the system outputs, observation initiation, flood warnings, and river heights would be retained. At suitable periods all data will be permanently archived either in digital or hard copy form.

The flood warning or forecast message is the ultimate external product of the subsystem. Using information prepared within AFFS, the message formulation and dissemination subsystem would be used to prepare and distribute the warning.

The volume of flood warning and forecast will depend on the severity and duration of flooding in the season or year. The number of flood warnings in a state in any 1 month has ranged from 0 to 541 (Queensland in February 1971). River height bulletins are provided daily in most states and are supplemented by additional reports during flood periods. These are mainly used for water management and irrigation.

6. COMPUTER REQUIREMENTS

Computer resources necessary for AFFS can be considered in two classes: operational requirements and development requirements.

6.1 Operational Requirements

The proposed operational system is outlined in section 3. The working core will need to accommodate the various programs and modules used in RBFCST. The size required is therefore dependent on the largest combination of modules likely to be loaded at any time. Table 2 gives the program size (not including system support software), disc space,

TABLE 2 Summary of operational hydrologic model programs.

Program	Function	Size (K byte)	CPU time (sec)	Temp. disc space (K byte)
UGMODEL	Given loss values, determines rainfall excess from gross rainfall hyetograph and calculates hydrograph of surface runoff using a unitgraph	15	2	—
FLDROUT	Routes upstream hydrograph through a river reach using one of three methods	15	2	—
SACMODEL	Uses the Sacramento model to produce a forecast of the streamflow hydrograph from a gross rainfall pattern	25	5	—
ROMODEL	Uses a runoff-routing model to produce a forecast of the surface runoff hydrograph from a rainfall excess hyetograph (Mcin *et al.* 1974)	25	5	—
REGMODEL	Uses the regression equations developed by the Bidwell procedure to produce a forecast of the streamflow hydrograph from a gross rainfall pattern (Bidwell 1971)	20	5	20

and central processor unit (CPU) time for a typical operation (IBM 360/65) for typical programs currently available. The table suggests that a working core of 32K bytes would be a reasonable minimum to accommodate the necessary modeling programs.

The size of the disc pack required for operational use will be determined by the volume of data to be handled and the size of the program modules to be stored, as discussed in section 3. Table 3 gives estimates of the capacity required for each of the disc files in the system. Their capacities are defined only as the number of items of information. The eventual space required will depend on the structure and format of the data records. However, assuming a fairly simple format the table suggests that a volume of approximately 0.5M bytes will be required.

During periods of routine operation two visual display units (VDUs) will be needed for 2 hours from 0900 hours and occasionally for about 1 hour at 1600 hours, to perform the daily data entry and monitoring functions.

6.2 *Development Requirements*

The programs required for the development and calibration of models will necessarily be larger and more complicated. Table 4 shows a range of programs used in model development which are currently run on an IBM 360/65 computer. Some of these are quite large. However, because they currently operate on a large capacity machine, little attempt has been made to reduce their size. It is expected that versions of most of these programs can be developed to operate in a single partition of the proposed mini-computers of 112K bytes. Estimates of CPU time (IBM 360/65) for typical applications and the required temporary disc space are given in Table 4.

During the calibration of models to catchments in system development work, it is necessary to analyze considerable amounts of historical data. These data need to be retained on disc for the duration of the system development, in some instances up to several months. Estimates of these data are given in Table 5 for different types of models.

7. ADVANTAGES OF THE AROS FLOOD FORECASTING SUB-SYSTEM (AFFS)

Implementation of the AROS Flood Forecasting Sub-system will allow the Bureau to provide a greater variety and number of forecasting products, with considerable improvements in timeliness and reliability.

A much faster and more accurate examination of river systems is possible. As more rivers become potential flood

TABLE 3   Estimates of capacities for disc files.

File	Item	Max. no. items
RAWFILE	River stage	200
	Outflow rates and storage levels	50
	Point rainfall	300
	Station temperature (max. and min.)	70
BASFILE	River stage	13,000
	Outflow rates and storage levels	3,000
	Point rainfall	10,000
	Station temperature (max. and min.)	200
	Rainfall forecast	100
AVFILE	Average (sub)catchment rainfall (100 x 8 x 5)	4,000
	Catchment moisture index	200
MODFILE	Model carryover details, hyetographs and hydrographs (10 records of 200 bytes x 30 catchments)	60^{a}
HYDCHR	Rating tables; store as a functional expression (50 rated stations x 10 records of 100 bytes)	50^{a}
	Storage-discharge tables (30 records of 200 bytes)	6^{a}
	Critical heights (3 per forecast point x 100 forecast points)	300
	Model parameters; 20 per catchment x 100 catchments	2,000
	Areas, lengths, etc.; 10 per catchment x 100 catchments	1,000
	Nomograms; functional expressions and look-up tables	10^{a}
	Rainfall weights; 8 combinations/catchments x 100 catchments	800
	Subcatchment reference dictionary; 100 catchments x 200 byte record/catchment	20^{a}
	Historical profiles; 30 catchments x 3 events/catchment x 200 bytes	18^{a}
	Incidentals	

[a] Refers to number of K bytes.

TABLE 4 Summary of programs used in model development.

Program	Function	Size (K byte)	CPU time (sec)	Temp. disc space (K byte)
INDUNIT	Derives unitgraphs by method of least squares	40	20	—
AVUNIT	Averages single storm unitgraphs to produce a catchment average unitgraph	38	20	10
ROUTER	To calibrate one of three standard flood routing procedures to a river reach	12	5	—
RORM	To calibrate a runoff routing model to a catchment	100	20^{a}	10
STRSIMUL	To calibrate the Sacramento catchment model to a headwater catchment	100	30^{a}	—
BIDREG	To calibrate the Bidwell regression model to a number of storms	100	120	20
HYDRAU	To develop storage-discharge relationships from hydraulic modeling of river reaches, junctions, dams, bridge waterways, etc. (Morris 1976)	200	20 min	930

[a]These times apply to typical runs where trial parameter values are tested. Automatic optimization runs can take from 2 to 4 minutes.

TABLE 5 Estimates of data requirements for model development.

Model	Data required	Space (K byte)
INDUNIT	5-20 storm events	10
ROUTER	5-20 corresponding upstream and downstream hydrographs	5
STRSIMUL	10 years daily streamflow 10 years daily rainfall at four or more stations	100
RORM	5-20 storm events	10
BIDREG	5-20 storm events	10
HYDRAU	2 storm events of high and medium stages and river cross-section data	700

hazards, the general overview required by the forecaster becomes the most difficult task. More rivers can be examined more quickly, thereby reducing the present mental strain on the forecaster and consequently increasing his efficiency.

Data handling is minimized since all observational data received are immediately accessible and are presented in the most pertinent format to the forecaster. Similarly all catchment parameters can be recalled and presented as required.

All routine calculations (e.g., daily catchment assessment) are carried out automatically.

The computer allows the use of more complex models in the forecasting systems. This leads to the following advantages:

● Continuous soil-moisture accounting models (e.g., the Sacramento model) provide a more comprehensive monitoring of the catchment moisture status and provide a complete forecast of all components of the flood hydrograph

● A more objective forecast can be made as the forecaster can quickly assess the consequences of a wider range of forecast rainfalls

● Modeling is not necessarily restricted to a constant time interval

● The availability of a wide range of modeling procedures will allow the most appropriate routine to be selected for each application

● The use of theoretically sounder models should lead to greater confidence when predicting extreme events and allow the effect of physical changes within the catchment to be anticipated

The availability of a computer will hasten the development of new forecasting systems and allow for more comprehensive post-flood performance analysis.

In addition to flood forecasting, AFFS could provide a more comprehensive range of streamflow forecasts to assist various water management authorities (e.g., in drought forecasts, in reservoir management decisions), and AFFS could act as an advisory service to industry (e.g., advising on the timing of pollutant releases into natural watercourses).

8. COST-BENEFIT CONSIDERATIONS

It is difficult to make a cost-benefit analysis of flood forecasting by itself, and it is even more difficult to establish the marginal difference of computer-produced flood forecasts over those produced manually. In the case of the AROS proposal the Flood Forecasting Subsystem will be one of six subsystems contributing to the benefits of the system. Therefore the marginal costs of AFFS will consist only of several more VDUs, additional disc space, subsystem program development, and the calibration of the more sophisticated computer-based models proposed (Table 6).

This is one of the advantages of having a combined meteorologic and hydrologic forecasting agency where a computer system is designed and dedicated to real-time forecasting and includes a number of common modules. For comparison purposes an independent computer system set up solely for flood forecasting is also considered. These additional costs are given in Table 6.

The AROS proposal provides for all hardware to be duplicated to give nearly 100 percent reliability. Since computing equipment, particularly the computer itself, is now very reliable, for the purpose of this analysis only one computer system is considered rather than two parallel computer systems. In the event of a failure in a flood period, simpler manual versions of the flood forecasting models can be used as a backup.

The annual cost of manually operating the flood forecasting system is not included. As the rate of development of forecasting systems under AFFS increases, capital, maintenance, and operational costs will also increase. These costs have not been included in the table as they are more

TABLE 6   Potential cost-benefits of a computer-based flood forecasting system in a major flood-prone state.

Costs		Benefits	
Component	Cost ($A1,000)	Component	Potential annual savings ($A1,000)
As a subsystem of AROS			
Three VDUs (one with hard copy)	14	Increased accuracy and reliability	100
Additional disc space (1 Mb)	2		
Program development	30	Quicker development of forecasting systems	250
TOTAL	46		
Computer subsystem maintenance	2	Other economic benefits derived from more comprehensive stream-flow forecasting	?
As a separate computer-based system			
Computer, disc, printer/plotter, communication interfaces, and other hardware	78		
Program development	30		
Data gathering program development	48		
Forecast dissemination program development	15		
TOTAL	171	TOTAL	350
Computer system maintenance	8		

NOTE: $A stands for Australian dollars.

than offset by the savings in automatic data collection, message switching, etc., which are introduced as part of AROS.

As is usually the case, the benefits are much more difficult to quantify. The benefits stem from the advantages given in section 7 and can be grouped as follows.

By using AFFS to develop flood forecasting systems, there will be an increased capability and speed of development of these systems. There is a large backlog in this development in Queensland, for example, where about 50 percent of the basins still require a quantitative flood forecasting system. Using AFFS it is anticipated that these systems can be developed at twice the rate, primarily through having a computer available in an interactive mode. Thus, instead of taking 20 years to develop the required systems, the systems can be completed in 10 years. Heatherwick and Quinnell (1976) conservatively estimated that flood forecasting can save 10 percent of the annual flood damage in Brisbane. On the basis of an estimated $A20m annual flood damage in each of the major flood-prone states (New South Wales and Queensland), the potential annual savings from flood forecasting is $A2m. The possible increase in savings from flood damage over the next 20 years due to the increased rate of system development with AFFS can be calculated as follows:

Total damages without AFFS = (50% x $A2m) x 20 years/2 = $A10m

Total damages with AFFS = (50% x $A2m) x 10 years/2 = $A5m

Potential mean annual savings = (10 - 5)/20 = $A0.25m

The operational productivity of the flood forecaster will increase. This increase provides an improvement in the timeliness and allows for a more thorough examination of the available data. The result is greater objectivity of the forecasts provided by the available systems. As more systems are developed the capacity of the forecaster to accommodate the extra workload will be enhanced by AFFS thus reducing the need for additional staff. However, the savings here should be balanced against the increase in development capacity provided by those staff.

The accuracy and reliability of forecasts should be increased through the use of better forecasting models leading to better forecasts. In turn this leads to increased public awareness and confidence and a greater and more active response to flood forecasts. This will particularly be the case where flood levees are involved and the breaching or holding of these may be determined by only a few centimeters in flood height. Increased public response will lead to a reduction in flood damages. A modest improvement in flood forecasts and public response using AFFS would represent a potential annual savings in damages of say 5 percent ($A0.1m).

The speed of getting flood forecasts to the public will be increased in those basins with a short time of concentration. In a flood situation these would be dealt with first and might mean the difference of 1 hour earlier warning in a basin that peaks in say 10 hours. Earlier warnings should reduce flood damage and are included in the 5 percent improvement above.

There are a number of economic benefits other than those accruing to flood plain occupants, e.g., navigation, the scheduling of hydroelectric power with thermal power generation, and water supply for agricultural and industrial use. It is not possible to quantify these benefits. However, any improvement in the accuracy of streamflow forecasts should have a considerable beneficial effect on the national economy.

To enable a benefit/cost ratio to be determined, it is necessary to calculate the present worth of the costs (PWC), i.e., the initial cost plus the discounted maintenance cost. This is given by:

$$PWC = C_i + \left[R(1 - R^N)/(1 - R) \right] C_m$$

where C_i is the initial cost, C_m is the mean continuing cost over the project life of N years (10 years) and $R = 1/(i + 1)$, and i is the discount rate (10 percent). The present worth of the costs of AFFS is thus \$A58,300. If a separate computer is used the present worth of costs is \$A220,200.

The present worth of the annual savings or benefits (PWB) is given by:

$$PWB = \left[R(1 - R^N)/(1 - R) \right] S_a$$

where S_a is the expected mean annual savings. For a discount rate of 10 percent over 10 years this represents a present worth of benefits of \$A2,150,000.

Thus on the basis of these estimates, AFFS has a potential benefit/cost ratio of 39 over the existing manual system. If a separate computer system is required this is reduced to 9.

If full reliability is required from two parallel computer systems the benefit/cost ratio is still greater than 4. If it were possible to quantify the other economic benefits derived from streamflow forecasting, these ratios would be considerably higher.

9. CONCLUSIONS

This paper has endeavored to show the complexities in developing a computer-based flood forecasting service for a

large region such as Australia. It involves data collection
on a large scale, real-time hydrologic modeling with an
emphasis on flexibility, and forecast dissemination to the
public. The forecasting system must also be geared to seek
and receive public response to its forecasts (including updating and correcting) and to act accordingly. This situation needs to be contrasted with the hydrologic modeler who
handles one catchment at a time (instead of up to 32) in a
non-real-time or design mode. This paper has enumerated the
necessary activities of a flood forecasting service to highlight these differences and to provide guidance to those who
are considering introducing similar computer-based systems.

A fairly superficial cost-benefit analysis suggests
that the introduction of a computer-based flood forecasting
system as part of a computer-based national weather service
would have considerable economic advantage (benefit/cost
ratio of 39) over an existing manual forecasting service.
If a separate computer is dedicated to flood forecasting the
benefit/cost ratio is still over 9. Furthermore, the use of
computers will avoid an increase in staff (at a time when no
staff growth is government policy) but will achieve a considerable increase in forecasting productivity during flood
periods.

ACKNOWLEDGMENTS

This paper is published with the permission of the
Director of Meteorology, Australia.

REFERENCES

Bidwell, V.J. (1971) Regression analysis of non-linear catch-
    ment systems. Water Resources Research 7:1118-1125.

Burnash, R.J.C., R.L. Ferral, and R.A. McGuire (1973) A Gen-
    eralized Streamflow Simulation System: Conceptual Mod-
    elling for Digital Computers. Washington, D.C.: U.S.
    Department of Commerce, National Weather Service, and
    Sacramento, California: Department of Water Resources.

Heatherwick, G., and A.L. Quinnell (1976) Optimising Benefits
    to Urban Residents of a Total Flood Warning System for
    the Brisbane Valley. Paper presented at the Hydrology
    Symposium held by the Institution of Engineers. June.
    Sydney, Australia.

Mein, R.G., E.M. Laurenson, and T.A. McMahon (1974) Simple
    non-linear model for flood estimation. American Society
    of Civil Engineers, Hydraulics Division Journal 100(HY11):
    1507-1518.

Morris, K.J. (1976) The Mathematical Modelling of Rivers.
    Paper presented at the Hydrology Symposium held by the
    Institution of Engineers. June. Sydney, Australia.

EFFICIENCY OF THE REAL-TIME HYDROLOGICAL FORECASTING SYSTEMS IN POLAND SINCE THEIR IMPLEMENTATION IN 1975

E. Bobiński, T. Piwecki, and J. Żelaziński

INTRODUCTION

The development and implementation of real-time hydrological forecasting systems for water management is the main task of the Hydrometeorological Service in Poland. These systems will soon be used to operate some 12 major water reservoirs and to manage the navigable reaches of the two largest rivers in Poland; the Vistula and the Odra.

Development started in 1971, and the first system, for forecasting the flow of the Soła River at the Żywiec cross section, was put into operation in 1973. A similar system for the Dunajec River at the Kowaniec cross section commenced operation in 1974, and one for the Krościenko cross section in 1975. In 1976, the river stage and depth hydrograph forecasting systems for the Lower Vistula were put into service. Information on these systems was documented and presented at several international symposia and meetings (see Bobiński *et al.* 1974, 1975, 1976, and 1977). Therefore, only a brief description is given here.

This paper emphasizes the experience gained in implementing and operating the systems, specifically in data collecting, transmitting, and processing, in employing hardware and staff, and in forecasting efficiency.

DEVELOPMENT AND OPERATION OF THE SYSTEMS

Description of the Systems

Information on the Soła and the Dunajec river systems, and on the Lower Vistula system is presented in Tables 1 and 2, respectively. More detailed information can be found in Bobiński *et al.* (1974, 1975, 1976, and 1977).

TABLE 1 Information on the river flow hydrograph forecasting systems.

River	Cross section	Catchment area (km²)	Altitude range (m above sea level)	Number of reporting posts Rain gage	Water level	Travel time during flood conditions (h)
Soła	Żywiec	780	340-1,500	14	1	4- 8
Dunajec	Kowaniec	680	580-2,500	11	1	3- 6
Dunajec	Krościenko	1,589	420-2,500	17	2	4-12

NOTES: *Input:* the rainfall amount and the river flow values in the catchment area recorded on the gages every three hours for the past 24 hours; recorded air temperature, wind speed, air humidity deficit, and total radiation for the past 24 hours; quantitative precipitation forecast (QPF) and four other meteorological variables for the coming 48 hours. *Output:* forecasted hourly values of the river flow and runoff volumes for the coming 12, 24, 36, and 48 hours, given in three variants of the quantitative precipitation forecast (QPF), runoff volume, rainfall amount, and the actual evapotranspiration computed for the last 24 hours. *Computer:* the forecast is computed by the ODRA 1305 computer. Machine time is three minutes and input and output data transmission is done by teletype. *Model:* modified SSARR version.

TABLE 2 General information on the river stage and depth hydrograph forecasting system for the Lower Vistula.

River stage reporting post	Distance from the dam (km)	Travel time (h)	Stage variation range[a] (m)	Input data	
				Specification	Time interval (min)
Włocławek dam	0	0	1.5-2.0	Q	after each change
Włocławek river gage	4.5	0.5	1.5	H	15
Toruń	60	12	1.0	H	60
Fordon	100	24	0.5	H	60

[a]For the river flow < 2000 m^3/sec.

NOTES: Q stands for river discharge; H stands for river stage. *Output:* river stage forecasts at Toruń and Fordon for the coming 24 hours with a 1-hour time-step; critical depth values for two chosen cross sections of shallows with the same lead time and time-step. *Input and output transmission:* teletype line. *Computer:* ODRA 1305. *Model:* a cascade of equal nonlinear or linear storages together with linear channel (Dooge model type), 1976-1977 version. In 1978 replaced by the model described by the integral equation (1).

The forecasts produced by the Soła and Dunajec systems are used by the control offices of the reservoirs located downstream of the river catchments' closing cross sections; those of the Vistula river system are used by the local water management office and the navigation dispatcher at Toruń city. The observation network incorporated into the three river systems is part of the basic network of the Hydrometeorological Service. The Soła and Dunajec systems' reporting posts are equipped with recording gages and radio transmitter/receivers. The river stage reporting post at Włocławek is equipped with a punch tape digital gage which records the stage every 15 minutes, as required by the system. All other river stage gages are equipped with the customary analog type recording gages. The observers at the reporting posts are locally hired part-time workers. The staff at the collecting stations is highly qualified and full-time.

The telecommunication facilities and the computer center serving the systems transmit and process the observational data. These facilities are used for developing and operating the hydrological forecasting systems. Since the hardware capacity of the center is adequate for real-time handling of meteorological information according to World Weather Watch (WWW) standards, it is also adequate for the real-time operation of the hydrological forecasting systems in Poland. Therefore, implementation of the systems has been smooth and they operate with no serious troubles. The staff is accustomed to the routine operations of the meteorological service, and the additional duties caused by the hydrological systems do not pose any special problems.

Improvement of the Soła and Dunajec Systems

A series of improvements, described in Bobiński *et al.* (1974, 1975, 1976, and 1977), have been made. The most recent improvement is the recalibration of the model parameters, made after new data sets were stored. The original model version was calibrated using historical data sets of poor quality. In 1975, a computer with greater capacity was installed, thus enabling input and output data to be stored successively on magnetic tape. The data are regularly checked and updated. The 1975 and 1976 data files were used for the recalibration and the 1977 data files were used for verification. A special program, MAKSYM, was prepared for executing the recalibration. It enables identification of parameters using both the Gauss-Seidel optimization method and the trial-and-error method. The program has a wide variety of control outputs that monitor and evaluate the performance of several of the model's components.

A mean-square-error (MSE) criterion was applied in the optimization procedure. Improvements in the model's performance are shown in Figure 1, where the "old" and "new" sets of parameters are shown. Besides the constant parameters, a function $s = f(WN)$, where s is a runoff coefficient and

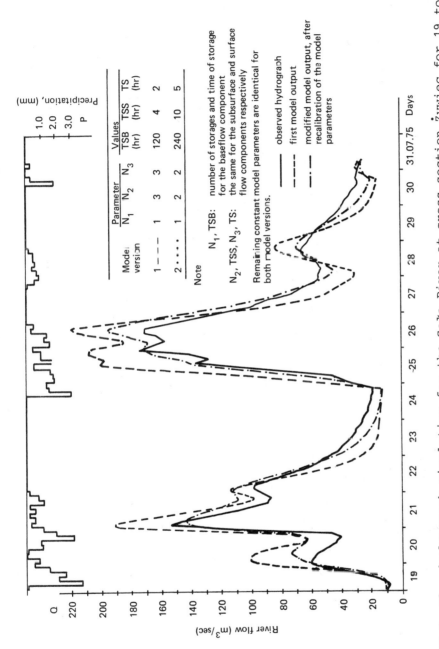

FIGURE 1 Flow hydrograph simulation for the Soła River at cross section Żywiec for 19 to 31 July 1975.

WN is a soil moisture index, has changed shape after recalibration. The recalibration resulted in better runoff simulation. However, overall operational forecast accuracy
still depends on the quantitative precipitation forecast
(QPF), on correctly evaluating the initial conditions, and
on the updating procedure as well.

In future development of the system, emphasis will be
placed on the control of input data and analysis procedures.
Control and analysis procedures already account for the
greatest part of the computer programs but improvement in
the handling of the real-time data is needed. Since the
systems will be expanded, different models can be applied
to include other catchments where the control and analysis
blocks should be standardized so that they can be easily
adapted to any catchment in the country and to the model
structure substitution or modification. Another task is the
improvement of the systems' reliability, i.e., decreasing
the amount of missing data and data errors and accelerating
the data flow. This is mainly a hardware modernization
problem.

The Lower Vistula System

In June 1978 a new model was implemented. The inputs
and outputs of the new model are the same as those of the
previous model (see Table 2) and the hardware also remains
the same. The model transforms an input $q(t)$ into an output
$Q(t)$ using a systems approach. The river reach is considered as a nonlinear dynamic system described by the integral
equation

$$Q(t) = \sum_{r=1}^{R} \left[\int_0^p \cdots \int_0^p h_r(\tau_1, \tau_2, \ldots, \tau_r) \prod_{i=1}^{r} q(t - \tau_i) d\tau_i \right]$$

(1)

where

t is time

τ is an integration variable

p is the memory of the system

R is the order of the system

$q(t)$ is an input function

$Q(t)$ is an output function and

$h_r(\tau_1, \tau_2, \ldots, \tau_r)$ are kernel functions

Kernel functions $h_r(\tau_1, \tau_2, \ldots, \tau_r)$ are identified on observed input and output data sets, assuming that a nonlinear system can be approximated by a combination of linear systems. The kernel functions of the linear systems were approximated by Meixner's orthogonal polynomials. The first river reach section, which is 4.5 km long and directly downstream from the dam, is represented by the nonlinear system of the second order ($R = 2$), whereas two remaining sections (see Table 2) are represented by the linear system ($R = 1$). An output from the upstream section model forms an input to the downstream section model.

This adaptive model identifies the parameters before each forecast run, taking into account the data observed from the last 120 hours, which results in a better performance than that of the previous model. More detailed information on this model can be found in Piwecki and Szymkiewicz (1974) and Szymkiewicz (1976 and 1978).

PERFORMANCE OF THE SYSTEMS

Forecast Efficiency Criteria

The systems' performance is estimated after each season of operation. Forecast error statistics are computed following the criteria used during the WMO Intercomparison of Conceptual Models Project (1975). Results of the computation are discussed in Bobiński *et al.* (1977). To estimate forecast efficiency, the following approach was adopted based on considerations presented below in the section on the efficiency of forecasting models.

(i) Compare the empirical probability distribution plots of two forecast errors: one obtained from the system under consideration, another being the result of an inertial or a "mean value" forecast (see Figures 2 and 3). If these plots show some similarity, examine the forecast efficiency estimate E

$$E = \sigma_M / \sigma_0 \tag{2}$$

where

σ_M is the MSE of model forecast, and

σ_0 is the MSE of "zero model" forecast, i.e., inertial or "mean value" forecast

(ii) Compare the normalized distribution autocorrelation functions of the forecast errors of two models as in (i). Some examples of application of such an approach are presented below.

50

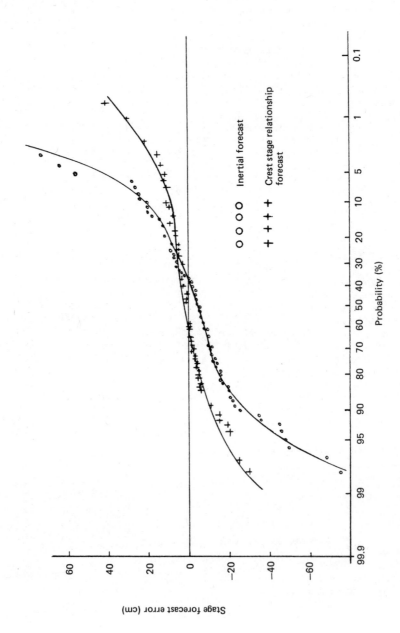

FIGURE 2   A stage forecast errors' empirical probability distribution for the Vistula River at cross section Warsaw for June 1974, June 1975, and June 1976. Forecast lead time is 3 days.

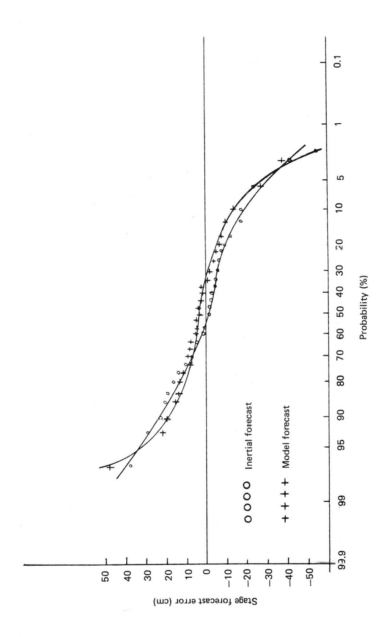

FIGURE 3 A low-water stage forecast errors' empirical probability distribution for the Vistula River at cross section Toruń for November 1976.

In addition to the forecasts obtained from the systems under consideration, an example of the river stage forecasts performed by conventional method is discussed as a certain reference level to the simulation model forecast efficiency.

The Soła and the Dunajec River Systems

The latest version of the model was made after several modifications produced acceptable forecasts. Since the lag time of the catchments is a few hours (see Table 1), the flow hydrograph forecast for the next 48 hours depends heavily on the QPF and on proper estimation of initial soil-moisture conditions. Information on this subject is presented in Bobiński et al. (1976 and 1977). As to the efficiency estimate for these catchments, it was stated that the inertial forecast errors are less than "mean value" forecast errors. Therefore, estimate E was examined in relation to inertial forecasts after comparison of the empirical probability distributions of the errors.

For most of the 1975-1977 forecast records the value of estimate E is 0.5-0.8. In the few months when the QPF showed higher errors, the value of E approached 1. Therefore, in general, forecast efficiency was fair enough. However, since no major flood occurred in the 1975-1977 period on the Soła and the Dunajec Rivers, the problem will have to be examined again under flood conditions.

The Lower Vistula River System

Two examples of the system's performance in 1976 are shown in Figures 4 and 5. The forecast for the lower gage at Fordon is fairly accurate, the forecast errors being mostly within 10 cm, whereas for the middle gage at Toruń the forecast is accurate for the initial 12 hours but shows more discrepancies for the next 12 hours. This is because the real flow of the hydropower station differs at times from the scheduled flow. These differences have practically no influence on the lower gage, where the travel time is about 24 hours; however, they cannot be neglected at the middle gage where the travel time is 12 hours. For the users in this case the most important forecast is that of the extreme stages and depths as well as the time of the critical stage (depth) occurrence. It is impossible to obtain a forecast during unsteady flow conditions by any of the conventional methods.

The forecast efficiency in relation to mean water forecast or inertial forecast, assuming that the river stage during the whole forecast lead time (24 hours) is equal to that observed at the initial moment, is very good, i.e., $E < 0.1$. However, flow variations induced by hydropower station operation are of a cyclic diurnal nature depending on the day of the week and on the season. For this reason other "zero model" forecast schemes were proposed.

53

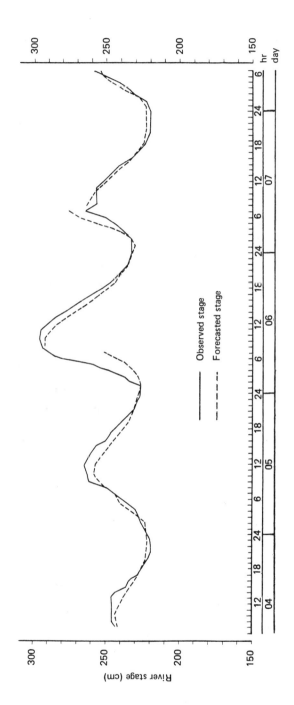

FIGURE 4   System output plot for the Vistula River at cross section Toruń for 4 to 7 November 1976.

LBUMM - E

54

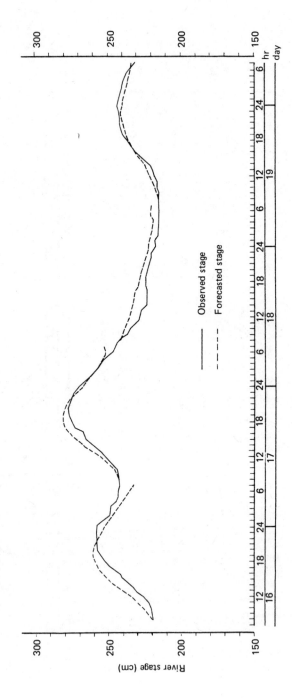

FIGURE 5   System output plot for the Vistula River at cross section Fordon for 16 to 19 November 1976.

MEAN VALUE FORECAST

Mean values of the highest and lowest stages (H_{max} and H_{min}) and the times of occurrence (T_{max} and T_{min}) based on the November 1976 data were computed. These values were assumed as a forecast for November 1977 and the forecast errors (MSEs) were computed. The errors were then compared to the system forecast errors according to equation (2) after a similarity of the errors' empirical probability distribution was proven. The results are shown in Table 3. As can be seen, the system forecasts are better for the stage forecasts only and are far worse for the time of occurrence in relation to the "mean value" forecast.

TABLE 3 E estimate values—"mean value" forecast.

| River gage | Forecasted variable | | | |
	T_{min}	T_{max}	H_{min}	H_{max}
Toruń	1.39	1.26	0.32	0.52
Fordon	1.76	0.57	0.44	0.46

INERTIAL FORECAST

The inertial forecast is based on the following assumptions. During 1 week in November, reservoir inflow is assumed as a constant; the outflow on the other hand depends on the weekly power load variations that are kept the same as those from the previous Monday through Sunday. Using the same procedure as above, the E estimate values shown in Table 4 were computed. The E estimate values for T_{min} and T_{max} in this case were even worse than for the "mean value" forecasts.

TABLE 4 E estimate values—inertial forecast.

| River gage | Forecasted variable | |
	H_{min}	H_{max}
Toruń	0.96	1.22
Fordon	1.34	0.90

The errors' empirical probability distribution plots (see Figure 3) are considerably similar. They were also similar when the Kolmogorov-Smirnov test was used. The errors of successive forecasts—model and inertial—were uncorrelated. The above examples illustrate a high dependence of the efficiency E estimate on the applied reference level, i.e., "zero model", and on the length of the statistical series used for the model identification and the estimate computation. In these examples the series lengths were very short—about 1 month. Moreover, during the identification period the mean-square deviations simulated from observed hydrographs were mostly within 5 cm for the stage variations range of about 150 cm, whereas during an operation period the MSE of the forecast rose to about 20 cm due to several errors in input data.

THE VISTULA RIVER STAGE FORECASTS AT WARSAW (CONVENTIONAL METHOD)

The forecasts are computed using crest stage relations 1, 2, and 3 days ahead. The procedure has been done over 50 years and the forecasts have been published. A set of 90 three-day forecasts for the month of June from the years 1974, 1975, and 1976 were examined. Among "zero models" a "mean value" forecast showed greater errors than the inertial forecast and the latter was chosen for the examination. The errors' empirical probability distribution plots are shown in Figure 4. One can see that the crest stage forecasts have a lower probability of great error. The estimate $E = 0.2$ means that the MSE of published forecasts is 80 percent less than that of inertial forecasts.

The successive crest stage forecast errors appeared to be uncorrelated, whereas successive inertial forecast errors are highly correlated, i.e., for $\Delta t = 1$ day, $r = 0.96$. This example shows that the conventional method is highly accurate and efficient despite its well-known limitations. The high standard of this method must be borne in mind when developing a more modern and sophisticated forecasting system.

EFFICIENCY OF FORECASTING MODELS

A Reference Level for the Forecasting Models

Let us consider the information gained from the forecast. Through the application of a forecasting model the number and magnitude of errors in a quantitative estimation process can be reduced compared with those of estimation without the model applications.

In water management practice it is impossible to assume that no attempt will be made to predict the behavior of a process. Therefore, as a lower bound of information or "zero model", we assume a prediction that is made without a forecasting system. Since in most countries observational

data records are kept, the mean and extreme values as well
as the probability distribution of the predicted variable,
i.e., river flow, are almost always available. Thus, the
"mean value" forecast is a possible "zero model". A distribution of predicted variable deviations from the mean usually
shows a great dispersion. Nevertheless, such a reference
prediction tool is quite useful in some cases. All hydrometeorological processes are nonstationary and their stochastic characteristics are subject to cyclic seasonal variations. For this reason "mean value" prediction should account for the seasonal variations in the mean. The findings
of Garrick *et al.* (1978) should be noted in this context.

Garrick *et al.* propose an efficiency criterion that
relates the model error variance to the variance of the
seasonal prediction based only on date. They demonstrate
that for the Sanaga River catchment, which experiences highly
seasonal stage variations, the SSARR simulation model is less
efficient than the simple seasonal prediction. The succes
sive in-time values of river flow are usually highly correlated. Keeping this in mind another forecast model may be
applied. In this case the basic assumption is that the
forecasted variable will remain unchanged from the last observation through the forecast lead time. This is an inertial forecast for which, in contrast to a "mean value" forecast, some observation and transmission system is necessary
to provide real-time information. In most cases the water
management control centers have such a system, even in the
simplest form, at their disposal. Therefore, an inertial
forecast is available almost everywhere with no additional
investment, and it can be used as another alternative "zero
model" to which a forecasting model under consideration may
be related.

Both "zero models"—an inertial forecast model and a
"mean value" model—have a very essential drawback: they
prevent the possibility of a correct forecast. A "mean
value" forecast, by definition, is practically useless in
most operational cases. An inertial forecast, by definition, prevents changes through the forecast lead time.

An Approach to the Forecasting Model Estimation

Two main features of a "good" forecasting model may be
postulated:

(a) Small forecast errors, or more strictly, a low
probability of committing great errors

(b) Lack of correlation between the errors of successive in-time forecasts

From (a) follows a verification method—comparing the
empirical probability distribution plots of errors produced
by two forecasting models, i.e., a "zero model" and the model

in question. If both distributions appear to be normal then the MSEs of both models may be compared and the outcome will be quite sound.

However, most of the forecast errors' probability distributions of the models used in Poland are far from normal distributions (see Figures 4 and 5). The forecasts of hydrometeorological variables, such as flow volumes, flow hydrograph ordinates, 24-hour precipitation amount, mean daily wind speed, etc., show the nonnormal error probability distribution plots with strong curvature in the great errors interval. This means that the probability of committing great errors in both underestimating and overestimating is far greater than that deducted from the normal distribution having the same value of MSE. Another feature of the studied errors' distributions is their generally moderate asymmetry.

Taking these features into consideration one must be cautious in drawing a conclusion about the forecast efficiency estimation based on examination of MSEs, mean absolute, mean relative errors, and similar criteria. A conclusion may be accepted only when both compared forecasting models show similar error probability distributions. If the distributions are similar, an estimate E, equation (2), can be examined. The estimate E is a variation of an estimate discussed in Nash and Sutcliffe (1970). The E value is assumed to vary over the interval $(0,1)$, although it can happen that $E > 1$. The lower bound means a perfect forecast, whereas $E \geq 1$ indicates that the model forecast is equivalent to or worse than the one obtained from the "zero model". In Poland values $E = 0.6-0.8$ are regarded as indicators of a fair forecasting model performance, whereas $E = 0.2-0.3$ indicates a very good performance.

We now consider the (b) postulate, i.e., independence of errors of successive forecasts. It is obvious that a high correlation between these errors is unacceptable. Some distinction, however, should be made between one time-step and several time-steps ahead forecasts. If at the time origin t_0, we predict the state of a variable at the times $t_0 + \Delta t, \ t_0 + 2\Delta t, \ldots, t_0 + n\Delta t$, then we consider an n-steps ahead forecast, i.e., flow hydrograph. Usually, the forecast error increases as n increases. These errors are mutually correlated and for such a case, (b) is not feasible. On the other hand, for the one time-step ahead and for the successive n-steps ahead forecasts, the forecast errors are uncorrelated. To verify this a comparison of the error autocorrelation functions of two models can be made. Since the error probability distributions are nonnormal, the autocorrelation functions should be computed after normalization of the error probability distributions.

An examination of the error autocorrelation is a good tool for improving the forecasting model. If autocorrelation of errors exists, then the model performance can be improved without changing the model structure and as a result, a decrease in the errors as well as their autocorrelation can be obtained.

If a model decreases the probability of the great error commitment and at the same time lowers the errors autocorrelation, it is certainly better than the mean value or inertial model or any previous model. In a case where one criterion is improving and another deteriorating, the ultimate estimation should be performed together with an analysis of the whole forecast response process and its overall efficiency.

REFERENCES

Boliński, E., T. Piwecki, and J. Żelaziński (1974) The mathematical simulation model for the Soła River flow forecasting. Journal of Meteorology and Water Management 2(3).

Bobiński, E., T. Piwecki, and J. Żelaziński (1975) The mathematical simulation model for the Soła and Dunajec Rivers real-time flow forecasting. Proceedings of the International Symposium and Workshops on the Application of Mathematical Models in Hydrology and Water Resources Systems, Bratislava. IAHS Publication No. 115. Washington, D.C.: IAHS.

Bobiński, E., T. Piwecki, and J. Żelaziński (1976) Real-Time Hydrological Forecasting Systems in Poland. Paper presented at IIASA, Laxenburg, Austria, 18 to 20 October.

Bobiński, E., T. Piwecki, and J. Żelaziński (1977) Real-Time Hydrological Forecasting Systems in Poland. Paper presented at the Second UNESCO/WMO Meeting on Hydrological Problems in Europe, Brussels, 19 to 22 September.

Bobiński, E., and J. Żelaziński (1977) A River Stage and Depth Forecast System for the Lower Vistula Downstream from Włocławek. Paper presented at the Ninth Conference of Danube Countries on Hydrologic Forecasts, Budapest, 5 to 10 September (in Russian).

Garrick, M., C. Cunnane, and J.E. Nash (1978) A criterion of efficiency for rainfall-runoff models. Journal of Hydrology 36(3/4):375-381.

Nash, J.E., and J.V. Sutcliffe (1970) River flow forecasting through conceptual models. Part 1—A discussion of principles. Journal of Hydrology 10:282-290.

Piwecki, T., and R. Szymkiewicz (1974) A linear model of a flow routing. Arch. Hydrotechniki 4 (in Polish).

60

Szymkiewicz, R. (1976) A non-linear model of a flow routing. Arch. Hydrotechniki 1 (in Polish).

Szymkiewicz, R. (1978) A mathematical model of the river stage and flow forecast downstream of the hydropower station. Arch. Hydrotechniki 2 (in Polish).

World Meteorological Organization (WMO) (1975) Operational Hydrology Report No. 7. Intercomparison of Conceptual Models Used in Operational Hydrological Forecasting. WMO Report No. 429. Geneva.

OPERATIONAL HYDROLOGICAL FORECASTING BY CONCEPTUAL MODELS IN SWEDEN

S. Bergström

BACKGROUND

The economic consequences of the discharge fluctuations from Swedish rivers are substantial. About 60 percent of the total demand for electric energy is met by hydroelectric power. The power plants rely on the proper operation of reservoirs. Thus, hydrologic forecasts are important.

Flooding is a problem not immediately associated with Sweden. However, intense spring floods, such as the one in 1977, can cause heavy damage and costs for the society. Therefore, flood forecasting is of particular interest in river areas, where the damping effect of lakes is small. During extremely dry summers, such as the summer of 1976, forecasting is important for water supply planning in certain areas.

Since 1972 the Swedish Meteorological and Hydrological Institute (SMHI) has been engaged in the development of a conceptual runoff model suitable for operational forecasting and for other applications under Scandinavian conditions. The model is now in operation in 10 catchments in Sweden, and forecasts are issued regularly during spring and on some occasions during autumn and winter. The work is financed almost entirely by river regulation companies and local authorities in the river basins concerned. At present, the SMHI has no public hydrological forecasting service.

MODEL STRUCTURE AND CALIBRATION

Due to limitations in the available data base, a very simple model structure had to be accepted. By the end of 1975 a model was developed and applied experimentally to 11 catchments in Sweden and Norway. The results justified proceeding with its operational use. The model was named the

61

"HBV-model", after the section of the SMHI in which it was developed. A general outline of the model structure is shown in Figure 1. More detailed presentations have been made by Bergström and Forsman (1973) and Bergström (1976).

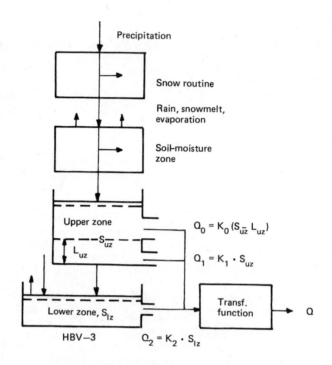

FIGURE 1   Structure of the HBV-model.

The structure of the model can be separated into three main components:

(1)   A snow accumulation and ablation routine based on a degree/day approach and individual computations in 10 elevation zones.

(2)   A soil-moisture accounting routine based on values of potential evaporation that are reduced to actual evaporation according to the present soil-moisture state. The present soil-moisture state is also a determining factor for the response of the model to input in the form of snowmelt or rain.

(3)   A response function with three near-linear components and a schematic time-area transformation.

The model is run on a daily basis with daily mean air temperatures, daily totals of precipitation, and monthly standard values of potential evaporation computed for a 30-year normal period.

The HBV-model is indeed a very simple conceptual runoff model. Detailed studies of the model's sensitivity to changes in its empirical coefficients were made in order to restrict the model's complexity. Therefore, the model is also comparatively easy to understand and handle and requires only small computer facilities.

The model has 13 empirical coefficients (parameters) which have to be estimated during its calibration. Many of these parameters have, however, proved to vary little from catchment to catchment. This simplifies the calibration procedure markedly. Calibration is based on subjective visual inspection of plotted hydrographs and is supported by a sum-of-squares criterion of fit. Normally, less than 20 test runs are needed if the model is calibrated by an experienced hydrologist.

APPLICATIONS FOR OPERATIONAL FORECASTING

In the spring of 1978 the HBV-model was in operation for forecasting in 10 catchments in Sweden. Catchment sizes, number of climate stations, and main purposes of the forecasts are shown in Table 1. Locations of the catchments are shown in Figure 2. An example of the model's performance is given in Figure 3.

DATA COLLECTION AND PROCESSING

When operating the HBV-model we rely on the ordinary network of meteorological stations in Sweden. The data from the major part of this network are reported to SMHI on a monthly basis. Therefore, special arrangements have been made for the hydrological forecasting project to collect data by telephone whenever needed. So far no automatic data collection and processing system is in operation, but work is in progress to minimize the amount of human interaction as far as possible. It is strongly felt that data collection and processing problems can easily limit the capacity of a forecasting service. The development of efficient systems is therefore of utmost importance.

UPDATING THE MODEL

Updating the model means running the model with the latest meteorological and hydrological data and preparing it for a forecast. If the computed discharge values deviate from the recorded ones on the day of the forecast, the persistence of the errors will disturb the forecast. This is also the case if the model is run during a snowmelt period but had not been run during the previous snowmelt. Thus the forecasts are made on the basis of a biased snow budget.

TABLE 1   Operational applications of the HBV-model in 1978.

River	Catchment	Size (km²)	Number of precipitation stations	Number of temperature stations	Main purpose
St. Luleälv	Porjus	2,863	4	2	regulation for power production
Ångermanälven	Kultsjön	1,109	3	1	regulation for power production
Ångermanälven	Malgomaj	1,862	3	1	regulation for power production
Ångermanälven	Ströms Vattudal	3,851	4	2	regulation for power production
Ljusnan	Svegsjön	5,860	5	5	regulation for power production
Dalälven	Trängslet	4,483	5	3	regulation for power production
Dalälven	Stadarforsen	4,136	5	2	regulation for power production
Svartån	Karlslund	1,284	7	4	flood forecasting
Emån	Blankaström	3,700	6	5	flood forecasting
Tidan	Moholm	1,172	6	4	flood forecasting

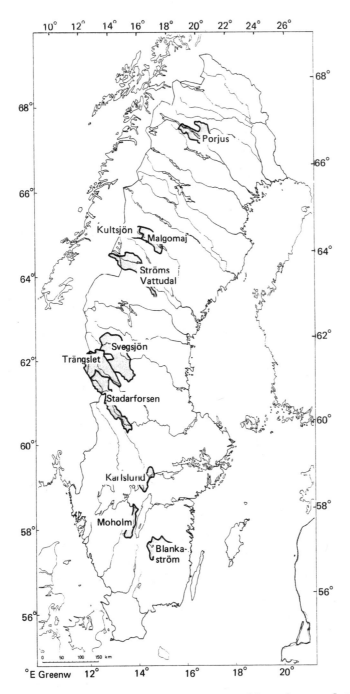

FIGURE 2   Locations of operational applications of the HBV-
model in Sweden.

66

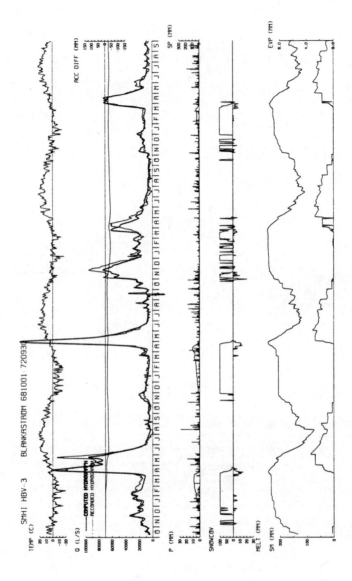

FIGURE 3 Example of the performance of the HBV-model in Blankaström. TEMP is air temperature
(°C); Q is discharge (l/s); ACC DIFF is accumulated difference between computed and
observed discharge (mm); P is areal precipitation (mm); SP is computed areal snowpack (mm water equivalent); SNOWCOV is computed snow covered area (%); MELT is computed snowmelt (mm); SM is computed soil-moisture state (mm); EVP is computed actual
evaporation (mm).

In order to avoid these sources of errors, the model is adjusted to the latest discharge values before a forecast is issued. This can, of course, be done in many different ways. We have chosen to adjust input data during the updating period until the observed hydrograph and the computed hydrograph are in close agreement. During snowmelt periods, updating is generally based on temperature corrections, but sometimes the latest precipitation values can be subject to adjustments. The advantages of this method are that it is easy to handle and to understand and that it takes into account the adjustments in all the different storages of the model simultaneously.

The updating procedure has so far been run manually with subjective decisions of which meteorological variable to adjust. This part of the forecasting procedure requires a high degree of hydrological judgment and experience and is therefore difficult to handle by an automatic algorithm. An example of a proper updating is shown in Figure 4.

FORECASTING PROCEDURES

The three main types of forecasts are given below.

(1) Short-range forecasts: these are mainly based on meteorological forecasts over 5 days but are sometimes supplemented by alternative simulations with different weather conditions.

(2) Forecasts of remaining spring flood volumes: these are based on alternative simulations using historical recorded climate series starting from the actual snow, soil, and runoff conditions as computed to date by the model.

(3) Forecasts of estimation of risks of high floods: alternative simulations described under (2) are made and the simulated peaks are studied to estimate the risk of flooding. Sometimes these simulations of peaks are based on the conditions in the model at the end of a short-range forecast.

An example of computer output from forecasts of the two latter types is shown in Figure 5. Each of the plotted hydrographs represents a simulation based on the updated state of the model and a recorded climate series for 1 previous year. The simulations thus provide us with alternative forecasts that can be used for the estimation of probabilities. The last simulation is made with zero precipitation during the period in order to arrive at an absolute minimum forecast. This simulation is normally excluded from the statistical analysis of the simulations.

68

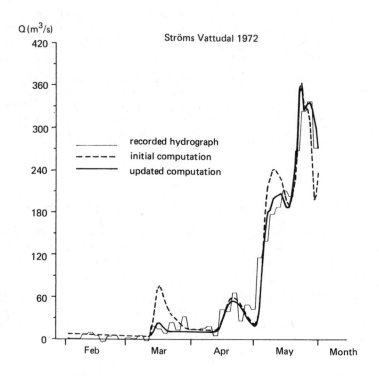

Q(m³/s)
420
360
300
240
180
120
60
0

Ströms Vattudal 1972

——— recorded hydrograph
— — — initial computation
——— updated computation

Feb   Mar   Apr   May   Month

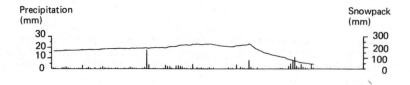

Precipitation
(mm)
30
20
10
0

Snowpack
(mm)
300
200
100
0

FIGURE 4   Example of the effect of the updating routine
during a snowmelt season.

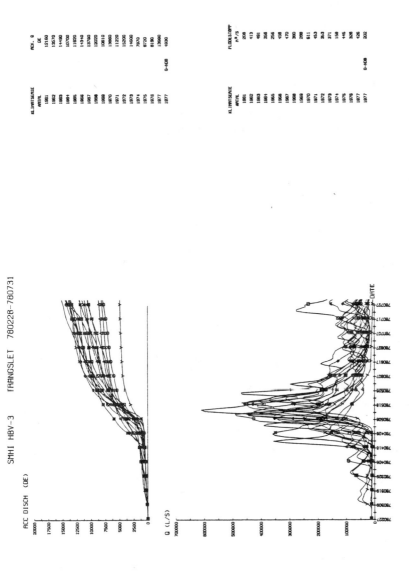

FIGURE 5   Example of long-range forecasts of remaining inflow (ACC DISCH) and flood peaks (Q) by simulation with 17 climate series in Trängslet. The eighteenth simulation is based on the temperatures in 1977 and zero precipitation.

70

RESULTS

In 1977 and 1978 forecasts by the HBV-model were issued on 133 occasions in the 10 catchments shown in Figure 2. On most of these occasions both short-range [type (1)] and long-range [types (2) and (3)] forecasts were produced, although some river regulation companies were interested only in long-range forecasts of volume. On a few occasions only short-range forecasts were issued. Some of the forecasts are evaluated below.

Short-range Forecasting

Figure 6 shows the results of the short-range forecasts of inflow to Lake Sveg (Svegsjön) during the spring of 1977. As can be seen, the model, supported by good meteorological forecasts, managed to predict the start of the spring flood and followed the development of the flood fairly well.

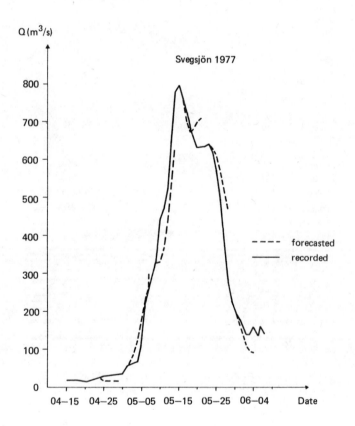

FIGURE 6   Summary of the short-range forecasts of the inflow to Svegsjön in 1977.

Forecasts of Remaining Spring Flood Volumes

Figure 7 shows a summary of the forecasts of remaining local inflow to Porjus in 1977. The forecasted period is from the date of the forecast until the end of June. Each vertical line represents one forecast with its minimum, mean, and maximum among the simulations. (The simulation with zero precipitation is excluded.) The earliest forecasts were the most accurate, while a bias in the snow accumulation of the model caused an overestimation of the remaining inflow for the last forecasts.

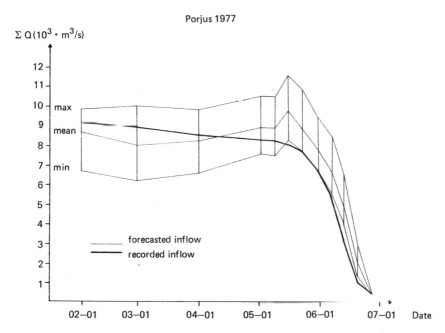

FIGURE 7   Summary of the long-range forecasts of the remaining inflow to Porjus from the date of the forecast to the end of June 1977. Each forecast is based on seven simulations.

It is important to note that a close agreement between the mean forecast and the actual outfall, as shown in Figure 7, does not always indicate a good forecasting model. If, for example, the period following the forecast is exceptionally dry, the forecast will be an overestimation if the model is good. The most efficient way of telling whether the deviation from the forecast is caused by the model or by extreme weather conditions is to run the model with actual input data for the period in question. A poor model performance can then be revealed by comparing the recorded hydrograph with the computed hydrograph.

Estimation of Risks of High Floods

The estimations of risks of high floods in Stadarforsen based on forecasts of type (3) (excluding the zero precipitation simulation) are summarized in Figure 8. As can be followed in the figure, there was an increasing risk during the spring caused by abundant precipitation and late snowmelt. The highest peak lies within the 50 percent limit for four of the last five forecasts. The second flood peak, which caused some damage in the river basin, was the result of a combination of intense rainfall and snowmelt, i.e., rather extreme conditions.

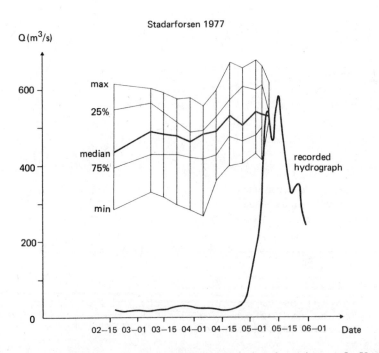

FIGURE 8   Summary of the long-range estimation of flood risks in Stadarforsen in 1977. Each forecast is based on 16 simulations.

Computer and Manpower Requirements

As stated, the HBV-model is a relatively simple model requiring only moderate computer facilities. It was developed on a SAAB-D22 computer and later transferred to a SAAB-D23. It is now on a UNIVAC 1100-21 at SMHI. A 4-year test run period of the model on the UNIVAC requires central processing unit (CPU) time on the order of 80 seconds. The simple structure makes it possible to use a desk calculator for shorter computations. At SMHI a Hewlett Packard 9821 with plotter is used for updating the model provided the period between updates has not been longer than a few weeks. Currently the hydrological forecasting system at SMHI is being revised, and in the future all computations and data handling will be made by the UNIVAC computer. During the most intense forecasting periods in spring, 2-3 hydrologists are engaged in forecasting. They are supported by one assistant who collects data by telephone.

Cost-Benefit

The cost of calibration of the HBV-model when made on contract is on the order of 60,000 Swedish crowns (US$13,000, 1978). The figure varies depending on the amount of data to be handled and on the complexity of the particular catchment. The cost for one forecast is also variable and depends on the number of meteorological stations, the length of the updating period, and the type of forecast. A realistic figure is around 1,000 Swedish crowns per forecast (US$220, 1978).

The costs for calibration and operation of the model are small compared to the value of the water, which today is leaving the hydroelectric power plants through the spillways instead of through the turbines. It is, however, very complicated to estimate exactly how much the losses could be reduced by better hydrologic forecasts. This question was discussed in Sweden by the VAST-group on hydrological models (VAST 1978). A very tentative estimation made by the VAST-group for the Dalälven River indicated that an average gain of 20 GWh per year might be a realistic figure for this particular river. The hydroelectric power production in Dalälven represents approximately one-fifteenth of the total Swedish hydroelectric power production.

This cost-benefit analysis is far from complete and can only serve as an example of the potential benefit of reliable hydrologic forecasts. The figures indicate, however, that the costs of model calibration and operation are small compared with the potential of increased hydroelectric power production.

A cost-benefit analysis for forecasts of high water levels and floods is even more difficult. It is, however, clear that the 1977 spring flood in central Sweden caused damage in the tens of millions of Swedish crowns and that some of the private property destroyed could have been saved if detailed forecasts were at hand for the critical rivers. Flood forecasting for the public is, however, not only a question of cost-benefit in a monetary sense, it also has a psychological aspect which must not be neglected.

74

REFERENCES

Bergström, S. (1976) Development and application of a conceptual runoff model for Scandinavian catchments. Hydrologi och Oceanografi RHO 7 (in Swedish).

Bergström, S. and A. Forsman (1973) Development of a conceptual deterministic rainfall-runoff model. Nordic Hydrology 4(3).

VAST (1978) Hydrologic Models. Stockholm: R&D Unit of the Power Stations Association.

THE RIVER DEE REGULATION SCHEME: OPERATIONAL EXPERIENCE OF ON-LINE HYDROLOGICAL SIMULATION

A.O. Lambert

THE RIVER DEE REGULATION SYSTEM

The flow of the River Dee headwaters in North Wales is partially controlled by three multipurpose river regulating reservoirs with a total storage capacity of $160 \times 10^6 m^3$ (Figure 1). One single-purpose direct supply reservoir (Alwen) of significant size ($15 \times 10^6 m^3$) is also sited in the headwaters. The total reservoired catchment area is $310 \ km^2$, being about 17 percent of the total catchment area of $1,816 \ km^2$ to the tidal limit of the Dee at Chester; however, because of the heavier annual rainfall in the uplands, about 36 percent of the annual average river flow at Chester arises from the reservoired catchment areas.

The objectives of the Dee system of multipurpose regulating reservoirs are as follows:

- Sustaining continuous river abstractions up to $10 \ m^3$/sec for potable and industrial use in Merseyside, North Wales, and Cheshire, in drought sequences of up to 1 in 100 years' severity

- Mitigating flooding in the Dee Valley

- Safeguarding valuable game fisheries (migratory Salmonidae

- Developing recreational use of reservoirs

- Generating hydroelectric power at Llyn Celyn

In 1966, the Water Resources Board (since 1974 the Water Research Centre) initiated a long-term research project aimed at improving the efficiency of operation of river regulation systems in the UK. The River Dee in North Wales, being the most significantly regulated upland river in the UK, with

76

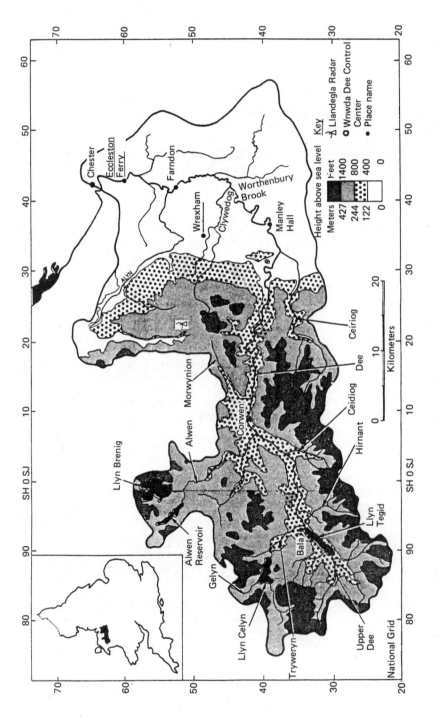

FIGURE 1 Topographical map of the River Dee Basin. Reproduced from Central Water Planning Unit (1977) with permission from the Controller of Her Majesty's Stationery Office.

integrated multipurpose operation of several large surface
reservoirs (see Figure 1), was selected as a natural testing
area for development of new methods of hydrological modeling,
real-time prediction and control, together with associated
instrumentation and telemetry systems.

Most aspects of the first 10 years of the Dee research
project, together with an extensive bibliography, are presented in Central Water Planning Unit (1977). This report
is recommended to anyone wishing to benefit from the experience gained from the Dee project.

In keeping with the stated objectives of this Symposium,
namely, that emphasis be on implementation and use of mathematical models including logistics and costs and benefits
(rather than on full descriptions of the models and their
developments), minimal reference is made to the detailed
features of the Dee system and the models used; wherever
such reference is essential in order to support a major conclusion, the detailed features are provided in the Appendix
to this paper.

The Welsh Water Authority has retained for operational
use many of the high capital cost installations (such as the
telemetry scheme) that were introduced to the Dee area as
part of the research project. While this paper does provide
some data on the costs and benefits of operating such installations, the principal benefits of the research project which
are presented here relate to experience gained on the logistics of real-time hydrological modeling, the choice of model
structure and its fundamental effect on data input requirements, the relative importance of measured and forecast rainfall, and similar matters. As one of the first generation
of sophisticated on-line hydrological forecasting systems,
Dee's major contribution is in the documentation of 3 years'
operational experience of real-time hydrological forecasting,
including the notable drought of 1976.

In the development and refinement of Dee system operation over the last decade, hydrological forecasting models
(used for short-term decisions) represent only a limited
part of the range of mathematical modeling techniques which
have been used to improve the management of the system.
Long-term policies based on seasonal reservoir control rules
and operational strategies for sharing regulation releases
between reservoirs with differing refill characteristics are
also essential; an off-line computer-based simulation of the
entire Dee system (to a 1-day time increment) has been developed and has proved invaluable in defining the precise yields
of the system and the scheme operation over historic or synthetic multiyear time sequences. Such models are not further
described in this paper.

REAL-TIME FLOOD FORECASTING

When the Institute of Hydrology was subcontracted by the Water Research Centre in 1974 to produce hydrological forecasting and telemetry system programs for the Dee, they recognized the fact that real-time operational forecasting presented quite different problems to those of non-real-time simulation. In a real-time system, data on rainfall, river flows, and reservoir levels are being continually received and updated at a control center, while varying forecasts of possible future rainfall for up to 24 hours ahead may be provided at irregular intervals. The reliability of valid data telemetered from outstations cannot reasonably be expected to exceed 90 percent without excessive investment in equipment duplication or standby installations. A robust hydrological model requiring limited data, designed for frequent updating, and capable (if necessary) of commencing operation partway through a storm event, is required for real-time operation.

The Inflow-Storage-Outflow (ISO) rainfall-runoff model (Lambert 1972) was preferred to the DISPRIN model (Moore 1975) which, although considered the most realistic hydrologically, was felt to be unduly complex for real-time work since it has between 11 and 23 parameters. The unit hydrograph/catchment losses model of the Institute of Hydrology (Institute of Hydrology 1975), which was suitable only for modeling complete flood events, was also considered unsuitable for real-time operation. The ISO model uses the water balance equation and incorporates a "route and lag" process, assuming a unique relationship between catchment storage and rate of river flow (outflow); since subcatchment outflows are continually telemetered to the control center, such basic river flow information supersedes the need for specific soil-moisture storage accounting procedures within the hydrologic model.

A brief description of the ISO model is given in the Appendix to this paper. If the storage/outflow relationship happens to be logarithmic or linear, it is possible to produce a set of predictive equations incorporating a single routing parameter. In most cases, however, the storage/outflow relationship will be complex and successive approximation techniques may be used to solve the water balance and storage/outflow relationships; alternatively the single routing parameter may be allowed to vary with rate of river flow.

The most important feature of the ISO model, which makes it eminently suitable for real-time flood forecasting, is that a subcatchment runoff rate after time period T may be predicted using only the initial runoff rate, the assumed rainfall rate over the time period T, and knowledge of the storage/outflow relationship (or the single routing parameter if appropriate). The method is used recursively to calculate successive points on subcatchment hydrographs, using $T = \frac{1}{2}$ hour.

It is necessary to incorporate a time-shift constant L which is determined from subcatchment analysis. L represents the amount of time by which calculated outflow hydrographs (derived from instantaneous routing of rainfall through catchment storage) have to be shifted to match the corresponding subcatchment runoff hydrographs as measured at the tributary gaging stations located at the downstream end of the subcatchments.

The relatively simple ISO model has been proved, by non-real-time simulation of past rainfall events (see Figure 2), to be a reasonably reliable means of representing the rainfall-runoff process during wet catchment conditions for the Dee area. These analyses also showed that the subcatchment time shifts L are remarkably short, being $2\frac{1}{2}$ hours for upland subcatchment areas of the order of 185 km^2, and only 1 hour for a 54 km^2 tributary of Llyn Tegid. For real-time forecasting of tributary flows, up to time L in the future, recorded rainfall (over $\frac{1}{2}$-hour intervals) for the past L hours is used as the model input. For tributary flow forecasts more than L hours ahead, forecast rainfall must be used.

The important conclusions arising from the development and real-time application of the ISO model may be itemized as follows:

(a) *Defining the relative importance of measured, as opposed to predicted, rainfall, in flood forecasting:* The ISO model demonstrates, possibly more clearly than most hydrologic models, that measured rainfall can provide a direct forecasting benefit (in terms of rising subcatchment river flows) no greater than the maximum subcatchment time shift L. If, as in the case of the Dee, L is small in relation to the time period required for operational control or flood-warning purposes, provision must also be made for using rainfall forecasts (in addition to measured rainfall) as input to the hydrologic model. The Dee system has only five telemetering rain gages (not located specifically to measure subcatchment rainfall) and the experimental weather radar installation (which was successful in real-time measurement of areal rainfall) has been moved elsewhere in the UK, where it will be of greater national benefit.

(b) *Defining the requirements for operational telemetered hydrometric data:* The ISO model assumes that the measured rate of subcatchment river flow represents the final result of all hydrologic processes acting upon the subcatchment up to L hours ago. If L is small, then evaporation during time L (in temperate climates) will be insignificant, and there is no requirement for telemetering climate stations for assessment of measured evaporation. By contrast, forecast evaporation over any future period may need to be input to the hydrologic model. As mentioned, forecasts of rainfall over the next 6-24 hours are of equal importance to measured rainfall on the Dee system. Since rate of river flow is the most fundamental parameter of the ISO model, it is not surprising that there are no fewer than 14 Dee outstations

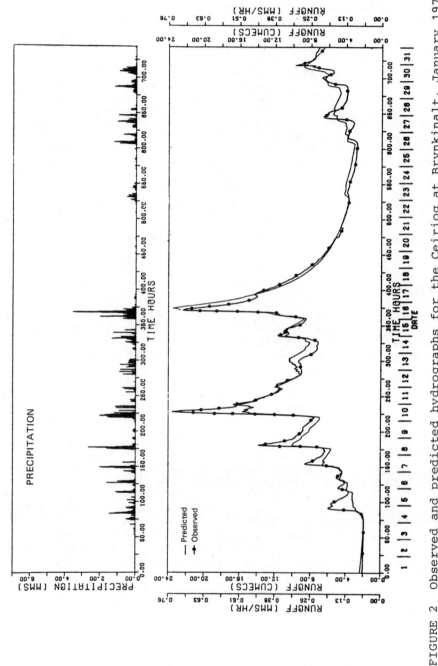

FIGURE 2 Observed and predicted hydrographs for the Ceiriog at Brynkinalt, January 1974. Reproduced from Central Water Planning Unit (1977) with permission from the Controller of Her Majesty's Stationery Office.

providing high quality telemetered data on river flows (in
addition to four outstations measuring the principal reservoir levels). Seven of these river gaging stations, particularly those on the main river, are purpose-built high accuracy river gaging structures; there is one ultrasonic gaging station and six river sections with informal control
sections and relatively stable stage-discharge relationships. Note also the importance of having a representative
subcatchment measuring rate of inflow to the major reservoired catchment areas. This is particularly necessary for
forecasting reservoir inflows using the ISO model, as the
estimated rate of reservoir inflow from measured incremental
reservoir storage changes is not sufficiently accurate or
consistent to use as input to the ISO model.

(c) *Defining the accuracy requirements for hydrologic
models used for on-line flood forecasting:* When a hydrologic model is used on-line for forecasting subcatchment
behavior from accurate input data (measured rainfall over
the last L hours or rainfall over a future period which can
be forecast with near certainty), the accuracy of the model
in simulating catchment behavior must be adequate for the
requirements of the particular flood-forecasting application.
When the model input is a quantitative precipitation forecast
(QPF) with inherent random errors, there is little justification for seeking to develop the accuracy of the hydrologic
model to a degree of refinement that is significantly
greater than the accuracy of the QPFs. To put this into
perspective, it is thought possible that scientific studies
of UK rainfall systems, based on deterministic rules and
radar-based rainfall data, will bring 6-hour QPFs within
an accuracy factor of 50 percent. The relatively simple
ISO model, subject to some minor refinements, has proved
of acceptable accuracy in real-time flood forecasting on
the Dee system, using both measured and forecast rainfall
data. Operational experience has shown that flood peak
forecasts for the lower Dee are generally within ±10 percent
of actual values.

(d) *Defining the requirements for operational presentation of river management data:* The river manager at a control center, being continually responsible for taking decisions on releases from reservoirs and issuing flood warnings
during a flood period, can suffer from the disadvantage of
too much data, which may be equally as problematical as too
little data. The computer-controlled telemetry system and
the four principal methods of data presentation are summarized later in this paper. For flood prediction purposes,
based on measured rainfall (sometimes supplemented by entering a QPF into the computer), the preferred form of data
presentation for the predicted hydrographs of river flows
and reservoir storages (for the next 24-48 hours) is via
color television monitors. This form of visual presentation
is rapidly assimilable by the river manager, and the somewhat moderate accuracy of presentation is consistent with

the fact that the hydrograph forecasts are partly based upon a forecast rainfall pattern that is unlikely to occur precisely as predicted.

The conclusions given in (a)-(d) clearly demonstrate that all the important investment decisions in an on-line flood forecasting system (computing capacity at control center, reliability of telemetry scheme, type and number of hydrometric outstations, data requirements, and requirement for QPFs) depend fundamentally on the choice of hydrologic model and the way in which the model simulates the rainfall-runoff process. This makes the correct choice of model the most important single investment decision from which all other investment decisions naturally follow.

Consideration of flood-forecasting models is of course incomplete without channel routing models. The Dee system incorporates, on line, Price's Variable Parameter Diffusion model for the upper and middle reaches of the Dee. The lower Dee is modeled as two quasi-linear channels with linear reservoirs in series. Schematic diagrams of the complete on-line modeling system and the main components of the hydrological forecasting model are given in Figures 3 and 4, respectively.

Real-Time Low-Flow Forecasting

The principal objective of low-flow regulation on the Dee is to maintain a prescribed flow at a control point on the lower Dee. The prescribed flow must be sufficient to guarantee a design minimum residual flow to the estuary and to permit continuous abstractions between the control point and the tidal limit. At present about two-thirds of the prescribed flow is abstracted, leaving one-third as residual flow to the Dee estuary. During dry weather up to 85 percent of the prescribed flow consists of regulation releases from the reservoirs.

It takes up to $1\frac{1}{2}$ days for regulation releases to travel the 100 km from the reservoirs to the lower Dee control point under low-flow river conditions. This travel time rules out the option of using QPFs for forecasting future variations of low flows, particularly because any under-release of regulation water (in anticipation of future rainfall which might not occur) could result in a serious deficiency of residual flow to the estuary, further resulting in water quality problems and possible saline intrusion at the abstraction points during high tides.

All low-flow forecasting is therefore based on the application of mathematical models that are in turn based on recession curve analyses assuming zero rainfall. The operational problem consists of continually trying to predict, as accurately as possible, the rate of flow from the unreservoired catchment area up to $1\frac{1}{2}$ days ahead. Because the

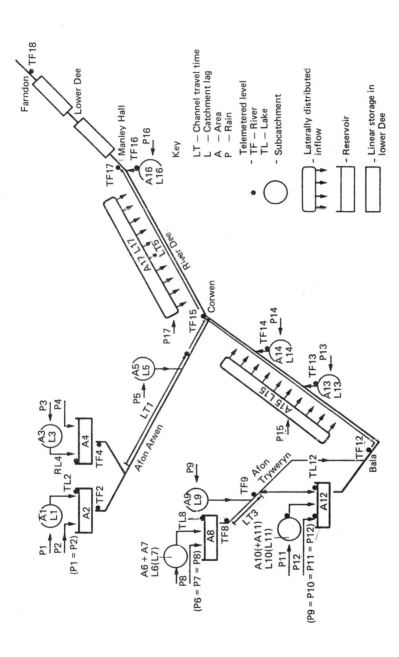

FIGURE 3   Schematic diagram of the River Dee model. Reproduced from Central Water Planning Unit (1977) with permission from the Controller of Her Majesty's Stationery Office.

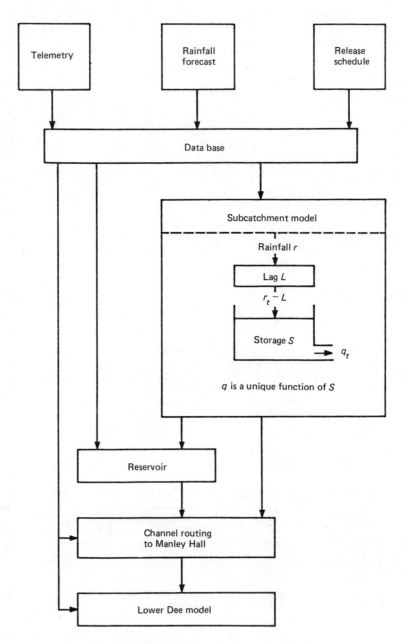

FIGURE 4   Main components of the hydrological forecasting
model including the ISO subcatchment model. Reproduced from Central Water Planning Unit (1977)
with permission from the Controller of Her
Majesty's Stationery Office.

substantial regulation releases are being constantly adjusted
and the regulation discharge hydrograph is modified by channel routing, it is essential in dry weather to operate an
on-line mathematical model that routes the regulation releases downriver and thereby continually calculates the
present values of regulation water at principal gaging stations downriver. Comparison with telemetered values of total
flow at these gaging stations enables inflow rates from the
uncontrolled middle and lower Dee catchments to be continually derived.

By on-line application of further mathematical models
representing the natural recession processes of the middle
and lower Dee catchments, the predicted component of flow
at the control point from the unreservoired catchment areas
in 1½ days' time is calculated and regularly output on hard
copy for the river manager at the control center. The on-
line prediction system has been developed to cope with the
regular occasions when the lower Dee control point is subject to unsteady flow conditions due to the hydraulic effect
of high tides.

This method of low-flow forecasting requires high capital investment in good quality river gaging stations at
reservoir outlets and on the main river, with accurate and
reliable stage-discharge relationships. The six gaging stations needed on the Dee for this method represent a capital
investment of approximately £200,000, with running costs of
the order of £5,000 per year. A telemetry scheme with appropriate computing capacity for the low-flow regulation
function only would represent a capital investment of the
order of £40,000, with an annual running cost of approximately £10,000.

At the start of the Dee Research Project, it was considered that excess regulation releases wasted due to inefficient forecasting of low flows might represent as much as
15 percent of the storage capacity provided. Operational
experience on the Dee system has shown that, using on-line
low-flow forecasting models, the true wastage in drought
summers on the Dee can be reduced to slightly less than 5
percent of regulation storage; the "saving" of 10 percent of
storage capacity represents a capital value of £3m, based on
the average cost of providing storage at the Dee reservoir
most recently constructed. Alternatively, the additional
safe yield of the system consequent upon the more efficient
use of storage could be calculated and given a monetary benefit value.

The actual cost-benefit situation on the Dee is more
complex than indicated by the simple presentation above, but
the quoted figures will perhaps be of general interest.

THE COMPUTER-CONTROLLED TELEMETRY/SIMULATION/FORECASTING SYSTEM

The operational system for control of the Dee Telemetry/ Simulation/Forecasting system is based upon a PDP 11/35 computer with 56K words of core memory and a backup disc of 1.2 megawords storage, programmed in FORTRAN 4, and sited at the Bala Control Centre. Data from 14 river gaging stations, four reservoir level stations, and five rain gages are commanded and temporarily stored by the computer every 30 minutes by GPO telephone, landline, and UHF radio system using repeater stations.

The following are the requirements of the system.

● The presentation of existing states of river flow, rainfall, and reservoir contents

● The retention by computer of hydrometric data over the past 24 hours, for forecasting river flows and reservoir contents

● The production of a printed record for as long as may be required in the evaluation of the system performance

Figure 5 helps to explain the Bala computer's function as a telemetry controller and data handler when the Llandegla Radar Station was operational. The prime functions were:

● The automatic calling or recalling of outstations

● The receipt, validation, scaling, and storage of data

● The printout of data in hydrometric engineering units, with date and time and the flagging of errors

● The presentation of the latest values from 10 outstations on a large diagram of the River Dee Basin

● The production of up to 12 inputs for a multipoint chart recorder

● The transmission of rainfall data from the rain gage cluster sites to the Llandegla Radar Station

● The presentation of a radar-derived rainfall map on a color video display

● The operation of a hydrologic model of the catchment

● The presentation of the output of the hydrologic model on a color video display. After every 30-minute scan, 24-hour forecasts of principal river flows and reservoir contents were automatically displayed, using measured rainfall only. QPFs could also be input by the operator at any time

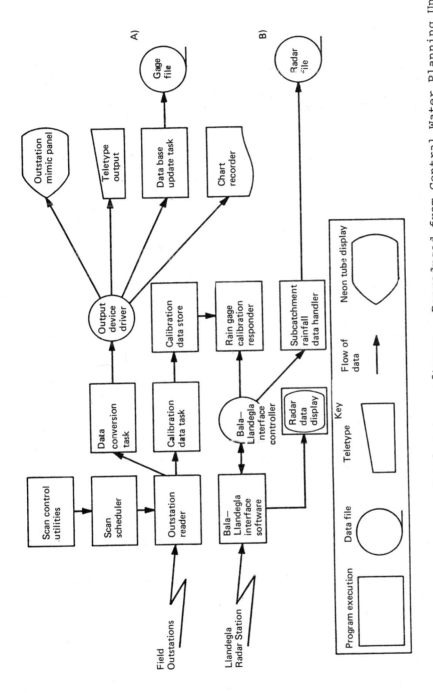

FIGURE 5   Major components of telemetry software.   Reproduced from Central Water Planning Unit (1977) with permission from the Controller of Her Majesty's Stationery Office.

in order to assess the effect of future rainfall on forecast river flows and reservoir levels.

The computer and its peripheral equipment are shown schematically in Figure 6. Attached to the core store is a range of input and output devices to control the machine, to receive data, and to display results in an easily assimilable way. The exchangeable disc input is used mainly to hold data and instructions for which there is insufficient capacity in the computer. The cassette tape unit is used to temporarily store information when transferring data between discs as is necessary whenever changes are made to any of the computer software.

The remaining inputs and outputs require an interface between the device and computer to send or accept information at the correct rate and in the correct form. The telemetry outstations are called by the computer through the station control unit. Data transfer between Bala and Llandegla was through rented line and PO modems.

At the Control Centre there are two teletypewriters, one used solely for outputting telemetry values and hard copy of forecasts, the other by the operator for inputting commands to the system. There is also a Texas 700 ASR which is used for recording telemetered values and information from the hydrologic model, including predictions. The remaining equipment includes a variety of special displays to assist the engineer in understanding the state of the system and comprises:

● A 12-track chart recorder, showing river stage and reservoir level

● A mimic panel of the river with digital display of river stage and reservoir level

● Two color television monitors. While the radar was operational, one was dedicated to displaying maps of radar-derived rainfall, the other was used for displaying hydrographs. Subsequently both have been used for displaying hydrographs.

The software in the Bala computer is under the control of a proven real-time systems executive (RSX-11M), which looks after all the problems of

● Disc-accessing (for both data and programs)

● Scheduling of programs at specific times or under specific circumstances

● Core and processor utilization so that the computer does not waste time waiting for an event to occur when there is other work it could do

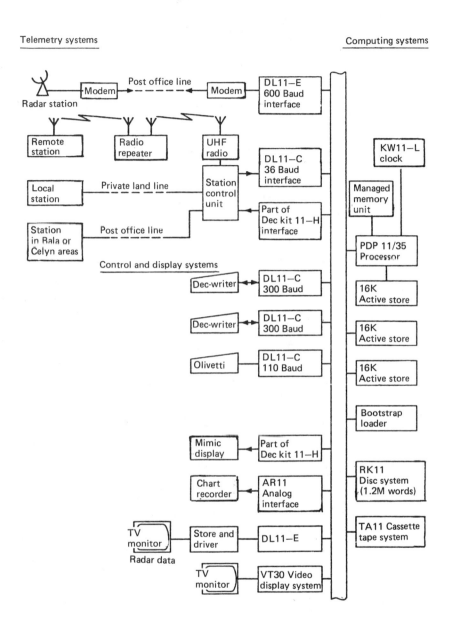

FIGURE 6   Block diagram of the complete system.   Reproduced from Central Water Planning Unit (1977) with permission from the Controller of Her Majesty's Stationery Office.

Wherever possible, the programs written for the computer at Bala were written in the high level FORTRAN language so that the operating staff could see more easily the functions and ramifications of any individual program within the system. While it could be argued that FORTRAN is not really a suitable language for real-time applications, it was chosen partly because there was no other acceptable alternative (CORAL 66 was not due to be available on the PDP 11 range until early 1976) and partly because by using FORTRAN the software could be developed on a variety of computers. Excluding the system software, the software in the Bala computer can be divided into three main areas: telemetry software, hydrologic model software, and display software.

In real-time forecasting the software performs a series of tasks, which are run sequentially. These tasks are

- Controlling acquisition of data through the telemetry

- Running the model

- Updating the data base

- Outputting the graphical displays

There is insufficient space within the core store of the computer for all tasks to be in core at once. It is therefore necessary that some tasks be introduced from disc store at the time of each forecasting run. Methods also have to be devised by which several tasks can act on the same data or by which one task can set up data to be used by another. The organization of the tasks and data files used to produce a hydrological forecast is shown in Figure 7.

The center of the system is the master data base that, at any time, contains recorded values of river stage and discharge, reservoir level, and rainfall for a period of 24 hours into the past. On occasions the master data base holds incomplete information when the computer fails or an outstation fails to report. There are tasks in the system that recognize such occurrences and that put estimates of missing values based on previously forecast values into the master data base. These estimates are used in place of measured values when the model is next run.

Further data files exist within the system. The gage file holds the latest telemetry input before it is put into the master data base. The model file holds some data from the master data base in a form that is acceptable to the hydrological forecasting model and also the forecast hydrographs for the next 24 hours. A further data file contains copies of the forecast hydrograph data for input to the graph generation program.

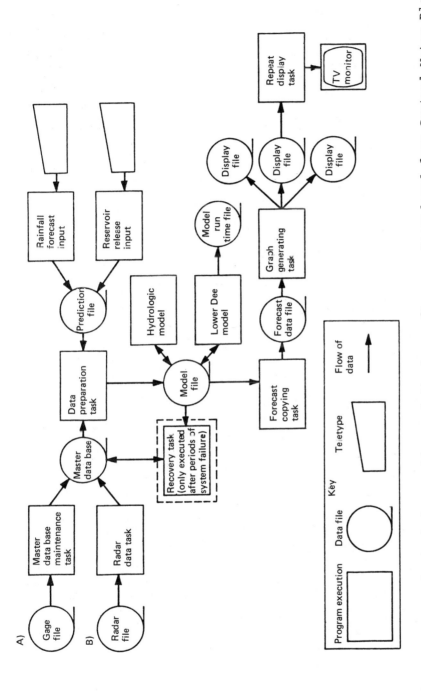

FIGURE 7 Hydrological forecasting and display software. Reproduced from Central Water Planning Unit (1977) with permission from the Controller of Her Majesty's Stationery Office

The tasks shown in Figure 7 are run to produce a hydrological forecast. The recovery task is run only after periods of system failure up to 6 hours in length to patch in missing data. The radar data task was initiated by the task which accepted data from Llandegla. The master data base maintenance task is run by the computer every 30 minutes and starts a sequence of actions in which the other hydrological and display tasks, except the reservoir release and rainfall forecast tasks, are run automatically. The last two tasks are run on demand and used to enter into the prediction file a series of intended reservoir releases and forecasts of rainfall. A list of the computer tasks which are run to produce hydrological forecasts is given in Table 1.

It is also possible to change values in the master data base itself by accessing the appropriate record by way of one of the utility programs. This action is necessary only when the computer system and an outstation have failed and if there is reason to believe that the default values were inadequate.

The Water Authority employs a full-time electronics engineer responsible for the maintenance of a small amount of special equipment at the control center and for all outstation equipment, including the radios but excluding the rented post office lines. The Authority seeks appropriate assistance for off-line repair of commercially manufactured items, and it was decided to use contract maintenance for the computer and its peripheral devices. As in any large telemetry system, items of equipment from different manufacturers are required to operate together. Therefore, clear interfaces were defined between equipment items. A manufacturer is not responsible for making his equipment work with another's equipment; this remains the responsibility of the Water Authority. A standby generator is provided at Bala to obviate a system "crash" caused by loss of mains power, which may last for a few minutes, a day, or longer. An inverter is also essential to provide a "smooth" mains supply to the computer. Regular technical support is given by the Institute of Hydrology on modifying and improving the system control programs.

The electronics engineer spends about 33 percent of his time visiting and maintaining outstations, including replacing defective equipment. The remainder of his time is spent at the control center, undertaking equipment repairs in the workshop or modifying and improving the system programs. Principal data stations are usually made operational within 24 hours of failure, but repairs on less important sites may have to wait for up to a week.

Only half a day's training is required to operate the facility of entering QPFs into the model on demand; restarting the computer after a complete system failure is also relatively simple. If the failure has been of short duration (up to 6 hours), the data base will not require modification,

TABLE 1 Computer tasks to produce hydrological forecasts.

Task	Frequency of running	Time of running
Software for Bala-Llandegla link	2-3 sec	
Telemetry scan and printout of data	30 min	On the hour and $\frac{1}{2}$-hour
Master data base maintenance	30 min	5 min after telemetry Starts automatically after the data base maintenance task
Hydrologic model	30 min or on demand	Starts automatically after the model finishes
Produce television display	30 min	
Ask Llandegla for radar-derived subcatchment rainfall totals	30 min	5 min before telenetry
Print error messages	30 min	10 min after telenetry
Print flow forecasts	1-6 h	12 min past the hour
Decide on season	24 h	0300 every day
Print master data base	24 h	0915 every day
Print rain gage reference levels and reassign zero to give daily rainfall totals	24 h	
Calibration scan	On demand from Llandegla	0900 every day
Entering forecasts of rainfall and reservoir release	On demand	
Change displayed hydrograph	On demand	
Run the recovery task	After system failure	
Change entry in master data base	Occasionally after system failure	

and the hydrological model will continue to produce reasonable forecasts. If, however, the system has been nonoperational for significantly more than 6 hours, the hydrological forecasts will be unreliable when the computer is restarted, unless the data base is deliberately manipulated by the operator to include actual river flows during the period of nonoperation; such manipulation requires detailed, specialist training. The hydrological forecasts are considered to be reasonably valid even if up to 50 percent of the telemetered data return is missing for short periods, or 20 percent for longer periods.

OPERATIONAL EXPERIENCE AND CONCLUSIONS

As a result of the Dee Research Project, the Welsh Water Authority now enjoys the benefits of a sophisticated telemetry system, with on-line hydrological simulation and forecasting capability, to assist in their multipurpose management of the River Dee system.

Operational experience has shown that it is advantageous to use relatively simple hydrologic models for on-line forecasting, the choice of models being specifically geared to the simulation problems requiring solution. In the case of the Dee, this philosophy has proceeded to the extent of utilizing entirely different mathematical models for low-flow and high-flow forecasting. The benefits of improved low-flow forecasting and more efficient river regulation arising from the use of mathematical models (channel routing and recession techniques) are relatively substantial on the Dee system. The telemetry and control system required for low-flow forecasting alone would require only six river outstations, compared to the 23 outstations of the present Dee scheme.

The on-line hydrological simulation for flood forecasting allows the river manager to make effective short-term use of existing flood control storage on the Dee and to issue reliable flood warnings to farmers, so that they may move their animals to higher ground. Because there are few communities in flood-prone locations in the Dee Valley, flooding does not carry heavy economic penalties. The reduction in flood costs that results from use of the on-line forecasting system, while not readily quantifiable in monetary terms, is not sufficient economic justification for the installation of a sophisticated telemetry and control system such as that which now exists on the Dee.

However, the flood-forecasting aspects of the Dee installation have resulted in significant benefits within the terms of the Dee Research Project. The research work on hydrologic models for real-time systems and the insights gained into the role of radar for rainfall measurement and prediction have been of great importance within the U.K. Insofar as the Welsh Water Authority has an obligation to control the river as efficiently as possible, there is no intention at present to significantly reduce the scope of the existing telemetry system now that the Dee Research Project is completed.

In trying to summarize the benefits of on-line hydrological simulation using mathematical models, with respect to the regulated River Dee, the inescapable conclusion is that the practical operation of the system demands the use of on-line mathematical models. The main questions relate to the economic justification of using ever more sophisticated models and associated telemetry schemes. The Dee experience should be useful in giving some guidance on the degree of sophistication that can be practically justified.

ACKNOWLEDGMENTS

Many organizations have contributed to the Dee Research Project and to the development of regulation of the River Dee. The author acknowledges his personal debt to all those whose work has been mentioned, implicitly or explicitly, in this paper. The paper expresses the personal views of the author.

The decade of research and development work in the Dee catchment area involved the following principal organizations: the Meteorological Office, Plessey Radar Ltd., the Institute of Hydrology, the Water Resources Board (until 31.3.74), the Dee and Clwyd River Authority (until 31.3.74), the Central Water Planning Unit (from 1.4.74), the Water Data Unit (from 1.4.74), the Water Research Centre (from 1.4.74), and the Welsh Water Authority (from 1.4.74).

REFERENCES

Central Water Planning Unit (1977) Dee Weather Radar and Real-Time Hydrological Forecasting Project Report, by the Steering Committee. Reading: Reading Bridge House.

Institute of Hydrology (1975) Flood Forecasting Report. Wallingford, Berkshire.

Lambert, A.O. (1972) Catchment models based on ISO-functions. J. Inst. Water Engineers 26:413-422.

Moore, R.J. (1975) DISPRIN—A Program Documentation. Internal Report. Marlow, Buckinghamshire: Water Research Centre.

APPENDIX

THE ISO MODEL—A BRIEF DESCRIPTION OF PRINCIPLES

The method assumes that a natural catchment area may be represented by a single unified natural storage S that controls the rate of river flow q, and that is intermittently replenished by inputs of rainfall at rates r considered constant over discrete time intervals; evaporation may be considered mathematically as negative rainfall. No subdivision of river flow into components (surface runoff, interflow, baseflow, etc.) is assumed.

The storage/outflow graph is derived from analysis of recession events. It is typically nonlinear

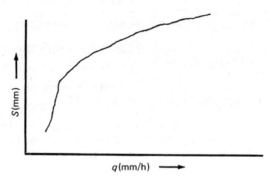

It is assumed that each subcatchment has a unique storage/outflow relationship. If the S/q relationship is complex and cannot be accurately represented by equations of the type

$$S = K_q + a$$

or

$$S = k \log_e q + b$$

or

$$S = k \log_e (q - c) + d$$

then the hydrological model uses the technique of successive approximation. For example, the water balance equation for a time increment T may be expressed as $\Delta S = R - Q$, where ΔS, R, and Q are respectively the storage change, rainfall, and runoff (mm) all over time period T. Assume a linear change in river flow from q_n (initial flow rate, mm/h) to q_{n+T} (final flow rate after time T); over the same time period, storage changes from S_n to S_{n+T}. Thus the water balance equation becomes

$$S_{n+T} - S_n = R - (q_n + q_{n+T})T/2$$

From any known initial values of storage S_n and outflow q_n and a rainfall input R over time T, the final values of storage and outflow are obtained by finding (by successive approximation using the storage/outflow relationship) the values of S_{n+T} and q_{n+T} that satisfy the above equation. The method is then used recursively to define successive points, T hours apart, on complete hydrographs.

If the S/q relationship can be approximated by an equation, such as

$$S = k \log_e q + b \qquad (k \text{ in mm})$$

then

$$dS/dq = k/q$$

and the water balance equation may be written as $dS/dt = (r - q)$. Combining these equations:

$$dq/dt = (dS/dt)(dq/dS) = (r - q)q/k$$

which may be integrated over time period T (assuming r constant) to give

$$q_{n+T} = q_n \left\{ e^{-rT/k} + (q_n + r)(1 - e^{-rT/k}) \right\}^{-1} \qquad \text{for } r \neq 0$$

and

$$q_{n+T} = q_n (1 + q_n T/k)^{-1} \qquad \text{for } r = 0$$

Once q_{n+T} has been calculated, the volume of runoff Q during the time period T may also be calculated from the equation

$$Q = rT - k \log_e(q_{n+T}/q_n)$$

It is possible to partially differentiate the equations (for $r \neq 0$ and $r = 0$) in order to calculate the percentage error in estimating q_{n+T} for any percentage error in q_n, k, or r. This is a most useful facility for sensitivity testing.

If parts of the S/q relationship are linear $S = Kq + a$ (K in hours), the equations become $dq/dt = (r - q)/K$.

$$q_{n+T} = q_n \left[e^{-T/K} \left\{ 1 - (r/q_n) \right\} + r/q_n \right] \qquad \text{for } r \neq 0$$

$$q_{n+T} = q_n \, e^{-T/K} \qquad \text{for } r = 0$$

Runoff volume $Q = R - K(q_{n+T} - q_n)$.

USE OF CATCHMENT MODELS FOR FLOOD FORECASTING IN CENTRAL AMERICA

A.J. Askew*

INTRODUCTION

In early 1976 the World Meteorological Organization (WMO) and the United Nations Environment Programme (UNEP) agreed to undertake a joint project, which bore the title "Selection of Hurricane and Early Warning, Including Flood Forecasting, Systems for Operational Application in Central America". The project was implemented over a 2-year period terminating in mid-1978, with WMO acting as executive agency in close collaboration with local experts and, more specifically, with the Comité Regional de Recursos Hidraulicos (CRRH). The project contained both hydrological and meteorological components, and within the former, one important task was an investigation of the feasibility of introducing catchment models as part of flood-forecasting systems in Central America. Preliminary surveys were carried out to assess the availability of data for the application of such models, and based on the surveys, models for use in the project were selected. For practical reasons only two models could be considered. Those chosen were the Sacramento model, as operated by the U.S. National Weather Service at its River Forecast Centers (Burnash *et al*. 1973), and the CLS model developed at the IBM Scientific Center in Pisa, Italy (Todini and Wallis 1977, Martelli *et al*. 1977). These were both readily available and yet they offered two quite different forms of catchment model.

PROJECT IMPLEMENTATION

The countries included in the project were Panama, Costa Rica, Nicaragua, Honduras, Guatemala, and El Salvador. The

---

*The views expressed in this paper are those of the author and should not be considered or construed as being the official views of the World Meteorological Organization.

hydrologic services in these six countries differ widely in size and in the administrative context in which they work. However, as a result of a past WMO/UNEP project in the region, strong links have been established between the services, and a certain degree of standardization has been achieved with respect to the collection and processing of hydrologic data.

The aim of this part of the project was to fit both models to one catchment in each of the countries, install both of them on local computers, introduce local experts to their potential for application, and, in the light of experience gained, to draw conclusions concerning the value of catchment models to flood-forecasting systems in the region. For this purpose the hydrologic services each chose, from within their countries, a catchment which was of interest to them and prepared the necessary data for fitting the models.

It was planned that one hydrologist from the region be trained at the River Forecast Center in Tulsa, Oklahoma, in the use of the Sacramento model and a second be trained at the IBM Scientific Center in Pisa, Italy, in the use of the CLS model. The two models were then to be taken back to Central America by these experts, installed on local computers, and, in cooperation with the centers in Tulsa and Pisa, fitted to the catchments in the six countries referred to above. Finally, the two experts were to tour the region installing the models on local facilities and demonstrating their use to colleagues in the other countries.

If all had progressed as planned, the project would have resulted in both models being installed in each of the six countries, fitted to local catchments, and yielding useful data from which it might even have been possible to draw conclusions concerning the performance of the models. However, as stated at the outset, the principal aim was not just to achieve the above results; this could have been accomplished far more surely, and even at less expense, by hiring overseas consultants to collate the data, fit the models in North America or Europe, and take the results back to the region as finished products. The intention was to work, as far as possible, with and through the staff of the local hydrologic services. If a forecasting system is to remain operational long after its installation, it must rely on local data, local computing facilities, and, above all, local expertise. The project was therefore designed to test, not only the feasibility of fitting catchment models to data from catchments in Central America, but also the extent to which local resources are adequate for supporting the long-term operation of forecasting systems based on catchment models.

There is no shortage of reports on the fitting of individual models to specific catchments and work has been done on the intercomparison of a number of models fitted to a range of catchments (see, for example, WMO 1975). Very little has been done, however, to investigate the applicability

of such models, most of which have originated in developed
countries in temperate climates, to catchments in developing
countries, most of which are in tropical or equatorial regions. It is encouraging to note the efforts being made to
study this question by the individual experts involved in
HYDROMATII (a group, affiliated with the International Association of Hydrological Sciences, which is concerned with
the operational application of mathematical models in developing countries.

Unfortunately, when one considers problems relating to
local logistic support for the application of catchment models, it is all too easy to take an "armchair approach" and
theorize on what is or is not feasible. "The data are being
collected, the personnel has been trained, the computers
have been installed, and therefore there should be no difficulties"—or so such arguments go. One of the objectives of
the project described in this paper was to challenge this
approach and to test the feasibility by practical example.
It is therefore not surprising to find that all did not progress according to plan. Nevertheless, the project was successful in that its main aims were achieved and much valuable
experience and information were gained on the problems to be
encountered in installing catchment models in developing
countries. This experience is summarized in the remainder
of this paper.

DATA

A coordinated network of hydrologic stations has been
established in Central America with assistance provided by
the WMO/UNEP project mentioned earlier. In addition, a reasonable degree of standardization has been achieved in the
processing and publication of the data gathered in the region. This provided a good starting point for the project.
However, in this instance specific data were needed on a
range of elements—precipitation, evaporation, and streamflow—for the individual catchments chosen for study.

The preliminary survey showed that most of the necessary
data were available; the problem was that they had to be col-
lated, presented in a specified format, and transmitted
safely as a cohesive set to the centers fitting the models.
Difficulties arose because of lack of appreciation of the
need to prepare the data within the few months available to
the project, i.e., to prepare all the data requested and to
prepare them to the format specified. *This illustrates the
need in such cases to work closely with the data suppliers
to ensure that they fully understand the requirements of the
models and the conditions relating to their use.*

Poor quality data and missing records are a constant
problem for hydrologic analysts the world over. The situation was aggravated in this instance by the shortage of
trained personnel for preparing the data, for reasons described below, and the impossibility of maintaining direct

contact between data suppliers and data users throughout the fitting process. *It is rare that a set of data will be without fault when first used to fit a catchment model and yet only those involved in the collection of the data are in a position to correct such faults with confidence.*

A second pervasive problem associated with hydrologic data concerns the nonrepresentativeness of many stations. In developing countries where there are few trained observers and where the communication facilities are not advanced, it is particularly difficult to install and maintain hydrologic stations at locations that, from a purely hydrologic/climatological viewpoint, are representative. On the Bayano River in Panama, for example, it was found that the simple regression techniques developed previously for flow forecasting gave better results than the model fitted during the project. This problem should, of course, be tackled at its source. *Nevertheless, if it is accepted that unrepresentative data will always be a problem to some extent, it is reasonable to suggest that those who develop catchment models should pay close attention to the manner in which their models handle such data: whether they do so explicitly or implicitly, logically or illogically.*

PERSONNEL

A number of the problems mentioned above can be traced to the shortage of trained staff at the local level. During the previous WMO/UNEP project a considerable number of people were trained, but there was still too few trained personnel to handle the vast amount of work to be done in the region. Professionals and well-trained technicians are at a premium in developing countries, and they are called upon to carry heavy work loads and considerable responsibility. If, for example, major construction work is being undertaken at a time when there is an urgent need for hydrologic information, there are frequently only one or two people in the country who can supply the information. In such circumstances it is hard for them to also keep up-to-date on the developments in hydrology or even to find time to spend on projects such as this. Added to this are the difficulties caused by the considerable mobility of professional staff in these countries, which on occasion may mean an unexpected transfer from one department to another or rapid promotion from technical to administrative posts.

All of these problems arose to a greater or lesser degree during the project. In the short term they can be overcome by calling on the services of overseas experts; this course of action was adopted to a limited extent. However, in the long-term it is necessary to rely on local expertise for the operation of forecasting systems.

The lack of trained personnel presents a problem, not only in the field of hydrology and water resources, but in

all technical assistance work in developing countries and
much effort is currently being expended in the search for a
solution.

COMPUTING FACILITIES

The original work on fitting the catchment models to
data from Central America was carried out at the River Forecast Center in Tulsa for the Sacramento model and at the IBM
Scientific Center in Pisa for the CLS model. This presented
few difficulties, apart from those relating to data referred
to above. However, at a certain stage it was necessary to
install the models on computers in the region. Surveys
showed that in some countries adequate facilities were available, while in others access to computers with sufficient capacity would have been difficult to obtain. The mere exis-
tence of the computers was not enough. None of the hydrologic services themselves operated machines capable of accommo-
dating both the Sacramento and CLS models. Once use had to
be made of computers operated commercially or by other government agencies, problems relating to their physical remote-
ness, limited hours of access, and financial considerations
arose. *The availability of adequate computing facilities*
therefore presented a number of problems for the project,
which could have become far more acute in any situation where
the models were to be used in a real-time operational mode.

An arrangement was eventually made for installing the
CLS model in Guatemala, with the assistance of staff from
the IBM Scientific Center in Mexico City and the Mexican
hydrologic service. At the same time, the Sacramento model
was installed on a computer in Cartago near San José, Costa
Rica, with the assistance of an expert from the center in
Tulsa. It took 1-2 weeks in each case for overseas experts
on the models to install them on the best local computers
available and to start them running with local data. The
original proposal of taking the models to and installing
them in each of the six countries was therefore out of the
question, and an alternative approach was adopted. WMO, in
conjunction with CRRH and the Escuela Regional de Ingenieria
Sanitaria of the University of San Carlos in Guatemala,
organized a 3-week seminar. For 2 weeks it was located in
Guatemala, the first week being devoted to a background re-
fresher course on catchment models in general and the second
to a workshop on the CLS model. In the third week the participants moved to Costa Rica for a workshop on the Sacramento model. Participants from all six countries attended,
and it was generally agreed that the meetings were a success.
It cannot be claimed that all participants returned to their
countries experts in the installation, fitting, and operation
of the two models, but they are certainly now well informed
in the fundamentals of the models, their potential for application, and their needs with regard to both data and

computing facilities—a very valuable basis for future work in the region.

It is worth noting that, if the basic structure and mode of operation of a model can be clearly explained, it is more likely to be understood by local experts who will then be in a better position to evaluate it, adopt it, and operate it.

In each of the countries in the region an HP 9830 computer was installed during the former WMO/UNEP project. These accept only BASIC and have 8K memories in five countries and a 4K memory in the sixth. These computers obviously offered an alternative basis for the regional installation of the models, except for their lack of storage and their inability to accept FORTRAN—the program language of the CLS and Sacramento models. A BASIC version of the Sacramento program has been developed by an overseas expert working in Panama. It was designed to suit the HP computers; however, it has some bugs which have yet to be removed and which, it is felt, can only be detected by someone intimately familiar with the model and its original FORTRAN version. The CLS program is far too big to be fitted on the HP computers in its full form. However, the major part of the program is the fitting and optimizing procedures and only a comparatively few program steps are needed for its operation once fitted.

There would therefore appear to be a good case to be made for the development of simplified versions of model programs, possibly limited to an operational mode, which can be made available in a variety of forms and languages for use on small local facilities. The full versions could be installed at national or regional centers to which the necessary data can be taken as and when the models are to be fitted to catchments.

In view of what has been said regarding the need for close collaboration between data suppliers, those fitting the models, and those using them, it is important to stress that, if possible, the data should be "taken" and not "sent".

CONCLUSIONS

The project is considered to have been successful in that it has provided valuable experience and information concerning the feasibility of using catchment models in forecasting systems in Central America. This paper has tended to dwell on the problems encountered because it is in consideration of these problems and the means used to overcome them that lessons can be learned. However, the project has yielded far more than a list of problems; both the CLS and Sacramento models are now securely installed at centers in the region and are available for use by local hydrologic services. A considerable number of local experts have gained first-hand experience in the use of the models and the feasibility of using them in local forecasting systems has been demonstrated, subject to the various conditions expressed in this paper. Thus a sound basis has been established on which future national and regional flood-forecasting projects can draw, and practical observations have been offered which are of relevance to work in all developing countries and even in many developed countries.

The short delay times typical of so many of the major river basins in Central America make it essential to base flood-forecasting systems on some sort of catchment model if the lead times offered by the forecasts are to be long enough for the local population to take effective action. Relatively sophisticated models could be utilized for this purpose in the region, especially if simplified versions are available for use in operational mode, and adequate allowance is made in future flood-forecasting projects for the necessary data analysis and computer support. The emphasis should not be on the extent of the analysis or on the power of the computers but more on the quality of the data control, the availability and reliability of the equipment, and above all, the development of a core of highly-motivated, local experts to ensure the long-term, efficient operation of the systems. In view of the continual shortages in the region of both financial support and trained manpower, it will not be easy to meet such demands. However, two important points can be made in any argument in favor of the use of catchment models in flood forecasting. The first is that the requirements for data, computer support, and expertise are very similar, if not identical, with those for all similar work in operational hydrology. Therefore, the introduction of the models would not itself lead to any significant increase or change in the requirements commonly set forth by national hydrologic services. Secondly, the value to be gained from the efficient use of available hydrologic data, especially in the development of nonstructural means of reducing the damage caused by flooding, regularly far outweighs the expenses involved. The cost of any project for installing a flood-forecasting system should, therefore, always be viewed in relation to the many large-scale agricultural or industrial projects, the investments of which the system is designed to protect.

ACKNOWLEDGMENT

The author wishes to express his appreciation to the World Meteorological Organization for permission to use the technical documents of the Organization in the preparation of this paper.

REFERENCES

Burnash, R.J.C., R.L. Ferral, and R.A. McGuire (1973) A Generalized Streamflow Simulation System: Conceptual Modelling for Digital Computers. Washington, D.C.: U.S.
Department of Commerce, National Weather Service, and
Sacramento, California: Department of Water Resources.

Martelli, S., E. Todini, and J.R. Wallis (1977) CLS: con-
strained linear systems. Pages 295-330, Mathematical
Models for Surface Water Hydrology, edited by T.A.
Ciriani, U. Maione, and J.R. Wallis. London: Wiley.

Todini, E., and J.R. Wallis (1977) Using CLS for daily or
longer period rainfall—runoff modelling. Pages 149-
168, Mathematical Models for Surface Water Hydrology,
edited by T.A. Ciriani, U. Maione, and J.R. Wallis.
London: Wiley.

World Meteorological Organization (WMO) (1975) Operational
Hydrology Report No. 7. Intercomparison of Conceptual
Models Used in Operational Hydrological Forecasting.
WMO Report No. 429. Geneva.

DEVELOPMENTAL AND OPERATIONAL ASPECTS OF GAMING-SIMULATIONS
FOR WATER RESOURCE SYSTEMS

G.L. Wright

INTRODUCTION

In the design of large and complex water resource systems, the engineer or planner will almost certainly be faced
with conflicting objectives, competition for the limited,
stochastic water resources among the various users, and perhaps conflict with the community itself—the very people he
endeavors to serve. Controversies continually arise over
such issues as whether a dam should be built in a wilderness
area or whether water used primarily by irrigators should be
diverted for industrial purposes. The gaming-simulation approach has, over the last two decades, become an accepted
method of modeling environmental systems (such as urban and
water resource systems and management situations), where
conflicts over and competition for a limited resource play
an important role. Examples of the various applications of
gaming-simulation can be found in Taylor (1971), Belch
(1973), and Wright and Sheather (1977).

This approach enlarges the boundaries of the system
being modeled beyond the physical and purely economic systems to include decision makers. Because of the complexity
of human nature, the behavior of decision makers usually
cannot be readily modeled in terms of ordinary dynamic equations but can be most successfully modeled by people playing
roles in a game. For this reason, the implementation of a
gaming-simulation presents difficulties not encountered with
a conventional computer simulation, even though they share
many common problems.

The developmental and operational problems likely to
occur during the application of the gaming-simulation approach to modeling a water resource system are outlined in
this paper. The requirements, in terms of manpower and computing facilities, for model implementation are also discussed. The Water Resources Allocation Game (WRAG), developed to examine the problem of allocating a stochastic supply

of water among competing users in the Upper Hunter Valley of
New South Wales, Australia, is discussed as an example of a
complex gaming-simulation.

INTERACTION IN SIMULATION MODELS

The process of simulation is an interactive one. A
decision set (representing policy decisions about the operation of the system being modeled) and data describing the environmental conditions (such as streamflows and rainfalls)
are fed into a computer model as input. A given period of
time is simulated, the response of the system is recorded,
and, based on that record, the decision set is modified, and
the whole procedure is repeated until a satisfactory system
response is obtained. The level and frequency at which interaction occurs between the user and the computer models is
perhaps one of the most important differences between the
three main approaches to simulation. The *traditional* approach is to use only historical records of environmental
data, which will probably be of 20 to 80 years' duration,
for each simulation run. The *synthetic* approach is to use
a long record (say 1,000 to 10,000 years total) that has been
generated from the historical record and (hopefully) has statistical properties closely approximating that record. This
enables the user to investigate a large sample of possible
system responses. The third approach is *gaming-simulation*.
A computer model is constructed, but, in addition, the key
decision makers in the real-world system are represented by
human players in a game. The players interact with the computer model by making decisions about its operation within
the rules of the game. The model is then run to simulate a
relatively short period of time, usually of the order of 6
months to 5 years. The results (i.e., system response) are
shown to the players, and the players then make another set
of decisions and the process continues.

The short (simulated) time between each modification of
the decision set and the fact that a number of players are
required to make the decisions create problems of implementation for the gaming-simulation approach. A group of people must meet regularly over a period of days, or in some
cases weeks, in order to simulate a sufficiently long record
for meaningful results to emerge. This in itself may seri-
ously limit the use of the approach in some cases.

THE WATER RESOURCES ALLOCATION GAME (WRAG)

The WRAG simulation (Wright 1971) provides a simulated
environment where players representing key decision makers
in the planning, development, and management of a real river
basin can formulate, implement, and test policies in order
to achieve their goals. These goals may be prespecified or
may be decided upon by the players during the game. The
simulated environment is simplified so that the players can

comprehend the fundamental factors that influence the system. On the other hand, the uncertainties of the environment caused by the stochastic nature of the weather and the behavior of other decision makers have been retained so that some degree of realism is achieved. The game attempts to abstract a few of the fundamental factors affecting the use of land and water resources in a river basin and to force players to operate within the constraints, both physical and political, imposed by these factors.

In the game, teams of players represent the major groups interested in the operation of a river system, e.g., farmers, government authorities, etc. They are considered to be the major decision-making groups in the Upper Hunter Valley, the study region.

The physical environment, the economy, and the community at large are represented by a digital computer model, which simulates the behavior of the system in response to player decisions and natural weather conditions. The game is played in rounds or cycles; each round or cycle represents a 5-year planning period and takes about 1 hour to play. During each round, the players make decisions that they feel will best advance their interests and aid them in their responsibilities. They are free to lobby and bargain with any other team in order to try to persuade others to pursue policies that are in their interests. Teams may also formulate long-term policies that require decisions to be made over a number of rounds.

At the end of each decision period, the computer model is run to simulate system responses for a period representing 5 years, using as data both the decisions of the players and weather conditions synthesized from historical data recorded in the study region. Results are presented to the players in the form of a computer-printed bulletin. The last step in each round is for the players to review how the system has responded to their decisions, so that they can plan policies for future decision rounds.

Development

The development of the WRAG simulation necessarily involved three main tasks. The first was the stochastic modeling of hydrometeorological inputs (the weather), the second was the digital computer simulation of the physical and economic systems, and the third was the formulation of game rules and roles to model the political and institutional structure of the system. The first two tasks are, of course, common to conventional simulations and entail the identification of a model structure that will adequately represent the processes involved, the collection of data sufficient to define the state of the system, and the testing of the model to ensure that it does, in fact, reproduce known conditions of the system under some given set (or sets) of inputs.

The third task, i.e., the formulation of game rules and roles, added a further dimension to the development process. It requires the analysis of the real-life political and institutional infrastructure of the system. In most cases, this is very complex. In Australia (and in most western countries) it most likely involves two or three levels of government [local, regional (state), and national (federal)], as well as agencies within each level, such as those concerned with water resource management, pollution control, and land-use planning. It also involves private-sector groups: water users (e.g., irrigators), resident action groups, private industry, etc. From all of these a subset is chosen that adequately represents the major interests in the decision-making processes in the water resource system under consideration.

The rules must constrain the players to make their decisions within a similar framework to the real-life one. These rules may be altered for different runs to investigate legislative strategies for water resource management. The rules include the delegation of authority to each team, fund-raising procedures, planning restrictions, and so on. All this must be done, not only to give a realistic representation of the system, but also to ensure that the rules and procedures are simple enough to be quickly comprehended by the players.

The development of a gaming-simulation also involves auxiliary tasks, such as the preparation of player instruction manuals and aids which give the players a written set of rules and guidelines for play. Other equipment may also be required. In WRAG there is a playing board which consists of a stylized map of the study region divided into approximately 100 land-use areas. Current land development, location of storage reservoirs, major towns, power stations, etc., are shown on the map. Thus, the players are able to visualize the state of development of the region as a whole, to establish land ownership, and to determine the suitability of each area for development. Each team has a form on which to record its decisions for each round. The design of this form enables the information to be quickly encoded onto computer punch cards or to be entered into the computer via a remote terminal.

The WRAG simulation initially took about 1 man-year to develop, although its progress was hampered by limitations on computing availability at some stages. A number of revisions and modifications increased the development time even further. It is estimated that this simulation would have cost up to 50 percent more in terms of time and money than a conventional all-computer simulation of similar complexity. Considerable additional programming effort was required for computing team accounts, land transactions, etc., and for printing a comprehensive output bulletin in an easily readable format for feedback to the players.

Implementation and Operation

When a conventional simulation has been developed, the use of the resulting model is most often limited only by computer availability and cost and the availability of one or two competent personnel. However, the implementation and operation of a gaming-simulation presents unique problems. In addition to the usual requirements of a computer of sufficient capability and personnel to collect data, run the program, and analyze the results, a gaming-simulation needs people to play the roles and a suitable room in which to play. These must be available on a regular basis over a period of days or weeks so that enough rounds can be played to obtain a meaningful output sequence. For example, the WRAG simulation requires 10 to 20 people to make up the seven teams. The decision round takes about 1 hour to complete, and about 30 minutes are required to collate, check, and enter the decisions, provided no serious errors have been made in filling out the forms. The number of rounds that can be played in a day varies from one to four. This is greatly dependent on the turn-around time of the program on the available computing facility, and on whether a batch station or remote terminal is situated in the vicinity of the game venue. This is often not the case.

Approximately six rounds of the game are required before meaningful trends begin to appear. This is equivalent to 30 years of simulated time and varies from game to game. This requirement could also vary substantially for other gaming-simulations, depending on the length of the simulated decision period, the degree of randomness in the simulated environment, and the consistency of the players in their decision making. This means that the gaming-simulation approach can be very demanding on both human and computer resources, and this could be a most influential factor when a planner is deciding whether to use the approach or not.

It is difficult to estimate the likely costs of implementation and operation of a gaming-simulation such as WRAG in any given situation. It depends not only on the computing costs and costs in terms of the user's salary, etc., but also on the cost of "employing" players. For instance, at university, students may be available to play; it may even be part of a curriculum. In a government body or a private organization where staff could be used as role-players, their salaries would, most likely, have to be taken into account. Additional personnel may also be required. The play of the game is overseen by a game "director". The director acts as a referee when disputes arise over interpretation, sets a time limit for the decision round, etc. He also completes a decision form, which is entered into the computer data about the particular game series (date, round number, etc.) for documentation purposes. He can also specify parameters that determine the economic climate in which the game will be run. In addition to a game director, one or more advisors

may be needed to explain the rules and to help the players
in their decision making, particularly if a group is unfamil-
iar with the game. Provision of these additional personnel
will increase game costs.

The program for WRAG is written in the Extended FORTRAN
language and can be run on CDC 6600 or Cyber 72 series computers. It contains approximately 2,500 executable statements. Synthetic data generation is carried out by a separate program in a job step preceding the main simulation.
This allows any multisite data generation program to be used,
provided it runs on the particular computer and its output
is compatible with the input requirements of the WRAG program.
The time taken for a complete run of the program, including
the synthetic generation of hydrometeorological input series,
is typically around 50 seconds on the CDC 6600 computer. The
cost of this amount of work is about $A20 (using 1977 commer-
cial rates). The central memory requirement is 150,000 (oc-
tal) words; however, this could be reduced by overlaying.
A number of data files and user-written utility programs are
also required.

Benefits

Gaming-simulation, despite its higher development and
operation costs, has a number of distinct advantages over
conventional simulation methods in certain cases. Because
of the expanded scope of the simulation, three factors are
considered: physical, economic, and political (political is
used in a very broad sense). In WRAG the physical and economic factors are simulated by a digital computer program.
The political factors are the various interactions between
teams as key decision makers, both in the public and private
sectors. As in real life, these decision makers will probably not be in complete accord since they will be pursuing
different objectives. Conflicts arise when decision makers
pursue objectives that can only be attained at the expense
of others' goal satisfaction. In a conventional simulation,
such conflicts have to be resolved (often arbitrarily) by
the model builder (or user) before the simulation is carried
out. In a gaming-simulation conflicts are resolved by lobbying, bargaining, and delegating authority during the simulation. For example, in the WRAG simulation, the State (Regional) Government and Local Government teams may come into
conflict, particularly when money is being sought by Local
Government to fund such projects as flood mitigation or sewage treatment works. Since the State Government has the
power to allocate funds for these purposes, it will probably
have the final say in these instances, but it may be swayed
in its decision by lobbying by the Local Government or other
teams.

In a river system, such as the Upper Hunter Valley, the
allocation of water among competing users is an important
policy to be decided. In a conventional simulation, this

policy could be tested by considering many alternatives and comparing them in terms of some criteria (e.g., the maximization of national economics efficiency). In WRAG, however, the water allocation policies are determined not externally, but by a Water Authority team within the simulation. In choosing its policies the Water Authority team must take into account not only the physical and economic consequences of its decisions but also the claims and arguments made by other teams. These last considerations may be neglected or improperly accounted for in a conventional simulation and this could result in a solution that may be optimum in an engineering or economic sense, but that may be "politically" unworkable because it creates conflicts that cannot be resolved readily.

The benefits of using a gaming-simulation such as WRAG, rather than a conventional all-computer simulation, must be considered in terms of the costs of making wrong decisions or, in other words, of adopting a solution that turns out to be cumbersome or unworkable because conflicts were improperly considered. By using the gaming-simulation approach for the solution of water resource planning and management problems, where conflicts are likely to play a major role, the risk of adopting an inappropriate solution is reduced, and hence expected benefits are increased.

CONCLUSIONS

This paper has discussed some of the problems associated with the development and operation of a gaming-simulation for a complex water resource system. In particular, reference has been made to the WRAG simulation which was developed for the Upper Hunter Valley of New South Wales. It has been seen that development and operation costs associated with a gaming-simulation are significantly higher than for a conventional all-computer simulation of similar complexity. However, where a simulation is to be developed to solve problems or to plan the development of a water resource system in which conflicts occur between parties interested in the planning and management of the available water and land resources, the benefits derived from a gaming-simulation may far outweigh the additional costs. These benefits principally derive from the extension of scope of a gaming-simulation to include not only the physical and economic aspects of the system but also many political and institutional aspects.

114

REFERENCES

Belch, J. (1973) Contemporary Games. Detroit, Michigan:
    Gale Research Company.

Taylor, J.L. (1971) Instructional Planning Systems: A Gaming
    Simulation Approach to Urban Problems. Cambridge:
    Cambridge University Press.

Wright, G.L. (1971) River Systems Modelling for Water Re-
    sources Allocation. Ph.D. Thesis. University of New
    South Wales, Australia.

Wright, G.L., and G. Sheather (1977) Gaming-simulation Mod-
    els for Environmental Systems. Proceedings of the Con-
    ference on Models for Modern Management. Sydney: Aus-
    tralian Society for Operations Research and Statistical
    Society of Australia.

MODEL FOR THE SELECTION OF APPROPRIATE TECHNOLOGY FOR A WATER RESOURCES SYSTEM

G.W. Reid

For many years developing countries have been working, with external assistance, to promote development of water treatment and waste disposal systems in their cities and towns. Adequate quantities of safe water and adequate sanitation measures are considered to be necessary but not sufficient conditions for social and economic development; however, up to this time programs simply have not succeeded in keeping pace with the problem of water and sanitation in less developed countries (LDCs). A breakdown has occurred where there have been direct technology transfers that resulted in the selection of treatment processes too sophisticated or costly for in-country construction, maintenance, or operation. A basic problem, then, relates to site-specific selection of appropriate technology in LDCs.

A 1971-72 survey by the World Health Organization (WHO) of community water supply and excreta disposal conditions in developing countries revealed that nearly one-third of the world's population (over one billion people) has no adequate water supply, and only 0.8 percent of the total population of developing countries is served by sewage treatment facilities (WHO 1977). As a result of this survey the United Nations Second Development Decade goals included the supplying of all urban populations with water, either by house connections or by public standpipes, and the provision of reasonable access to safe water for one-quarter of the population in rural areas by 1980. Based on achievements made up to 1975, percentage goals were increased to 36 percent of the rural population, and excreta disposal targets were established for the first time. However, despite great efforts, populations have increased more rapidly than new facilities have been installed.

The importance of the quality and quantity of water supply to human health and economic conditions has been clearly demonstrated and has been the target of international

115

development efforts in LDCs. Experience has clearly shown
that international investments have not been used efficiently
or effectively, i.e., selection and use has been made of inappropriate technology.

The approach presented in this paper to aid in the resolution of this problem is (1) to assist the LDC in using a
systems approach and in identifying the major alternatives;
(2) to devise ways to present the alternatives to LDC decision makers, thus facilitating diffusion; and (3) to assist
the LDCs in developing self-sufficiency in selecting or producing appropriate technology. In 1973 a study was undertaken to develop a model to select appropriate (low cost)
treatment methods for specific LDC sites. The model methodology has been tested for user and consumer acceptance and
methods are now being sought to implement its use.

THE ENVIRONMENTAL SETTING PROBLEM

In studying the problem of technology transfer, the
engineer/client relationship was seen to be of critical importance. The engineer striving to bring technology to an
LDC works in an alien, and in many ways, a very complicated
environment. Pictorially, one can identify at least eight
separable, frequently conflicting elements that he must take
into consideration or deal with in his work (see Figure 1).
In selecting an appropriate technology, the engineer operates
to meet national health standards and perhaps international
standards. The plan must fit into larger water schemes;
usually it must be designed without any long-term physical
data or national or local funding, and donors must be located.
The environment must be able to support operation and maintenance, and local political and business interests exercise
special requirements in many instances.

A study made in 1970 by Reid for the Avco firm and the
American Society of Civil Engineers included research on the
types of technology most often preferred by decision makers.
The results showed that 80 percent of the decision makers
wanted what everyone else was currently using; 15 percent
wanted older, cheaper solutions; and only 5 percent would
consider newer, innovative solutions. The decision maker
was concerned about the present; the problems of the future
and the problems associated with operation and maintenance
were considered to be problems for future decision makers.
The engineer's interest, too, was shown to be limited to the
immediate task of building the plant. This meant that neither the decision maker nor the engineer appeared to be interested in the ability of the site to keep the process going.
In response to this common problem, there have been attempts
to require the engineer to provide operational "follow-ons"
for completed projects, such as including in the contract
certain requirements for supervision and training for an initial period.

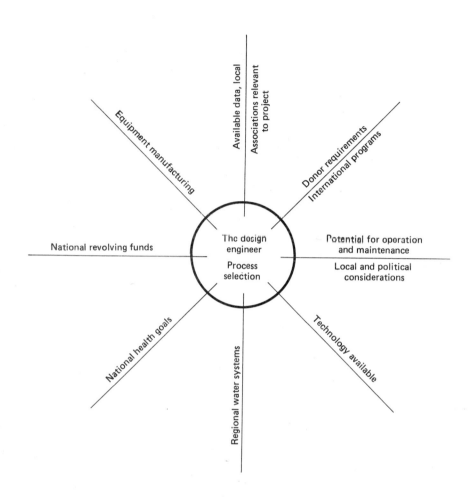

FIGURE 1   Conflicting elements affecting the engineer working in a less developed country.

    Quite often plants have been overdesigned technologi-
cally. Financing has been based on capital costs only (ig-
noring operation and maintenance costs). Proper operation
has been lacking and replacement parts and materials have
been nonexistent. If a piece of equipment failed, it was
repaired rather than replaced. If enough parts failed so
that the plant stopped functioning, a new plant was built.

TECHNOLOGY TRANSFER

The engineer/client relationship is important in technology transfer. Moreover, an improvement is required in communication between the areas of need in the LDCs and the sources of technology in developed countries (DCs) and LDCs. To develop in-country competence and self-sufficiency, it is helpful to establish local and regional centers of technology. The extent to which LDCs use research and technology developed abroad is directly related to the "absorptive capacity" of these countries, i.e., the readiness and capability of specialists and institutions to adapt, apply, and disseminate the technology. This capacity is important whether the technology is being transferred in the form of equipment, as technical information, or through exchanges of people. It embodies a capability to recognize the alternative technical approaches that are or could be available; to choose the technology that makes the most sense technically, economically, and socially; if necessary, to adapt the technology to local conditions; to understand the direct impact and the more subtle long-term impacts of the technology; and to operate and maintain the technology.

Institutional orientation is often the decisive aspect of a developing country's capability to absorb technology. For example, there are a large number of LDC students at most DC universities. But are their courses of study truly of relevance to interests back home, or will they give further impetus to the "brain drain"? While it is difficult for a United States university on an institutional basis to make sudden changes in the orientation of the content of its academic curriculum, individual professors and instructors can introduce elements into their courses that will enrich the experiences of developing country specialists and allow them to return home better prepared to face the realities of development. Many of our university professors maintain collaborative linkages with a large number of researchers abroad. The substantive aspects of those linkages—exchange of technical reports and joint research efforts—can do much to influence the orientation of research activities in developing countries.

It is difficult for a country that does not itself possess a reasonable number of trained scientific and technical personnel to know what usable technology exists elsewhere, to understand it, to adapt it to the country's special needs or peculiar conditions, to repair and maintain the necessary equipment, or indeed to operate it. If a country builds up its own scientific and technical capacity, it is in a much better position to utilize what exists elsewhere. Lack of appropriately trained personnel is often an obstacle to the wider application of technology that is already known and to some extent used in a country. In addition, each country is better able to hold its place in international competition if it has the capacity itself to introduce innovations (new products or less costly methods of production) based on existing technology.

Technical change affects man's entire way of life—how he makes a living, his habits, etc. It is inevitably disruptive of established attitudes and practices. All societies have some built-in resistance to change and a strong inclination to maintain the status quo. The capacity of a society to assimilate new technology depends on both its capacity to adapt the technology to its own conditions and its capacity to adapt itself to the needs of technology. Some technologies are readily accepted, but others require a massive education program. It has been observed by sanitary engineers for several decades that water plant designs based on current DC practice and which do not take into account local conditions are doomed to failure.

PROCESS SELECTION MODEL

The formulation of water resources strategies requires a full knowledge of and experience in dealing with the basic facts, traditions, and goals of the overall social and economic development of the region. Therefore, it is normal for decision makers to select the most recent, up-to-date, and proven methodology. This is true in both developing and developed countries. In selecting water and wastewater treatment processes, the most up-to-date process may not necessarily be the most recently developed technology but rather the model device being used by some advanced and better informed countries. It is desirable to "look like" one's rich neighbor or to strive to emulate the current and the popular; hence, one majestically arrives at the best solution to one's problem. However, this approach may be far from practical and optimal. For example, the correct sewage treatment in Chicago may not be applicable elsewhere, certainly not in Bangkok. In fact, the process selected for Chicago might not be technically optimal but is probably politically optimal.

In general, there is an urge to be with the advanced and the rich. This is particularly true for developing countries and it results too frequently in the selection of water or wastewater treatments that cannot be managed due to a lack of logistics, a lack of trained personnel, and a lack of proper chemicals. Therefore, it is obvious that a need exists to develop schemes whereby decision makers will be encouraged to select from an array of water and wastewater treatment processes that will optimize in-country capability —manpower and materials. This need can best be demonstrated by a treatment process selected and used in some developing countries that are not in-country compatible. There are ample examples of chlorinators that have no chlorine and filters with broken rate controllers, that are shut down due to lack of parts, or that are poor products because of improper chemicals and chemical dosages.

There is a great variety of processes that are effective in treating water and wastewater. Historically, in DCs more sophisticated processes were selected as countries grew in size, industrial capability, and wealth. Though generally so, industrial development does not necessarily correlate with levels of technology. There are suitable technologies available that are highly advanced but not acceptable (or should one say: not sufficiently proven to be acceptable) to a developing country. On the other hand, there are older, well-established technologies that are most suitable.

The author developed a predictive model to help planners select water and wastewater treatment processes appropriate to the material and manpower resource capabilities of particular countries at particular times. Through the use of this computerized model, a large amount of data can be processed quickly, and the resultant output will display the consequences of all the various actions, including all relevant costs. Such a display will, in most cases, enhance the design engineer's judgment. For those planners who do not have access to a computer capable of executing the model, a manual approach was developed.

The field validation work consisted of model runs made by selected users to ascertain that the appropriate data could be obtained to run the model, i.e., to ensure that input data requirements could be met in various developing countries where substantial data are not generally available.

This model was originally presented in a United States Agency for International Development (USAID) publication and a World Health Organization publication (Reid and Discenza 1975a, 1976), and a sample computer printout was included. In addition, a computer program was presented in a supplementary USAID publication (Reid and Discenza 1975b). Experience has shown that documentation beyond the logic diagram is not useful due to the variety of computer equipment that is available to prospective users. Therefore, this publication includes the logic diagram together with the step-by-step procedure presented in manual form. An understanding of these items will enable any programmer to tailor a program to particular equipment needs. Actually, the support tables and calculations are quite simple, and the manual procedure should suffice for most purposes.

Figure 2 is an overall view of the proposed planning model data flow for the selection of a combination of processes. (Figure 3 is a graphic representation of Figure 2.) This methodology uses 18 inputs that describe socioeconomic conditions, 31 inputs in five main categories that describe the indigenous resources, two inputs that describe the demographic profile, and three inputs that describe the raw water quality. These constitute the raw data. The method employed to assure selection of an appropriate process uses two categories of raw data (socioeconomic and indigenous resources) and reduces them through a weighting process to four sociotechnological levels and five resource capability categories. These categories are used with a matrix of

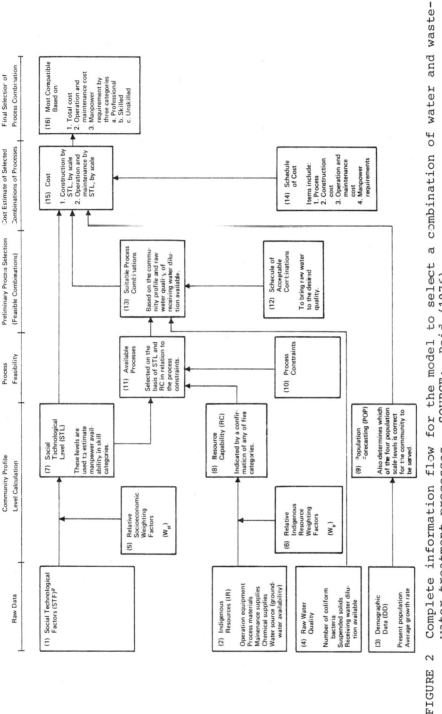

FIGURE 2   Complete information flow for the model to select a combination of water and waste-water treatment processes. SOURCE: Reid (1976).

122

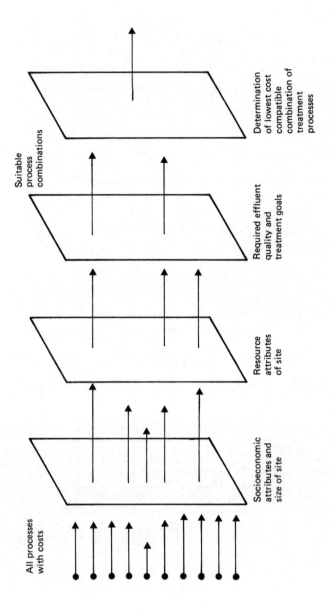

FIGURE 3   Types of screening involved in the selection of a compatible, lowest cost combination of treatment processes.

process constraints (in terms of manpower and material requirements) to screen for acceptable alternative processes
for future consideration. The model identifies basic individual treatment processes. In practice, however, basic
treatment processes are frequently utilized in varying combinations, depending on the conditions of the raw water to
be treated or on the condition of the received waste streams.
The individual processes determined acceptable by the model
are thus used to set up combinations of processes. The limitation on combinations, in the case of water, relates to
initial raw water quality, and the screened combinations are
designed to provide acceptable groups or sequences of treatments that will bring raw water to a potable level.

Next, the locations of the processes involved in the
suitable combinations are determined based on size of population group to be served or scale and on sociotechnological
levels, and a matrix of capital costs, operation and maintenance costs, and manpower requirements is applied. This
matrix is developed by empirical analysis of data from more
developed regions, regression analysis of regional or national data from developing countries, or real entries of
local data. The final step in the model will provide the
least cost process combination, in terms of total cost or
in terms of maintenance costs, as desired.

Since the perspective of the model is global, there is
a large array of treatment processes considered to be potential candidates for the treatment of water and wastewater.
The array of processes is open to expansion as new ideas are
tested through the global network on adaptive and innovative
technological transfer. However, in certain areas some processes lend themselves to greater probabilities for success
than others. To account for local variations, the model can
be adapted by the addition and elimination of processes as
needed.

The model initially was limited to organized communities or nucleated villages that range in population from
500 to 100,000 inhabitants. At the lower level the limit
was intended to include individual family systems, if they
are collectively managed. At the upper limit, high population concentration areas were excluded because they can
afford professional expertise and have generally been able
to develop adequate systems without the need for a planning
model (WHO 1977).

The model's data requirements are reasonable. The model is structured so that if information for up to 30 percent
of the sociotechnological items is lacking, reasonable community identification can still be achieved. In fact, one
alternative would be to arrive at a community level by consulting a series of scenarios developed for this purpose
(Reid and Discenza 1975a), thus bypassing the related data
requirements entirely.

Another limitation of the model is that it deals only with water and sewage treatment. Procurement and distribution methods and transportation of wastewater away from households are not presently considered, although they could affect treatment costs to some degree.

The model is relatively simple, the inputs flexible. It has a manual computational program and an automated computer program that are available in several computer languages. The model is limited to selected water treatments and a similar model is available for sewage treatment only. A model is being developed for the other elements of a water supply system: intake, reservoir, pipeline, and distribution systems for which alternative designs and materials are selected for each step, then aggregated in the most cost-effective way. There is also a prioritizing model under development. (A prioritizing model is a model that sets forth rankings.) In the consumer review process, these types of models were most frequently requested.

MODEL IMPLEMENTATION

In modeling the major concern and the source of many problems involves the relationships among client/donor and their agents, engineers, planners, bankers, etc. This is particularly true in developing countries, for which the models are intended, but it is also true in developed countries.

Most clients want to be identified with the most advanced technology and most engineers with their single and best solution; rarely do they feel obligated to look at alternatives. On the other hand, the selection of the most appropriate technology is the best assurance that the water system selected will be compatible with in-country development and natural and human resources.

To promote use of the model, the implementation approach envisioned by the author and the initial study sponsor has what might be called both "reactive" and "proactive" modes.

The reactive mode stresses bring the model to the attention of donor and regulatory agencies, USAID, the United Nations Development Programme (UNDP), World Bank, etc., as well as to individual governments charged with decisions. Professional and scientific organizations, such as the sponsors of this Symposium, could also be classed as reactive, but as proactive, too. In the reactive mode the hope would be "to get them" to develop an official policy requiring the use of the models, or at least to look at socioeconomic inputs and alternatives. It is also hoped that professional and scientific organizations will develop a sense of responsibility for the model.

In the proactive mode of implementation, emphasis is on education at an operational (county) level thru publications, demonstrations, short courses, etc., conducted or arranged for/by official groups such as WHO, the United Nations Educational, Scientific and Cultural Organization (UNESCO), the United Nations Environment Programme (UNEP), the Economic Commission for Western Asia (ECWA), USAID, or private groups such as universities.

The model has been presented at numerous conferences and published (see Reid 1974, Reid *et al*. 1974, Reid and Muiga 1975, Reid and Smisher 1975, Reid 1976, Reid and Discenza 1976, and WHO 1977).

USAID has financed the development of a text (Reid and Coffey 1978) covering client/donor relationships; appropriate technology; process selection and prioritizing models; the state of the art of water and sewage treatment in DCs; and cost and demand studies. It is further planned to use the text for a series of 1-week courses at USAID, World Bank, Inter American Bank, and other similar groups; these would be followed by four essentially global conferences for selected professional audiences, hopefully, in collaboration with WHO, UNEP, ECWA, etc. By global conference is meant one each in Africa, Asia, Latin America, and the Near East. These presentations would be progressively honed by audience feedback. Next, two LDC sites would be selected for a 4 to 6 month in-country demonstration, and again the results would be used to improve the next series of 5-day presentations in some 20 LDCs. The final step might well be for USAID to send a team on a country to country request basis to work with the country on developing the use of the model. WHO has also indicated an interest in a similar educational function, particularly in South America thru the Pan American Health Organization (PAHO).

At a preliminary conference in Columbia it was suggested that a two-step format be followed: presentations would be given at a conference and a workshop would follow bringing together interested people from the conference, who have collected the necessary data on their own problem. They would then go thru the operation of the model on their data. The conference approach is envisioned as a cadre system, where the model developer teaches other model builders and where teams from this group present the model to regional professional and international agency people and faculty members, who, in turn, present it to developing country professionals.

The author has had experience with an urban system model developed for the National Science Foundation (Reid 1977) and with the River I model, the property of the Environmental Protection Agency in Washington, D.C. One-week conferences of selected audiences were conducted. The audience went away with an understanding of the model; however, in

most cases not in sufficient depth to actively use it. The
5-day session included a hands-on computer program solution.
It is the author's opinion that at least a second follow-up
workshop or O.J.T. (on the job training) follow-on program
is necessary. Some of the participants saw the capabilities
of the model and wanted a central authority to provide the
analyses for them. Others were intrigued with parts of the
program and wanted a deck to take home.

Models have a rightful place in water resources development. The rather simple one developed for in-country compatible water treatment process selection, which is particularly applicable to developing countries, should become an
excellent addition to the LDC's water planning process.
Several avenues still need to be explored to expedite the
use. At present it appears that only agencies requiring re-
petitive access need be concerned about computerized operations. (Such agencies include consultants, official county
or state water authorities, universities, international agencies, and lending agencies.) All of these usually have sufficient staff and equipment to run the analyses. Perhaps,
the sooner the client understands the tool, the sooner he
will insist on the analyses by the consultant as a part of
the selection process.

The author developed water demand models for several
states in the USA, and for ECWA and UNESCO. The clients
wanted the model and results, but they also wanted us to run
the model and to continue developing it. Perhaps an initial
short course, followed by continuing working arrangements,
is appropriate.

The dual problem of user acceptance of modeling and appropriate technology has been dealt with here. As to acceptance of appropriate technology there are other avenues of
study that could be explored, such as consumer-perception
and clients' cognitive approach. The client/donor/modeler
relationship and possible proactive and reactive programs
have been explored. There is, however, an additional area
of vital importance. It relates to the modeler himself.
The author believes, and has for some time, that the modeler
must present his product so that it will maximize user acceptance and not increase his prestige among his peers, which
appears to be the present goal. Figure 4 illustrates the
problem (Reid 1972). The graph is essentially a bi-model
of polarization of interests. There is an evident mismatch
between the model builder and the consumer concerning goals.

A final point relates to the modeler's perception of the
role modeling plays in the problem solution; it must be put
in proper perspective. The model, perhaps, is only a tool,
to be used in the decision process. The decision must not
be given to the modeler. The decision maker needs to understand the power of modeling in the same way he understands
what chemical analyses or water samples can provide; he need
not run the analyses himself.

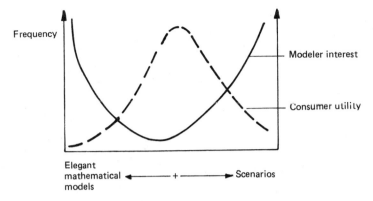

FIGURE 4 Polarization of interests. SOURCE: Reid (1972).

Although models can be very useful as an additional in-put to the selection process, they are not being used at present, and much of the problem rests on the shoulders of the model builder.

REFERENCES

Reid, George W. (1972) Water quality modeling for forecast-ive and planning purposes. Pages 383-390, International Symposium on Modelling Techniques in Water Resources Systems, Proceedings, Vol. 2, edited by Asit K. Biswas. Ottawa, Canada: Environment Canada.

Reid, George W. (1974) Importance of Low Cost Technologies in Water and Wastewater Treatment in Developing Coun-tries. Paper presented at the Conference on Environ-mental Health in the Arabic Cities, Bagdad, 6-11 April.

Reid, George W. (1976) Planning for Water and Waste in Hot Countries. Paper presented at the Third International Conference on Environmental Health Engineering in Hot Climates in Developing Countries, Loughborough Univer-sity of Technology, Loughborough, Leicestershire, UK, September.

Reid, George W. (1977) An urban model for the evaluation of alternative growth policies. Pages 335-340, Regional Environmental Systems, Assessment of RANN Projects, NSF/ ENV 76-04273. Seattle, Washington: Department of Civil Engineering, University of Washington.

Reid, George W., and Kay Coffey, eds. (1978) Appropriate Methods of Treating Water and Wastewater in Developing Countries. Norman, Oklahoma: Bureau of Water and En-vironmental Resources Research, University of Oklahoma. (Prints are available from the United States Agency for International Development, Washington, D.C.)

Reid, George W., and Richard Discenza (1975a) Predictive
    Methodology for Suitable Water and Wastewater Processes.
    Norman, Oklahoma: Bureau of Water and Environmental Re-
    sources Research, University of Oklahoma. (Prints are
    available from the United States Agency for Interna-
    tional Development, Washington, D.C.)

Reid, George W., and Richard Discenza (1975b) Predictive
    Methodology for Suitable Water and Wastewater Processes,
    Supplement II, Computer Program. Norman, Oklahoma:
    Bureau of Water and Environmental Resources Research,
    The University of Oklahoma. (Prints are available from
    the United States Agency for International Development,
    Washington, D.C.)

Reid, George W., and Richard Discenza (1976) Predictive Meth-
    odology for Suitable Water and Wastewater Processes.
    Technical Paper Series No. 8. The Hague, Netherlands:
    World Health Organization, International Reference Cen-
    ter for Community Water Supply.

Reid, George W., and Michael I. Muiga (1975) Aggregate Mod-
    elling of Water Demands for Developing Countries Using
    Socio-Economic Growth Patterns. Paper presented at the
    UNDP/UN Interregional Seminar on River Basin Develop-
    ment, Budapest, September.

Reid, George W., and Dale A. Smisher (1975) Low Cost Methods
    of Treating Water in Developing Countries. Paper pre-
    sented at the International Water Resources Association,
    Nag Pur, India, December. Also presented at the Confer-
    ence of the American Water Works Association, Denver,
    Colorado, April.

Reid, George W., Albert Talboys, and Dale A. Smisher (1974)
    Low cost methods of water and waste treatment in less
    developed countries. Pages 388-395, Water for the Human
    Environment, Proceedings of the First World Congress on
    Water Resources, Vol. 3, edited by V.T. Chow, S.C.
    Csallany, R.J. Krizek, and H.C. Preul. Champaign,
    Illinois: International Water Resources Association.

World Health Organization, International Reference Center for
    Community Water Supply (1977) A Report on the Global
    Workshop on Appropriate Water and Wastewater Treatment
    Technology for Developing Countries, Voorburg, Nether-
    lands: 17-22 November 1975. Bulletin Series 7.
    Netherlands: The Hague.

A COMPUTER SIMULATION MODEL FOR THE MANAGEMENT OF THE LAKE MAGGIORE WATER SYSTEM

G. Ambrosino, G. Fronza, and R. Soncini-Sessa

1. INTRODUCTION

Over the last 20 years, as an alternative or a complement to standard engineering techniques, cost-benefit analysis has often been used for water resource decision-making problems. (See Hall and Dracup 1970, Herfindahl and Kneese 1974, James and Lee 1971, Kneese and Smith 1970, Maass *et al.* 1962, and Wiener 1972. This list includes studies at different economic scales, ranging from the single-reservoir operation problem to complex environmental planning.) However, the application of cost-benefit analysis to real cases often encounters difficulties related both to the validity of the underlying economic assumptions (the partial equilibrium—purely competitive representation of the markets) and to evaluation problems (determination of demand curves, discount factors, etc.).

Moreover, in regions where resource use is not at an early phase, the decision maker's actual freedom of choice may be strongly restricted by previously granted rights of resource use. These rights, often of a complex form and sometimes even unwritten, may have established equilibria among conflicting objectives. Specifically, the situation in developed regions often exhibits the following characteristics.

● Complexity of the short-run operation, i.e., of the operating rules of the system, varies many times during the year and in each period of the year. The operational rules are described by complex functional relationships. This characteristic of the system regulation resembles the resource use rights and behavior mentioned above.

● Long-run modifications (new investments, new users) are infeasible if they imply too strong a change in the status quo

Hence, it is necessary to take into account the relative in-
flexibility of the existing situation. Such a viewpoint has
been accepted by the authors of this paper when dealing with
the opportunity for increasing the useful capacity of Lake
Maggiore, which has long been a multipurpose reservoir of
primary economic importance in northern Italy. The study
illustrated here consists of two steps.

The first step is to set up an interpretative model of
the present situation, namely, of the present operating rule.
We observed that even if the year is subdivided into a certain number of "seasons", an analysis of the past operation
does not point out a rigorous operating rule, i.e., a functional relationship between yield and resource availability.
Rather, in each season there is an average behavior (of complex form) that can be regarded as an operating rule plus
erratic (but at times relevant) real-time adjustments. These
adjustments represent empirical adaptations to unpredictable
situations of water availability or demand, subjective judgment and forecasts, etc. Identification of the operating
rule (in the sense of average behavior) was carried out by
means of a modified least-squares fitting technique.

The second step (see section 3) is to simulate the possible effects of different capacity enhancements under different exploitations of the extra capacity. Specifically,
two types of effects (one corresponding to economic benefits
and one to costs) were considered.

● The smoothing of deficit yields for downstream users

● The enhancement of storage peaks (in flood conditions) that cause damage to the recreational facilities located on the lakeside

These two aspects are predominant from an economic viewpoint
and, in fact, the present value of capacity results from a
difficult tradeoff between the different requirements of the
downstream users and of the recreation facilities on the
lake (De Marchi 1945, Citrini 1973). In turn, the complex
release policy is the result of a difficult (but long settled) tradeoff between the different requirements of the two
main downstream users: agriculture and hydroelectric power
production. Thus, the analysis illustrated here was carried
out under a basic "management continuity" assumption: the
present release policy (see section 2 for a description of
the procedure) keeps the amount of release within the range
of storages corresponding to the present value of capacity.

2. THE PRESENT MANAGEMENT: AN INTERPRETATIVE MODEL

In the system under consideration, water is released
downstream through gates located at the outlet of Lake Maggiore. The decision on the yield can be practically considered continuous in time. In fact, the position of the gates

is set in the morning of each day, and in most cases, it is
not changed until the next morning. However, it may be modified during the day in particular situations (e.g., incoming
flood).

Based on an analysis of demand and availability characteristics the year has been divided into the following eight
"seasons":

(1)   1 January-14 February
(2)   15 February-28 February
(3)   1 March-15 April
(4)   16 April-30 April
(5)   1 May-15 September
(6)   16 September-20 October
(7)   21 October-30 November
(8)   1 December-31 December

The seasons have then been considered during periods of different management behavior. In particular, the effect of
present legislation on lake operation has been taken into
account since it is established by law whether or not the
gates be kept open when a certain level is exceeded. The
certain level (measured with respect to the hydrometric zero
in Sesto Calende, by the lake outlet) is: $x_M = 1.00$ m during the summer period (1 March-1 November) and $x_M = 1.50$ m
during the remainder of the year. This constraint on lake
operation has the effect of limiting storages. It has been
imposed by the lakeside inhabitants in order to protect their
facilities from floods.

The decision maker's present behavior has been identified by the following procedure. Consider the lake continuity equation:

$$dx/dt = [a(t) - u(t)]/S(x(t)) \qquad (1)$$

where

$x(t)$ is the level at instant t (meters)

$a(t)$ is the inflow rate at instant t (m^3/sec)

$u(t)$ is the release flow rate at instant t (m^3/sec)

$S(x(t))$ is the lake surface at instant t (m^2)

The decision maker's behavior exhibits a "systematic component", which can be revealed by examining past operation
figures for each season; more precisely, by analyzing levels
and release flow rates at the beginning of each day in a
yield-level plane. Figure 1 illustrates the situation in
the third season; the situation is quite similar in the
other seasons. If the level is outside the regulation range
(namely, when $x(t) > x_M$), the release-level pairs remain on
the lake discharge-elevation curve, because of the legal
constraint mentioned above.

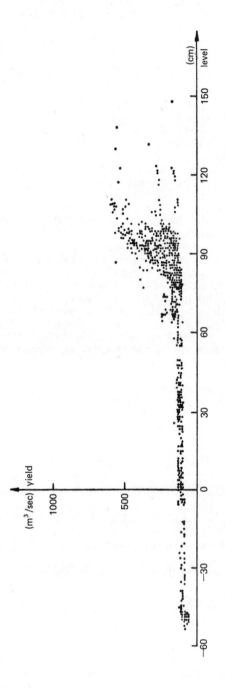

FIGURE 1   Past regulation figures in season 3.

In conclusion, the empirical analysis of past management considers the release the result of an underlying operating rule (specifically a yield-level relationship) to be identified by interpolating management figures, namely, by filtering the superimposed "random noise" (see Figure 1) corresponding to erratic real-time adjustments. It must be stressed that this is an *a posteriori* interpretation since no written or explicit prescription exists. Rather, there is a certain number of target releases of downstream users, but the figures represent only reference values, not actual supplies, and they are not enough for properly accounting for the whole management behavior.

In view of the empirical analysis, the operating rule has been postulated to belong to the following class (see Figure 2) ($S = 1, 2, \ldots, S_j$):

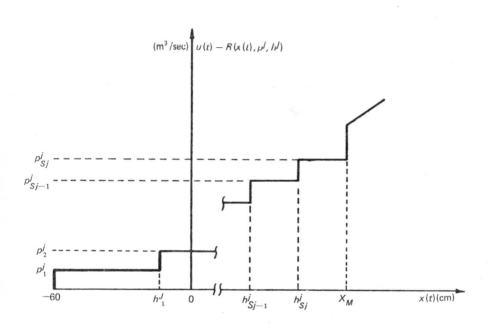

FIGURE 2   Operating rule.

$$
u(t) = R(x(t); \, p^j, \, h^j) = \begin{cases}
p^j_i & \text{if } x(t) < h^j_1 & (2a) \\[2mm]
p^j_s & \text{if } h^j_s \leq x(t) < h^j_{s+1} & (2b) \\[2mm]
p^j_{S_j} & \text{if } h^j_{S_j} \leq x(t) < x_M & (2c) \\[2mm]
N(x(t)) & \text{if } x_M \leq x(t) & (2d)
\end{cases}
$$

where j is the seasonal index $(j = 1,2,\ldots,8)$; $N(x(t))$ represents the lake discharge-elevation curve [see explanation of equation (2d)]; and $p^j = |p^j_i|$, $h^j = |h^j_i|$. Since the available data for identifying p^j and h^j are daily inflow volumes plus levels and release flow rates at the beginning of each day, it is necessary to use the continuity equation (1) with the operating rule equation (2) to calculate a daily mass balance:

$$x(k + 1) = x(k) + \int_{kT}^{(k+1)T} \left[a(t) - R(x(t); \ p^j, \ h^j)\right] dt/S(x(t)) \tag{3}$$

where $T = 86{,}400$, the number of seconds in a day; and $x(k)$ represents the level at the beginning of the kth day. Equation (3) can be simplified as follows.

(a) In a "nonflood" situation, for example when $x(k) < x_M$, the level variation in 1 day is not very relevant. Therefore, a good approximation can be obtained by setting $x(t) = x(k)$ in the integral of the second term in equation (3). Thus, the daily mass balance is

$$x(k + 1) = x(k) + \left[A(k) - T \cdot R(x(k); \ p^j, \ h^j)\right]\Big/S(x(k)) \tag{3a}$$

where $A(k)$ is the inflow volume in the kth day.

(b) In a "flood" situation, for example when $x(k) > x_M$, approximation (a) may lead to conspicuous errors. In this case, it is better to evaluate $x(k + 1)$ by using an interactive procedure; recall from equation (2d) that $R(x(k); \ p^j, \ h^j) = N(x(k))$, in this case:

$$x_{v+1}(k + 1) = x(k) + [A(k) - T \cdot N(x_v(k + 1) + x(k))/2]/S(x(k)) \tag{3b}$$

where $v = 1,2,\ldots,$ is the iteration index of the procedure; while $x_1(k + 1) = x(k)$ is the starting value of the procedure.

The inflow and level record of the period 1954-1975 has been considered. In correspondence with such data, identification of parameters p^j and h^j in equation (3) has been obtained using a modified least-squares fitting technique. Specifically, for each j, h^j and p^j have been chosen in accordance with the criterion:

$$\min_{h^j, p^j} \sum_k J(e(k; p^j, \ h^j)) \tag{4}$$

where $e(k;\ p^j,\ h^j)$ is the difference between the actual lake level and the level given by the model; $J(e)$ is the truncated parabola shown in Figure 3, and the sum is extended over all days of the jth seasons of the period considered. The use of equation (4) instead of the standard least-squares approach has smoothed the effect of totally irregular releases and given a more reliable result.

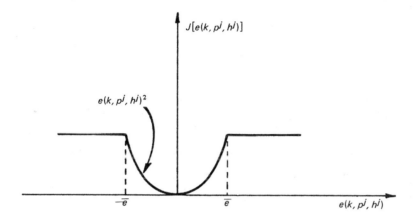

FIGURE 3   Performance index to be minimized in model identification.

The solution of the mathematical program of equation (4) has been done through an iterative algorithm; more precisely, through pattern search (see Himmelblau 1972) which has given a rather quick convergence. At each iteration of the algorithm in the space of the decision variables $(p^j,\ h^j)$, it is necessary to evaluate the sequence $\{e(k;\ p^j,\ h^j)\}_k$ by using equations (2)-(3). The optimal values of the decision variables (model parameters) are shown in Table 1. Such parameter

TABLE 1   Model parameters $(p_j\,(\text{m}^3/\text{sec}),\ h_j\,(\text{cm}))$.

Season	Variable								
	p_1	h_1	p_2	h_2	p_3	h_3	p_4	h_4	p_5
1	107	-28	114	-16	135	92	152	126	107
2	108	-32	136	36	149	87	164	—	—
3	85	-47	107	- 2	124	64	153	95	165
4	118	- 4	164	35	200	—	—	—	—
5	133	-29	181	25	210	75	228	—	—
6	90	-46	109	-39	128	55	146	88	179
7	90	-17	115	50	136	98	140	140	181
8	107	0	115	62	128	81	141	140	158

values are reliable, since a large amount of data has been used, and, moreover, the data have proved to be homogeneous. As a matter of fact, identification of the model by separately using only subrecords (of 1954-1964 and 1965-1975, respectively) has not given substantial differences with respect to the results shown in Table 1.

Table 2 gives some significant indexes of the quality of the fitting between the interpretative model and the actual management. As for deficit situations, different combinations of reference flow rates (targets) in the summer and winter periods have been considered. For each reference flow rate b, the sequence $\{d_{bT}(k)\}_k$ of deficit release flow rates $(d_{bT}(k) = \max (0, b - u_T(k)))$ in the actual regulation has been evaluated, as well as the sequence $\{\hat{d}_b(k)\}_k$ supplied by the model. If

$$\{D_{bT}(k) = T \cdot d_{bT}(k)\}_k$$

and

$$\{\hat{D}_b(k) = T \cdot \hat{d}_b(k)\}_k$$

TABLE 2 Indexes of the model fitting vs. the reality.

Modeled		Actual	
$\rho_u = 98$	$e_u = 0.0$ (m^3/sec)	$\sigma_u = 45$ (m^3/sec)	
$e_p = 0.0$ (cm)	$\sigma_p = 3.0$ (cm)	$e_{max} = 9.0$ (cm)	
$D^1_{110T} = 339$ $(10^8 m^3)$		$\hat{D}^1_{110} = 286$ $(10^6 m^3)$	
$D^1_{140T} = 15,170$ $(10^6 m^3)$		$\hat{D}^1_{140} = 13,481$ $(10^6 m^3)$	
$D^2_{170T} = 101$ $(10^6 m^3)$		$\hat{D}^2_{170} = 93$ $(10^6 m^3)$	

NOTES: The table shows the correlation ρ_u between model and actual releases, the average e_u and the standard deviation σ_u of the release error, the average e_p and the standard deviation σ_p of the lake-floods estimation error (that is, the error in estimating the levels exceeding 2.5 m), and the maximum value e_{max} of the lake-floods estimation error. D^l_{bT} and $\hat{D}^l_b$ are total deficit volumes, modeled and actual respectively, in the period l ($l = 1$ is the winter period; $l = 2$ is the summer period) for the reference flow rate b.

denote the sequence of deficit volume in the actual and simulated regulations respectively, the total deficit volume in
the period p_l (l = 1 corresponds to the winter period; l = 2
corresponds to the summer period),

$$v^l_{bT} = \sum_{k \in p_l} v_{bT}(k) \qquad \left(\hat{v}^l_b = \sum_{k \in p_l} \hat{v}_b(k) \right) \qquad \text{for various } b$$

has been evaluated (Table 2).

3. SIMULATION OF THE EFFECTS OF ENHANCING THE REGULATION
   RANGE

The interpretative model described in section 2 has
been used for determining the effects of enhancing the regulation range. Such effects are both positive (smoothing of
downstream deficits) and negative (more severe lake floods)
from an economic viewpoint. Two different regulation range
enhancements have been considered separately:

(α) x_M is set equal to 1.50 m also in the summer period
(1 March-1 November)

(β) x_M is set equal to 2.00 m throughout the whole year

Of course, it is necessary to make assumptions about
the management behavior in a condition of modified range.
Hence the following basic hypothesis has been made. In the
modified situation the present operating rule would be maintained within the range of levels corresponding to the present regulation range. This corresponds to an assumption of
a minimum perturbation of the pattern of releases and hence
of equilibria between downstream users.

Three different exploitation policies of the extra range
have been considered, both in situations (α) and (β). They
are shown in Figure 4, where it is clear that Policy I is
the less "careful" with respect to the effects of the extra
range on the enhancement of lake floods, while Policy III is
the most careful. For all possible combinations of extra
ranges and of extra-range exploitation policies, equations
(2)-(3), adjusted to the new x_M values and to the extended
operating rules of Figure 4, have been run. In particular,
the following indexes have been evaluated (see Table 3):
for various b (reference flow rate), the total deficit volume D^l_b in the summer and winter period ($10^6 m^3$). For flood
situations, Figure 5 shows observed and computed daily lake
levels during the flood periods, i.e., when $x(k) > 2.5$ m.

138

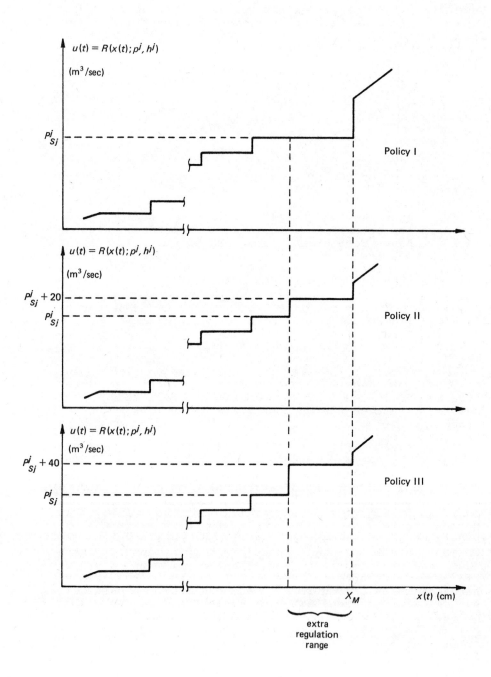

FIGURE 4 Different policies for exploiting the extra regulation range.

TABLE 3 Indexes of deficit for various extra regulation ranges and different exploitation policies.

	Policy I	Policy II	Policy III
Situation (α):			
	$D^1_{110} = 152 \ (10^6 \text{m}^3)$	$D^1_{110} = 160 \ (10^6 \text{m}^3)$	$D^1_{110} = 173 \ (10^6 \text{m}^3)$
	$D^1_{140} = 9,240 \ (10^6 \text{m}^3)$	$D^1_{140} = 9,686 \ (10^6 \text{m}^3)$	$D^1_{140} = 10,084 \ (10^6 \text{m}^3)$
	$D^2_{170} = 69 \ (10^6 \text{m}^3)$	$D^2_{170} = 71 \ (10^6 \text{m}^3)$	$D^2_{170} = 72 \ (10^6 \text{m}^3)$
Situation (β):			
	$D^1_{110} = 123 \ (10^6 \text{m}^3)$	$D^1_{110} = 144 \ (10^6 \text{m}^3)$	$D^1_{110} = 151 \ (10^6 \text{m}^3)$
	$D^1_{140} = 7,876 \ (10^6 \text{m}^3)$	$D^1_{140} = 8,647 \ (10^6 \text{m}^3)$	$D^1_{140} = 9,224 \ (10^6 \text{m}^3)$
	$D^2_{170} = 69 \ (10^6 \text{m}^3)$	$D^2_{170} = 69 \ (10^6 \text{m}^3)$	$D^2_{170} = 69 \ (10^5 \text{m}^3)$

FIGURE 5a   Present policy.

FIGURE 5   Observed (a) and computed (b-g) lake levels during flood events from 1 January 1954 to 31 December 1975 under different policies.

141

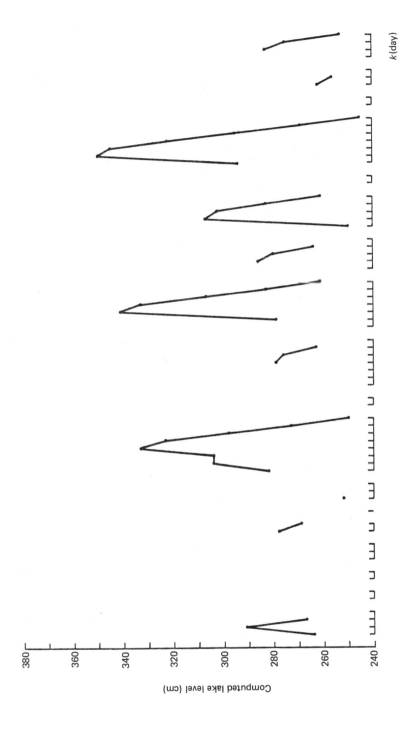

FIGURE 5b Policy Iα.

FIGURE 5c Policy Iβ.

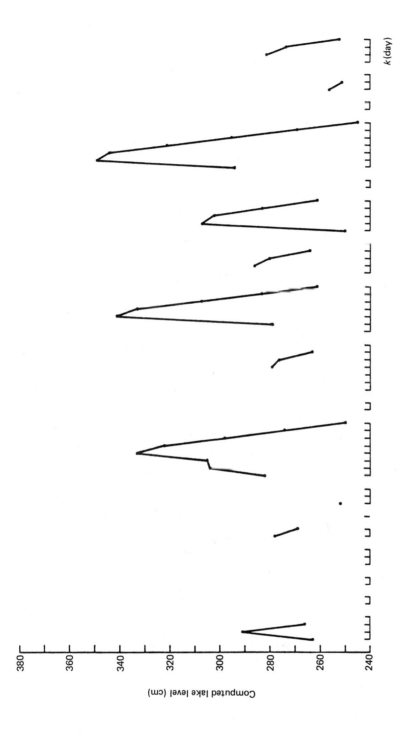

FIGURE 5d Policy IIα.

144

FIGURE 5e Policy IIβ.

145

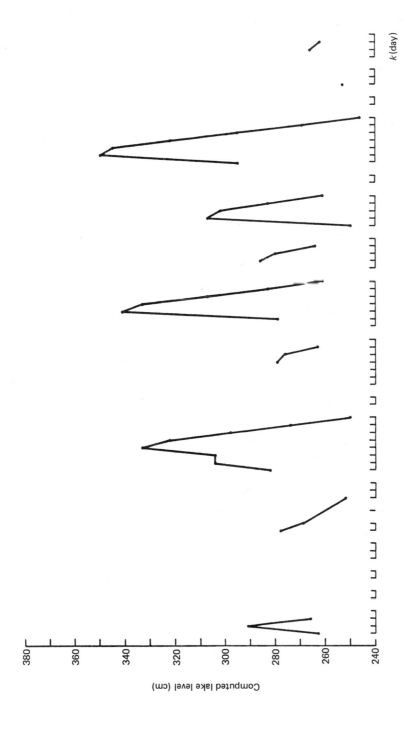

FIGURE 5f   Policy IIIα.

FIGURE 5g Policy IIIβ.

4. MODEL IMPLEMENTATION AND USE

As stated in the previous sections, the philosophy of the model described in this paper is quite simple: the model quantifies an existing complex situation with satisfactory detail and points out the effects of perturbations of the status quo. The model philosophy is scarcely questionable, namely, there is no realistic alternative (in terms of quantitative analysis) to the present model (in the specific case).

The model programming is not complicated since it consists of simulating the daily continuity equation in different conditions, though under a complex operating rule. The model computer costs are modest (for each 22-year simulation run, computer time is about 20 seconds).

In view of these positive features, the model has been favorably considered by the decision-making staff during its development. Moreover, the study is likely to be enlarged to include other lakes with similar management problems in northern Italy.

REFERENCES

Citrini, D. (1973) The Floods of Lake Maggiore and the River in the First Thirty Years of Regulation. Publication No. 14. Milano: Consorzio del Ticino (in Italian).

De Marchi, G. (1945) Determination of the Water Flows made Available for Utilization by the Regulation of the Outflows of Lake Maggiore. Publication No. 2. Milano: Consorzio del Ticino (in Italian).

Hall, W.A., and J.A. Dracup (1970) Water Resources Systems Engineering. New York: McGraw-Hill.

Herfindahl, O., and A. Kneese (1974) Economic Theory of Natural Resources. Columbus, Ohio: Charles Merril Publishing Company.

Himmelblau, D.L. (1972) Applied Nonlinear Programming. New York: McGraw-Hill.

James, L.D., and R.R. Lee (1971) Economics of Water Resources Planning. New York: McGraw Hill.

Kneese, A.V., and S.C. Smith (1970) Water Research. Baltimore, Maryland: Johns Hopkins University Press.

Maass, A., et al. (1962) Design of Water-Resource Systems. Cambridge, Massachusetts: Harvard University Press.

Wiener, A. (1972) The Role of Water in Development. New York: McGraw-Hill.

THE USE OF A GROUNDWATER MODEL IN THE DESIGN, PERFORMANCE
ASSESSMENT, AND OPERATION OF A RIVER REGULATION SCHEME

M.W. Liddament, D.B. Oakes, A.C. Skinner, and W.B. Wilkinson

1. INTRODUCTION

Abstractions for public water supply and industry, currently amounting to a net demand of 380 Ml/d, are withdrawn
from the River Severn, England (Figure 1). The total li-
censed abstraction rate is 850 Ml/d of which 500 Ml/d can be

FIGURE 1   Demand on the River Severn.

149

supplied by the Clywedog regulating reservoir ($49.7 \times 10^6 m^3$) located in the headwaters. The stored water is released to the river at times of low flow to meet the many demands on the river system. These demands are rising and by the early 1980s another source of storage for river regulation must be found. Having made extensive investigations the Severn-Trent Water Authority now proposes to develop the groundwater resources of the Triassic sandstone aquifer of North Shropshire for this purpose (Severn-Trent Water Authority 1977a). The River Severn and its tributaries flow over the outcrop of the aquifer.

Mathematical models of the groundwater system have been used in combination with surface water models to determine the feasibility of this proposal and to aid in well field design. Once the scheme becomes operational, the models will be used to assess performance, and following some modification to their structure, they will be used to assist in scheme management. As far as the groundwater system is concerned, this will involve phasing of abstraction between well groups during a regulation period and the control of compensation discharge water to the tributary rivers. This paper describes briefly this novel use of groundwater within a multiple water resource system and the way in which groundwater models have contributed to design; more particularly, it describes the proposed role and structure of a groundwater management model.

The Triassic sandstones comprising the aquifer are coarse- to medium-grained. By drilling it has been determined that they are at least 200 m thick, and geophysical surveys indicate that in places they may exceed 450 m. They underlie about 800 km^2 of the North Shropshire plain (Figure 2). Over large areas of the aquifer the sandstone is covered by glacial and more recent deposits of gravels, sands, and clays (usually referred to as drift deposits), in places up to 60 m thick. Typical aquifer transmissivity is in the range 200-500 m^2/d and the unconfined and confined storage coefficients are about 0.1 and 0.0001 respectively (Severn River Authority 1974).

The field investigations were designed to determine the amount of natural recharge to, discharge from, and storage in the sandstone aquifer, and to establish the yield that could be obtained by using the groundwater resource to contribute to the regulation of the River Severn. The groundwater models helped to resolve a number of difficulties and constraints in meeting the above objectives. For example, (i) the drift deposits covering the aquifer vary both in lithological type and thickness making it difficult to estimate infiltration, (ii) there are many existing groundwater abstractions in the area which are used for public water supply, industry, agriculture, and private domestic use, and the proposals had to ensure the protection of these or the provision of alternative supplies, (iii) if the abstraction wells for the scheme were not properly sited, the withdrawal of groundwater would reduce the baseflow of the surface streams to the extent that recirculation between surface

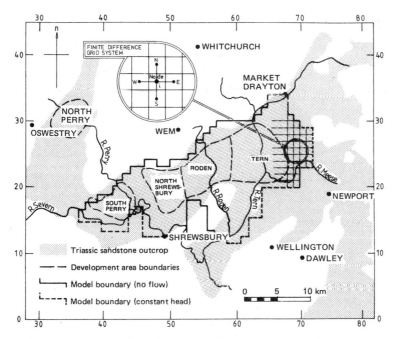

FIGURE 2   The model boundary, grid system, and extent of the
            Triassic sandstone aquifer of North Shropshire.

water and the wells would result, making the scheme inefficient for river regulation, and (iv) compensation water is
needed to support the tributary rivers at certain times when
there is no requirement for main river regulation and this
had to be quantified.

    The investigations have established a natural recharge
to the aquifer of some 200 Ml/d, of which about 80 Ml/d is
currently abstracted by existing boreholes. The Severn-
Trent Water Authority proposes to pump the groundwater from
the aquifer using about 70 newly constructed boreholes and
to discharge this to the River Severn to increase the net
yield available from the regulated river by 225 Ml/d. The
groundwater abstraction will only be required at times of
low flow, on average only once every 3 years, and thus this
large increase in the yield of the River Severn can be
achieved by imposing a long-term average demand on the
groundwater system of between 7 and 10 Ml/d, depending on
the method of management.

    The initial construction and calibration of the ground-
water model used much of the data on the hydrology and hydrogeology of the area collected during the investigation phase.
The scheme will be introduced in stages to meet rising demands and at each stage the groundwater model will be used
in its management and to assess operational performance.

The feedback from this analysis and the new data on aquifer properties and groundwater levels arising as each new stage is built and operated will be used to refine the modeling process, to provide better predictions of the next stage of development, and to improve management of the scheme.

Because of the large storage capacity and slow response of the groundwater system there is no requirement to use the groundwater management model in an on-line mode. In this respect it contrasts strongly to many surface water resource management models.

The costs of model development and operation and data collection and handling are presented in this paper. They are shown to be very small in relation to the estimated con- structional and operational costs of the scheme.

2. DESCRIPTION OF THE GROUNDWATER MODEL

A regional simulation model of the River Severn catch- ment incorporating both surface water and groundwater compo- nents is used to govern the operation of the river regulation scheme. In this regional resource model the groundwater com- ponent is treated as a simple storage reservoir. In practice the interaction of the groundwater system with surface water flow in the tributaries of the River Severn is complex; thus to aid the design and operation of the groundwater scheme, a separate model of the groundwater system has been produced. The structure of the groundwater model is briefly described in the following section.

The modeled area is illustrated in Figure 2. The short dashed lines denote constant head boundaries formed where there is good hydraulic contact with rivers. The remaining model boundaries, shown by solid lines, are formed by geo- logical faults and groundwater divides across which there is assumed to be no groundwater flow. This diagram also shows the regions in which the various well groups are sited. The North Perry region is not yet included in the modeled area. This region will be modeled at a later stage as the develop- ment of the groundwater scheme proceeds.

The major watercourses crossing the region are the Riv- ers Tern, Roden, and Perry. Of these, the Rivers Tern and Roden are in hydraulic contact with the groundwater system. The results of field studies have been used to determine the maximum induced leakage from these two rivers. The River Perry is several meters above the main water table on rela- tively impermeable drift cover, and no hydraulic contact is assumed.

In areas of outcrop and thin sandy drift it is assumed that aquifer recharge takes place directly by rainfall infil- tration. Over the remainder of the area, vertical leakage is assumed to be dependent on the permeability and saturated

thickness of the drift cover. In places the groundwater
level is confined by these drift deposits.

Perennial abstraction for local water supply, river
regulation, and compensation are represented in the model.
Regulation abstraction is controlled by strict rules governed
by the River Severn regional simulation model. This abstraction takes place from boreholes built for this purpose, and
the water is discharged into the River Severn and its tributaries. Compensation abstraction is introduced to compensate
fully for both the reduction in groundwater baseflow and the
induced riverbed leakage during regulation periods. At the
end of the regulation period when the River Severn no longer
requires support from the groundwater scheme, compensation
abstraction may also be required to supplement reduced river
flow in the tributaries. The quantity and duration of compensation abstraction is evaluated using the groundwater model.

These features are modeled by numerical solution of the
transient two-dimensional groundwater flow equation given by

$$\frac{\partial T}{\partial x}\frac{\partial h}{\partial x} + \frac{\partial T}{\partial y}\frac{\partial h}{\partial y} = S\frac{\partial h}{\partial t} - Q \tag{1}$$

where

      x, y are coordinates in the horizontal plane

    $h(x,y,t)$ is height of piezometric surface

    $Q(x,y,t)$ is source term, including infiltration, drift
        leakage, riverbed leakage, and abstraction

      $T(x,y)$ is transmissivity, and

      $S(x,y)$ is storage coefficient

It is assumed in this equation that the horizontal component
of groundwater flow is much greater than the vertical component and that changes in the saturated thickness of any unconfined part of the aquifer are small.

The area of the groundwater scheme was superposed by a
rectangular grid system corresponding to the 1-km United
Kingdom National Grid. The number of internal grid squares
thus formed was 375. Equation (1) was replaced at the cen-
troid of each grid square by its fully implicit finite different approximation (Figure 2). For a typical node, i, the
approximation is given by

$$(1/\Delta x)^2 \{ T_{iN}(h_N - h_i) + T_{iW}(h_W - h_i) + T_{iS}(h_S - h_i)$$

$$+ T_{iE}(h_E - h_i) \} = (S_i/\Delta t)(h_i - h_i{}') - Q_i \tag{2}$$

where

$T_{i\mathrm{N}}$ is harmonic mean transmissivity between node i and the adjacent North node

h_i is groundwater level at node i at time $t + \Delta t$

$h_i{}'$ is groundwater level at node i at time t

Q_i is source term at node i

S_i is storage coefficient at node i

Δx is finite difference mesh spacing = 1000 m

Δt is time increment, and

subscripts N,W,S,E refer to adjacent North, West, South, and East nodes

Thus a set of finite difference equations with a corresponding set of unknowns in groundwater level was formulated. These equations were solved by the method of successive over-relaxation (Varga 1962) for successive intervals in time Δt. In general the time interval is 5 days but it may be automatically adjusted to cope with varying aquifer conditions.

A clear understanding of the surface water-groundwater system is required if the model is to be successful. Thus great importance was attached to assessing accurately the regional hydrology and hydrogeology. The Tern and South Perry areas (Figure 2) were first selected for a detailed hydrogeological study and groundwater models of these catchments were produced prior to a model of the complete system. These areas were selected because of their contrasting nature. In the Tern area the Triassic sandstones are largely unconfined, there being little drift cover. In the South Perry catchment the sandstones are generally confined by thick, relatively impermeable drift deposits.

Six abstraction boreholes and associated observation boreholes were constructed in the Tern catchment. The catchment was also gaged and soil-moisture probes installed. The permeability of the bed of the River Tern was determined at several points along its length by taking cores from the riverbed for laboratory examination and by conducting *in situ* falling-head tests. Cores taken during drilling were also studied in the laboratory. Aquifer parameters were determined at individual locations by pump tests and analyses of cores. Eighty-four days of simultaneous abstraction from all the abstraction boreholes also took place. A similar detailed analysis was made in the South Perry area. The

155

survey was then extended to the other regions and permeability tests conducted along the River Roden.

The field data were used as input to the pilot models and to the model of the entire area. The models were calibrated by making adjustments to the aquifer parameters, particularly in regions where data were scarce or uncertain, so that observed sequences of groundwater behavior could be faithfully reproduced. During calibration use was made of regular water-level measurements from observation boreholes and river flows. Calibration periods included the modeling of groundwater flow for the 4-year period between 1 September 1973 and 30 September 1977 and the modeling of group pumping tests in the Tern and South Perry catchments. Figure 3 shows a typical comparison between observed and computed flows in the River Tern between 1 January 1974 and 31 December 1975,

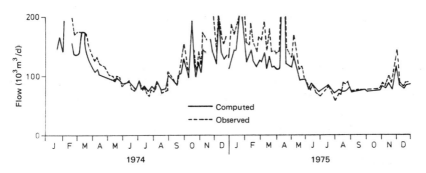

FIGURE 3   Comparison of observed and computed flows in the River Tern.

and Figure 4 illustrates the observed and computed drawdowns at the end of the group pumping test in the Tern pilot area.

3.   PLANNING AND DESIGN STAGE

It is not the primary purpose of this paper to describe the planning and design stages of the scheme, but rather to emphasize the developing role which groundwater models of the type described can play in the successive stages of resources investigation, design, and operation. The various phases of the design process where the model has been used are described below.

3.1   *Development of Control Rules*

The phasing in of surface and groundwater regulation of the River Severn during a relatively dry year is shown in Figure 5. A diagrammatic hydrograph at the Bewdley Control

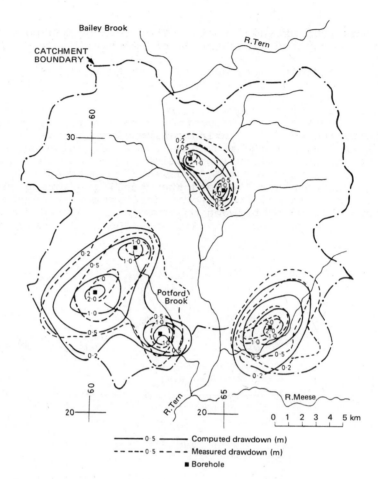

FIGURE 4   Comparison of observed and computed drawdowns in the Tern pilot area at the end of the group pumping test.

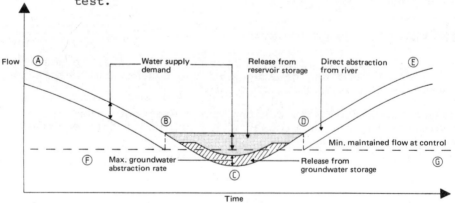

FIGURE 5   Meeting demand at Bewdley on the River Severn by reservoir release and groundwater abstractions.

is shown by the line ABCDE and the minimum maintained flow
by the line FG. To the left and right of B and D, respectively, water supply demands can be met by direct abstraction
from the unregulated river. Between B and D, regulation releases either from surface water or groundwater storage are
required to maintain the minimum flow at Bewdley and to meet
demands. The rules governing the operation of the various
components (reservoirs, groundwater storage, river abstraction, etc.) of the River Severn regulation system are evaluated on a regional resource simulation model.

The low frequency of groundwater used proposed, the
large groundwater storage, and the slow response time of the
groundwater system mean that the use of the groundwater is
primarily determined by the storage state and refill expec-
tancy of the surface reservoir component. There is therefore only a limited need to consider the storage state of
the groundwater system in the operation of the surface reservoir storage. This means that control rule development by
predictive simulation does not require interaction between
surface and groundwater models. The approach that has been
used is to develop simple empirical control rules for the
dual system, treat the groundwater reservoir in an analogous
fashion to a surface reservoir in the resource simulation
model, and apply the resultant demands on groundwater storage
to the groundwater model. This technique has proved to be
successful, but it is recognized that it may not be valid if
much greater load factors of demand are applied to the
groundwater system. In that situation the volume of aquifer
storage at the start of a regulation period may not be sufficient to allow groundwater abstractions to continue at the
maximum possible rate for an extended period. An interactive
surface water-groundwater model would then be needed to develop control rules.

3.2 Well Field Design

A major constraint on the efficiency of groundwater
regulation schemes is the net gain to the river system (Oakes
and Wilkinson 1972). Net gain may be defined as:

$$\text{net gain} = \frac{\text{augmentation of river flow}}{\text{groundwater abstraction rate}}$$

Clearly a scheme with a high net gain (close to unity) is
very efficient, whereas a low net gain (near to zero) indicates a high degree of baseflow interception or recirculation
and is very inefficient. An important factor influencing
net gain is the separation of the boreholes from the river,
since the more remote a borehole is the more it will develop
storage in the aquifer and the less it will intercept natural
drainage to the river system or cause leakage through the
streambed. The minimum net gain acceptable depends on the
cost of the water yielded compared with alternative schemes.
In practice, economic factors require that net gain be

158

greater than about 0.4. In the design of groundwater schemes there is an important economic exchange present, whereby siting boreholes further from the river increases regulation efficiency (net gain) and may therefore, up to a point, reduce operating costs but at the expense of the additional capital cost of longer pipelines to convey the water to the discharge points (Birtles 1977).

Without a reliable groundwater model to provide estimates of net gain for various borehole distributions, an economic analysis cannot be attempted. In the design of the Shropshire scheme, a study was undertaken of the Tern catchment. This study led to the choice of borehole sites remote from the watercourses.

Figure 6 illustrates the operation of the scheme as it affects one of the tributaries of the River Severn to which groundwater will be discharged. The demand is specified by

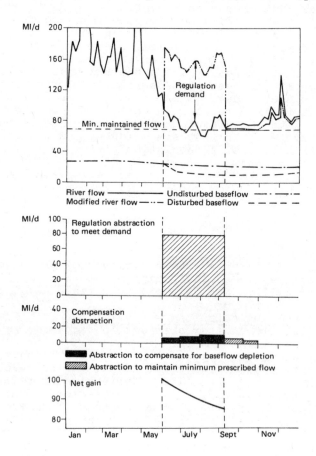

FIGURE 6   Operation of the scheme as it affects one of the tributaries of the River Severn.

the regional simulation model and is met by regulation abstraction. The depletion in the groundwater component of
baseflow to this tributary is determined by the groundwater
model and is fully compensated for by additional groundwater
abstraction. At the end of the regulation period the reduction in baseflow is sufficient to cause the flow in the river
to fall below a minimum desirable flow. Although there is
no requirement to meet a regulation demand on the River Severn, compensation groundwater abstraction is still necessary
for a limited period. For this particular regulation sequence and well field design, the net gain is shown to be
high.

3.3 *Setting of Abstraction Licences*

Under the United Kingdom Water Resources Act 1963, all
abstractions of groundwater must be authorized by a licence
that states the amounts that may be pumped in any specified
period. For boreholes that are only to be used intermittently but that may be used extensively in extreme drought
periods, this poses special problems. The licences must
permit sufficient water to be pumped in drought periods,
both for regulation pumping and for compensation. They
must not be too strict and thus unreasonably restrict other
potential users of goundwater from obtaining their supplies.
The groundwater model has been used to simulate groundwater
abstraction during the critical 5-year period determined
from the River Severn regional simulation model, and the
licences for the individual wells and for each well field
are set on the basis of the groundwater model results.

4. ASSESSMENT OF PERFORMANCE

It is envisaged that, during operation of the groundwater scheme, the model will play an important role in assessing the system performance. Because of the interference between well groups and because of the difficulties in assessing the effect on river flows of augmentation pumping, it
will generally be impossible to infer the performance during
operation of any well group from field measurements of
groundwater levels or river flows alone. Running the numerical model will allow the net gains of the various well
groups to be estimated and thus provide essential data for
planning the next stage of development and for making future
operational policies. Comparison of the model results with
observation will, additionally, highlight areas where
groundwater-level predictions are unreliable. The field
data collected will allow recalibration to proceed concur-
rently with development of the scheme, and thus better prediction of the next stage of development will be provided.
In this manner the model will not be required to make predictions of performance for pumping rates that are greatly
in excess of past usage. A possible computer-based system
for performance assessment and model recalibration is shown

in Figure 7. A fundamental requirement of such a system is
an up-to-date groundwater-level map as input to the numerical model [1].* The map will be updated perhaps on a monthly

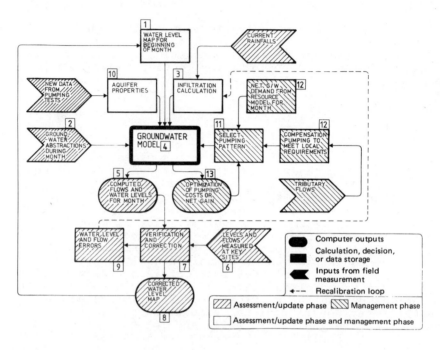

FIGURE 7 Computer-based system for performance assessment,
management, and model recalibration.

basis using actual abstractions [2] and calculated infiltra-
tions [3] during the month to drive the groundwater model
[4]. The levels and flows computed for the end of the month
[5] will be subject to errors because the model cannot represent fully the complexities of the aquifer system and because errors in calibration are inevitable. To prevent long-
term drift of computer water levels, groundwater levels and
river flows will be measured at a number of key sites [6]
and used to correct the computed water-level distributions
[5]. In the early stages of scheme implementation, it is
probable that all of the observation boreholes and river
gaging sites will be used in the correction routine. All
of the data will be of fundamental importance to the assessment of well field performance as well as to the continuing
calibration of the groundwater model and so will need to be
collected in any case. At full development the data collected and available to the computer model will comprise

---

*The numbers in square brackets refer to stages shown
in Figure 7.

abstraction rates from 64 abstraction wells, water levels from 91 observation wells, and river flows from 10 gaging stations.

The correction routine [7] will involve extrapolating the differences between observed and computed levels at the observation boreholes to the entire modeled area using two-dimensional trend analysis. These differences will then be added to the predicted water-level pattern to produce a current water-level map [8] that will be correct at each of the water-level measurement sites, and that will closely approximate the distribution obtained from the model alone.

The accuracy of the prediction program will be readily assessed in terms of the sizes of differences between the predicted and observed levels each month [9]. Additionally the flow hydrograph from the gage on each catchment will be obtained for comparison with the modeled baseflows. The observed flow hydrograph provides an integrated measure of groundwater systems response, and thus provides useful re-calibration data for the storage coefficient [10] and infil-tration rates [3] particularly. Infiltration data are dif-ficult to assess on a catchment with a sizeable runoff com-ponent, and data collected during the operation of the scheme will be valuable in refinement of groundwater recharge esti-mates. Because of the slow system response, data can be pre-sented manually to the computer each month. The process of recalibration to obtain better estimates of aquifer proper-ties [10] will probably also be done manually, rather than by an inverse technique, because of the complexity of the groundwater system and the wealth of hydrogeological knowl-edge that exists.

5. MANAGEMENT

The releases from regulating storage are designed to maintain a prescribed flow at the control point on the River Severn at Bewdley (Figure 8) and at the same time to ensure that the demands of abstractors upstream of the control point can be met. The release strategy is determined from known recession characteristics of the river and its tributaries and precipitation and abstraction forecasts. Analysis of operational experience in 1976 (Severn-Trent Water Authority 1977b), when only surface storage was used to regulate the river, has shown that of the 39,000 Ml released from storage only 82 percent was used to provide for demand upstream of the control point and to meet the minimum statutory pre-scribed flows. Of the remaining 18 percent of the released volume, some 2 percent was lost by seepage and evaporation, while 16 percent was excess regulation and can be attributed to a combination of errors in flow measurement, abstraction forecasting, and hydrological forecasting. For resource planning purposes, regulation losses and excess regulation have been assumed to be no greater than 10 percent. Im-proved hydrological simulation models are being developed by the Authority to predict the river flow at the control

162

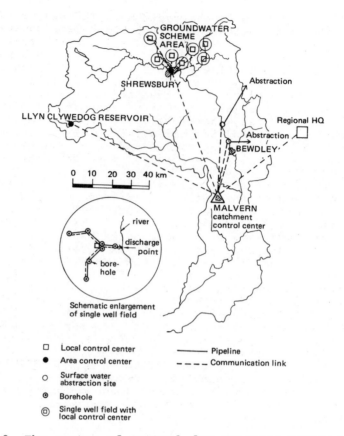

FIGURE 8   The system of control for resource management.

point.   Automatic scanning devices will also be used.   These
will interrogate up to 200 outstations and provide real-time
river-level and rainfall data, supplemented by areal rainfall information from weather radar.

Such a system alone places considerable demands upon
communication and forecasting facilities.   The incorporation
of a groundwater storage into the resource system substantially increases its complexity.   The large amount of data
that will be collected on pumpage, water levels, and rates
of discharge from individual wells and well fields, together
with data from observation boreholes monitoring both water
quality and water level, is comparable in volume to the data
obtained from the rest of the River Severn regulation control
system.   The control and communication facilities proposed
for the groundwater scheme are designed to provide only the
strategic information at catchment management level that will
be used to update the water-level map stored in the model in
the manner described above.   By this means an overview of the
whole groundwater storage system will be maintained in analogous fashion to information on the storage states of the

surface water components of the system. The system of control is illustrated in Figure 8. The catchment control center at Malvern will be the highest level of a three-level hierarchy of information and control. It is from here that the regional simulation model will be operated. The regulation demand and apportionment between the available storage sources are determined at this level. Instructions to meet demand by reservoir releases are sent to the control center at Llyn Clywedog, while instructions to meet demand by groundwater abstractions are sent to the area control center at Shrewsbury. The decision on how to phase in the well groups in order to satisfy the demand will be based largely on basic information concerning the condition of the boreholes, pumps, and pipelines received from the local control centers associated with each group of abstraction wells.

The predictive capability of the groundwater model will be needed during periods of regulation and compensation pumping to cope particularly with potential deterioration of local conditions such as low flows in the tributary streams. Various patterns of pumping can be tried on the model to determine which wells to pump for given conditions [11]. Because the aquifer has a relatively high storage, its response to pumping is quite slow. Similarly, water levels depressed by pumping will recover rather slowly. Water-level fluctuations are typically less than about 30 cm per month. The model is therefore well suited to help in the management of the groundwater component of the scheme. Operation of the model for 2 weekly or monthly predictions of water-level changes and net gains will give adequate warning of the need to revise pumping patterns in response to local or regional conditions. The computer-based scheme shown in Figure 7 includes the facility to do this. Because of the large storage coefficient of the model, predictions are relatively insensitive to infiltration rates so that for a monthly forecast the infiltration may be assumed to be zero. This will give the most pessimistic prediction of groundwater-level changes and will be relevant for management in drought events. For any given demand [12] on the groundwater system, the model may be used to seek some optimum strategy [13] by varying well distribution [11]. The optimum may be related to net gains or pumping costs for example. Either may be calculated from the model outputs. On the basis of the results of these simulations, advice will be given to area control on the pattern of pumping to be adopted. This system will operate most effectively in noncritical drought situations. At times when full use is being made of the groundwater scheme, particularly in low flow periods in the late spring when there is the overriding need to conserve surface storage in the event of an extended drought, the optimizing procedures will not be applicable. In these situations the model will be used to monitor the baseflow recession. This will have the dual purpose of assisting the planning of surface storage releases and providing information for use at the area and local control levels on the likely volume of compensation releases necessary in the event of a cessation of regulation. Without this latter facility, a long period

of gradual reduction of discharge would be necessary to ensure that flows in tributary streams were not allowed to
fall below prescribed minima.

When the scheme is fully operational and a number of
years' operating experience have been acquired, the number
of key site requirements to update the computed water levels
will decrease to perhaps 30, including 10 measurements of
river flow. About 20 groundwater-level measurements per
month will provide an adequate basis for extrapolation over
the whole model area. The most suitable sites for this purpose will become apparent during operation of the model in
the early stages of scheme implementation when all of the
available groundwater data are used. It may at some future
time be possible to discard the water-level map correction
routine or at least to use it less frequently than the prediction routine.

6.   COSTS AND COMPUTER REQUIREMENTS

It has taken 6 man-years' input, including data preparation during calibration and scheme design, to bring the
groundwater model to its present stage of development. This
has been achieved at a cost of £80,000. The computing costs
have been about £15,000. The total costs of development and
simulation to date are thus about £100,000. This is very
small in relation to the estimated cost of the groundwater
scheme of £8m.

Major field investigations in two pilot areas, including
drilling boreholes and test pumping, were made at a cost of
£600,000. Their purpose was to assess the size and best use
of the groundwater resource. The groundwater model has been
an integral part of these investigations. Therefore, it is
not possible to say what proportion of the data costs was
specifically assigned to the needs of the model. It is
clear, however, that large amounts of data are required at
this early stage to develop a reliable groundwater model for
design and subsequent management.

If the groundwater scheme proceeds, the continued use
of the groundwater model is necessary as it is the only means
of determining the performance of certain of the proposed
well groups during operation. A further 2 man-years' input
is required to enhance the present design model so that it
may be used in performance assessment and management (sections 4 and 5 and Figure 7). Once operating, it will require
relatively little attention other than at times when groundwater regulation is imminent. The manning and running costs
at this stage are estimated to be £3,000 per year. This may
be compared with the average annual groundwater pumping costs
of £40,000 per year.

The groundwater model is implemented on a CDC 6500 computer and requires 32,000 sixty-bit words of central memory.

The central processing time for program compilation is 12
seconds, and the time for execution is 43 seconds for each
year of simulation. The cost of a year's simulation is about
£12. The assessment and management routines shown in Figure
7 are not yet complete, but will require little additional
computer storage. Since the update routine will be used only
infrequently, it will be stored on disc or magnetic tape and
called into central memory when required. The biggest demands on computer storage and central processing time will
result from simulation with the groundwater model.

7. CONCLUSIONS

   A groundwater model has been developed that has aided
in (a) determining the size of a groundwater source, and
(b) the detailed design of a scheme to use this resource to
regulate the River Severn. The model development and computing costs have amounted to £100,000. This is a very small
amount in relation to the total capital cost of £8m for the
groundwater regulation scheme.

   A regional simulation model for the River Severn Basin
allocates demands between groundwater and surface water
storage. Because of the slow response time of the groundwater system, it has been shown that there is no requirement
for direct interaction between the regional simulation model
and the detailed groundwater model, at the level of groundwater use envisaged.

   For a small additional expenditure the existing groundwater design model may be readily adapted to deal with performance assessment and operational management. There is no
requirement for real-time operation of the groundwater model.
Continued use of the model is necessary as the scheme develops if the operating efficiency of the scheme is to be properly assessed. Additionally, during the years of scheme implementation the model will provide essential guidance to
the planning of the staged development of the resource.
Benefits will increase if the load factor on groundwater use
is increased.

   A large quantity of data, collected at a cost of several
hundred thousand pounds, has been necessary to calibrate the
groundwater model. Substantial amounts of new data will also
become available as the resource is developed and will be
used to improve model performance. However, the need for
data input will diminish as operational experience is gained.

   The computer requirements for the groundwater model are
by today's standards small. A year's simulation costs £12
and needs central memory storage of 32K words.

166

ACKNOWLEDGMENTS

The authors wish to thank the Director of Operations of the Severn-Trent Water Authority and the Director of the Water Research Centre for permission to publish this paper. The authors also wish to acknowledge the assistance of their colleagues from the former Severn River Authority and the former Water Resources Board.

REFERENCES

Birtles, A.B. (1977) Siting of Groundwater Abstractions for River Regulation. Optimal Development and Management of Groundwater. Presented at the Thirteenth Congress of the International Association of Hydrogeologists, Birmingham, England.

Oakes, D.B., and W.B. Wilkinson (1972) Modelling of Groundwater and Surface Water Systems. 1—Theoretical Relationships Between Groundwater Abstraction and Baseflow. Reading Bridge House, Reading, England: Water Resources Board.

Severn River Authority (1974) Shropshire Groundwater Investigation. First Report. Sheldon, Birmingham, England: Severn-Trent Water Authority.

Severn-Trent Water Authority (1977a) Shropshire Groundwater. Report of the Investigation and Proposals for Development. Sheldon, Birmingham, England: Severn-Trent Water Authority.

Severn-Trent Water Authority (1977b) Regulation of the River Severn—1975 and 1976. Sheldon, Birmingham, England: Severn-Trent Water Authority.

Varga, R.S. (1962) Matrix Iterative Methods. Englewood Cliffs, New Jersey: Prentice-Hall.

MATHEMATICAL MODEL OF THE UPPER NILE BASIN
(COMMENTS ON LOGISTICS AND BENEFITS OF SIMULATION MODELS)

J. Nemec and G.W. Kite

INTRODUCTION

A large number of symposia all over the world have witnessed the development of a great number of simulation models of water resource systems by consultant engineering companies, research institutes, and universities. The very
same symposia have also witnessed the efforts by the authors
of the models to prove the correctness of their model's
structure and of its algorithmic formulation and, by more or
less complicated verification criteria, to prove that the
results obtained are good. While the need for a scientifically sound and reasonably structured model is not questioned,
when a need for it arises in hydrologic and water resource
development projects and activities, this scientific sub-
stance is often overshadowed by logistics in the model's
application. Under these logistics the data base, the hardware available, the skill of the user, and the cost of the
model's development and continuous use are considered most
important. However, the importance of logistics is rarely
stressed in the above-mentioned symposia and authors of models often ignore them.

The World Meteorological Organization (WMO), in addition
to its project on intercomparison of conceptual hydrologic
models for purposes of forecasting (WMO 1975), has used several models in its field projects in Africa, Asia, and Latin
America. The importance of logistics has been amply demonstrated by WMO's experience. The most salient example of
this is perhaps the planning, development, and use of a simulation package for the water resource system of the Upper
Nile Basin, including Lake Victoria, Lake Kyoga, Lake Mobutu
Sese Seko, the River Nile, and many other rivers. The model
is being used by the Hydrometeorological Survey Project, an
international endeavor described below.

THE MATHEMATICAL SIMULATION OF THE UPPER NILE BASIN

The Hydrometeorological Survey Project originated in 1967 as a cooperative venture of the governments of Egypt, Kenya, Sudan, Tanzania, and Uganda with WMO acting as executing agency for the United Nations Development Programme (UNDP). The objective of the first phase of the project from 1967 to 1972 was to collect and analyze hydrologic and meteorological data from the lake catchments. The desire to find an explanation for the unprecedented rise in the levels of the lakes in the early 1960s provided a major stimulus for collecting these data.

In 1974 it was decided that sufficient data had been collected to enable a mathematical model of the Upper Nile Basin to be made. As a consequence, a second phase of the assistance to the Project was agreed upon between UNDP/WMO and the riparian countries (now including Rwanda and Burundi). The objectives of this second phase include the development of the model and the investigation of various alternative patterns of regulation for the lakes to increase benefits to the riparian countries. The building of the model was entrusted, after an international bidding procedure, to the Snowy Mountains Engineering Corporation (SMEC) Pty. of Cooma, Australia, a consulting company, with Australian Government participation.

The mathematical model of the Upper Nile Basin simulates the hydrology and hydraulics of the River Nile, its lakes, and its tributaries from the headwaters in Rwanda and Burundi to a point about 20 km north of the outlet of Lake Mobutu Sese Seko. The total catchment area simulated is around 410,000 km^2 and includes portions of Burundi, Kenya, Rwanda, Tanzania, Uganda, and Zaire. To carry out this task the overall model, which consists of 37 FORTRAN computer programs, is divided into three main components:

● A catchment component which converts precipitation and potential evapotranspiration inputs into runoff in the rivers flowing to the lakes and to the main Nile

● A lake water balance component which performs an accounting function to balance the inputs to the lakes (precipitation and evaporation over the lakes and runoff from the land area) with the outflows from the lakes

● A channel component which simulates the movement of water through the river channels between the lakes

These three components are brought together by a master program which calls the individual programs as they are required. The catchment component, a variation on the U.S. National Weather Service Sacramento model (Burnash *et al.* 1973), takes daily precipitation and evaporation as input and, by means of an internal simulation of the processes of infiltration, percolation, drainage, and soil-moisture storage, produces daily streamflow as output. Before the model is used for problem solving, the numerical values of about 20 parameters are identified through a calibration of the model using recorded streamflow. As well as the main Sacramento model program, the catchment component contains programs for a Thiessen weight determination of mean basin precipitation and evaporation, a statistical analysis program (WMO 1975), a parameter optimization subroutine, and other programs to assist in parameter identification.

The suite of programs for the lake component utilizes lake data to simulate the natural behavior of the lake system and provides data for the assessment of various alternatives of lake regulation. The programs can utilize either lake levels L, inflows I and outflows O, or precipitation P and evaporation E over the lakes and runoff R from the land area as input data. Either set of data can be used to compute net basin supplies (NBS) to the lakes. They are defined as

$$NBS = R + P - E = S + O - I$$

where S is the change of storage calculated from the differences in the lake levels L at the beginning of each month. There is also a model subroutine for utilizing generated synthetic sequences of net basin supplies. Ancillary programs provide statistics of the regulation plans tested and plots of recorded and regulated levels and outflows.

The channel model component was to be capable not only of simulating the natural channels but also of simulating the proposed changes in the water regime and morphology. The contractor therefore selected to use an implicit method of solution of complete equations of unsteady flow in open channels based on a numerical method described by Amein and Fang (1970). This method uses a fixed grid solution plane and determines the values of the variables (depth of flow, width of channel, velocity) for the complete channel reach at one time interval using implicit relationships existing among the variables at that time level. The advantage of this method is that it is numerically stable and relatively insensitive to the magnitude of the distance and time-steps used.

The three components of the overall system contain a total of 36 individual programs (subroutines). The master program controls the selection of these programs in sequence. Each program is a FORTRAN subroutine which is cataloged in the relocatable storage library and placed by the linkage editor, together with all other required subroutines, into phases of the core image library. The master program, in response to a request on a punch card, transfers the phase required from the core image library to the central processing unit (CPU). The master program and all necessary library programs are kept in the CPU throughout the operation. Since the successive phases replace each other, the maximum storage requirement in the CPU is that of the master program plus the largest single phase.

In operational use, the operator specifies on a punch card his choice of programs and defines the jobs he wishes these programs to carry out. Basic data are read from cards or magnetic tapes and placed on disc files. In general, each program will then read its data needs from the discs and return its computed results to discs again. This extensive use of disc files gives speedy and safe completion of the simulation with a minimum of operator intervention. In all, 10 disc files are used. To simplify operations, the job control cards describing these disc files are cataloged in the procedure library so that only one input card is needed for execution.

The mathematical models were foreseen as serving two basic needs.

● Evaluating alternatives of water resource development in an operational way

● Training staff of the participating countries in water resource system modeling

The project is presently using the model for two studies.

(1) Various methods of regulating the Lakes Victoria, Kyoga, and Mobutu Sese Seko to give increased benefits to riparian users are being investigated. A common data base of monthly lake levels and outflows for the period 1912-1974 is being used. Since no economic input data are available at the moment, proposed regulation plans are being compared using simple criteria based on the operational hydraulic needs of various interests and based on keeping plans within a set of agreed ranges of lake levels and outflows.

(2) Regulation studies are being made using a set of net basin supplies based on historical levels and flows. At the same time it is recognized that the water demands of the riparian countries will increase more rapidly in the future. A study is therefore under way to estimate the magnitude of water demands and consumptive uses for each country in the years 1980 and 2000. This information will then be used to modify historic periods of net basin supplies, to check the sufficiency of water supplies, and to evaluate the long-term effects on the hydrologic regime of the lakes and rivers.

Training of national staff is an important component of the use of the model. Ten engineers have already been trained by the subcontractor for a total of 18 weeks; 8 weeks at the subcontractor's headquarters in Australia and 10 weeks in Nairobi, where the modeling unit of the Project is located. In addition, five of these engineers have worked for almost 6 months on an improved calibration of the catch-

ment model. All 10 national specialists can operate the
model competently and can make the minor changes needed to
incorporate specific water resource projects into the simulation runs.

The mathematical model is operated on the Kenya Government's IBM 370/135 computer in Nairobi. The model uses one
tape drive and space on two disc packs. Tn total 507 tracks
are used, of which 147 are retained permanently and 360 are
used for retention of data only during job processing. The
370/135 operates using four partitions and most system jobs
can be run in the background with execution times of 15 minutes or less. As mentioned, all programs are cataloged as
is the job control language. Backup tapes are kept of all
source decks and all disc file contents. In the event that
disc contents are wiped, recovery can be made from these
tapes.

Job throughput time in Nairobi depends on the time of
the month. At the beginning of the month turnaround time
is generally about 12-18 hours. However, in the third week
of the month when government payrolls are being processed
turnaround time is on the order of 24-48 hours. As can be
expected, a job using two or three tapes tends to be avoided
by the operators because it takes considerably longer to perform.

CONSTRAINTS ON MODEL SELECTION AND BUILDING

Dozens of water resource models have been produced over
the last 10 years; this development has changed the planner's
task from finding a model to selecting the model best suited
to his project. This selection is carried out subject to a
number of constraints, such as availability of data, location of project, hardware availability, degree of sophistication required and, most important, finance. If models are
used by projects that do not have extensive experience in
modeling, which is the case in most developing countries, an
economic solution is to transfer and adapt models, or their
parts, used elsewhere. This transfer is most often done by
subcontractors—commercial consulting companies, research
institutes, or universities. Thus the selection of the model is linked with the selection of the subcontractor. This
should not exempt the user or his representative from having
at his disposition some independent expertise in modeling.
(In the case of projects assisted by multilateral or bilat-
eral technical cooperation, the representative is most frequently an international governmental organization or a
national institution for technical assistance to a donor
country.)

The experience of WMO indicates that the selection of
the model and of the subcontractor is reasonably successful
only if the specifications of the job to be done and the
requirements of the end results are very detailed and sufficiently technically worded to permit the elimination of all

proposals by subcontractors that do not correspond to the
required performance and end product. In the case of the
Upper Nile model these specifications amounted to 30 pages
of technical text with tables and diagrams giving a detailed
description of the physical conditions and administrative
framework of the project, of the terms of reference of the
subcontractor, of requirements on transfer, installation,
and training of personnel, and of prescribed resources. Evi-
dence of the capability of the subcontractor was also required. The requirements and specifications are, of course,
subject to all the above-mentioned constraints.

As has been stated, the output of a model is only as
good as the input data. More importantly, the model selected
should only be as good as the data available. A 6-hour iteration is of no value for daily data. Depending on the time
and financial scale of the project, it may, however, be desirable to include in the model the option of using data at
shorter time increments should they later become available.
Model application should be considered in two phases: an
initial phase in which the model is used to evaluate the
data (for example, by comparing data from individual rainfall stations with mean basin precipitation, by plotting
rainfall and runoff on the same graph, by comparing computed
with recorded runoff) and a second stage of true calibration
and operation. The assessment of the availability and quality of the input data should always be a part of the specifications since many subcontractors, quite naturally, condition
the performance of the model by the amount and quality of the
input data. It is up to the subcontractor to propose a model
that is able to give appropriate performance with the available data.

The next three constraints—location, hardware, and
degree of sophistication—are all linked. In the experience
of WMO, it is not necessarily true that developing countries
will have a lower quality of computer hardware; in many cases
the reverse is true. However, it is often the case that
the off-the-shelf software packages used without difficulty
in many industrialized countries may not be available in
developing countries because of insufficient demand. The
model must always be developed by the subcontractor on the
same type of computer that will be used, and the model developer, from the beginning, must tailor his model to the
exact machine, operating system, and library routines and
facilities of the user. This will eliminate many of the
problems encountered in transferring a model from one computer center to another.

In designing the system the capabilities of the users
should be taken into account. It may be preferable to make
multiple use of direct access disc files rather than to specify frequent use of tapes. The accounting and bookkeeping
systems used often influence the procedures to be followed.

Very often, of course, the shape and complexity of a
model change as the design progresses and the builder

familiarizes himself with the facilities available in the country of use. Comparison of Figure 1 from the chosen contractor's bid for the Upper Nile model showing the original idea of the system and Figure 2 from the contractor's final report on the same model showing the actual system demonstrates this development very clearly. The functions of the programs shown in Figure 2 are listed in Table 1.

The financial constraints are, of course, most important in the selection. Very rarely are the available funds exactly tailored to the task to be performed, although some flexibility always exists. Even with very detailed specifications of requirements and performance, the cost of building a model that allegedly satisfies the specifications can vary widely from one subcontractor to another, depending on the country and internal organization of the subcontractor. In the case of the Upper Nile model, 10 companies, research institutes, and universities submitted bids for the job. The proposed prices varied by a ratio of 1:3 with the lowest being 50 percent below the average, the highest being 160 percent over the average. It is obvious that not all 10 bids satisfied all the conditions of the specifications. Nevertheless, five of them, satisfying the specifications reasonably well, displayed prices still in a ratio of 1:2. It should be noted that a very careful technical selection by a panel of six independent experts, using not less than nine criteria, of which cost was only one, identified two subcontractors that both offered satisfactory services with only marginal differences in quality and acceptable price. As in many other cases, the cheapest bid was not satisfactory, while the most expensive one was not the best in quality. This experience has shown that, in addition to the price, the general approach, experience, and capability and flexibility of the subcontractor are of great importance.

GENERAL COMMENTS ON LOGISTICS

Any model, no matter how well designed, will eventually need modifications. These may be necessary to better suit the model to local conditions (since the user knows these conditions better than any contractor) or to increase the utility of the model (for example, by adding optimization routines to a simulation model or by including the capacity for real-time forecasting in a multiuse model).

The mechanism of effecting these changes depends on the relationship between designer and user. If the model is designed and built in-house, the organization must ensure an adequate carry-over of competent personnel from the design phase to the application phase. If the model design is contracted, the task of the user can be greatly eased by including a number of simple specifications in the contract. Full descriptions not only of input requirements but also of the detailed programming procedures followed must be provided in the model documentation. After development of the model,

174

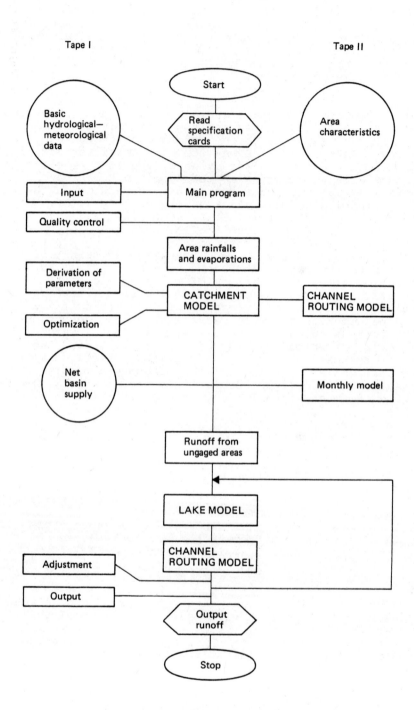

FIGURE 1 Diagram of the model (first proposal).

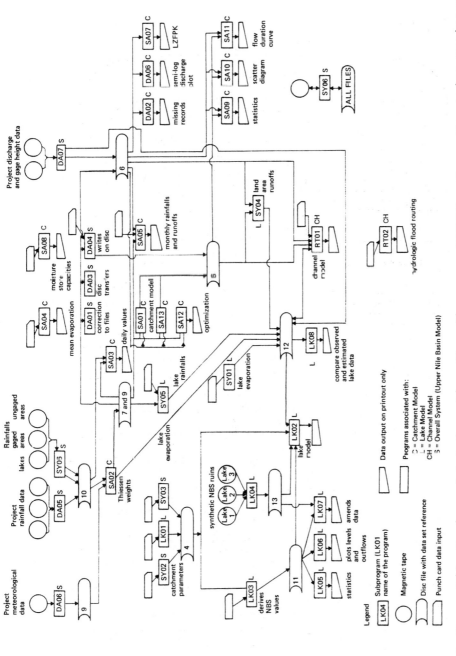

175

FIGURE 2   Upper Nile Basin model information flow diagram.   SOURCE: Snowy Mountains Engineering Corporation (1977).

176

TABLE 1 Computer programs of the Upper Nile Basin model.

Title	Function
HMET MAIN	Master program
HMET DA01	Corrects errors in the data disc files
DA02	Searches for missing discharge records
DA03	Transfers data from one disc file to another
DA04	Lists daily values and transfers from card to disc
DA05	Transfers rainfall data from tape to disc
DA06	Transfers evaporation data from tape to disc
DA07	Transfers discharge data from tape to disc
HMET SA01	Applies Sacramento model
SA02	Computes Thiessen weights and mean values
SA03	Lists daily station and mean values from SA02
SA04	Computes mean monthly evaporations
SA05	Lists monthly and annual rainfalls and run-offs
SA06	Plots daily discharges on semi-log scale
SA07	Computes estimates of lower zone drainage rates, etc.
SA08	Computes estimates of capacity of moisture stores, etc.
SA09	Computes evaluation statistics
SA10	Plots scatter diagram of monthly runoffs
SA11	Computes daily flow-duration curves
SA12	Optimizes model parameters
SA13	Applies Sacramento model in predictive mode
HMET RT01	Carries out channel routing by implicit method
RT02	Carries out channel routing by Muskingum method
HMET LK01	Transfers characteristic curves to disc file
LK02	Carries out lake water balance and operational studies
LK03	Derives net basin supplies for the historical period
LK04	Transfers synthetic net basin supplies from tape to disc
LK05	Computes statistics of lake level and outflow sequences
LK06	Plots lake levels and outflows
LK07	Amends or lists long-term lake data
LK08	Lists net basin supply values from Mode 1 Operation

TABLE 1 *Continued*.

Title	Function
HMET SY01	Prepares monthly lake evaporations
SY02	Transfers catchment parameters to disc file
SY03	Writes sequence of catchments to be processed
SY04	Derives runoff for the land areas
SY05	Prepares monthly lake rainfalls
SY06	Transfers data from tape to disc and disc to tape

statements, variables, or routines no longer used in the programs should be eliminated, statement numbering should be cleaned up, and, if card decks are to be retained, the cards should be numbered sequentially. Training of personnel must be extremely thorough and must include details of program construction and procedures for later modification. In general, the users cannot expect to operate a model without having in-house personnel that is sufficiently trained to modify the model, although not necessarily able to build it. Thus, training becomes a very important part of the logistics.

Of course, the ideal situation would be if models could be built in modular form, so that enough simple modules are available for assembly by in-house experts. Such modules would have to be interfaced to be compatible mutually as well as with the different data handling and hardware systems. A plan for international transfer of technology used in hydrology and exchange of information and views among those involved in developing and applying the technology is being developed by WMO's Operational Hydrology Programme. The project, called Hydrological Operational Multipurpose Subprogramme (HOMS), is in its preliminary design stage and the plan for its implementation will be submitted to the next WMO Congress (Geneva, May 1979) for consideration and funding.*

CONCLUSION

Although the model of the Upper Nile Basin has been in operation for only a limited time, potential benefits have already appeared. The operation of the power plant at the outlet of Lake Victoria (Jinja) is a water use for which benefits can be most easily quantified, although, of course,

*HOMS was approved by the WMO Congress in May 1979 and is being implemented on the basis of a detailed plan of action drawn up by the WMO Commission for Hydrology in Madrid in April 1980.

178

other water uses within the basin are equally or possibly
more valuable. Under existing conditions the power plant
operates as run of the river and does not influence the
level of Lake Victoria. The model has shown that if Lake
Victoria were regulated keeping lake levels within the historically (1912-1974) recorded range, the yield of the lake
would equal the long-term mean with a reliability of 70 percent, and if the minimum lake level is allowed to go 2.5 m
below the lowest recorded level, the reliability would be
100 percent. This increase in yield compared to the natural
flows gives a major increase in power output. A sample run
of the model using simulated costs and benefits showed a
gain of 36 percent over recorded conditions. If put into
operation, this plan would repay very quickly the whole cost
of the model. The cost/benefit ratio of models and related
logistics is not always evident, *prima facie*. However, a
simple evaluation of this ratio may prove the overwhelming
benefit that can be derived *if* the results of simulation
are used in the management of and investment activities in
water resources, particularly in developing countries.

ACKNOWLEDGMENT

The authors wish to express their appreciation to the
World Meteorological Organization for permission to use the
technical documents of this Organization in the preparation
of this paper. The views expressed here are those of the
authors and not of the World Meteorological Organization or
the United Nations Development Programme.

REFERENCES

Amein, M., and C.S. Fang (1970) Implicit flood routing in
    natural channels. American Society of Civil Engineers,
    Hydraulics Division Journal 96(HY12):2481-2500.

Burnash, R.J.C., R.L. Ferral, and R.A. McGuire (1973) A
    Generalized Streamflow System: Conceptual Modelling
    for Digital Computers. Sacramento, California: U.S.
    Department of Commerce, National Weather Service, and
    State of California, Department of Water Resources.

Snowy Mountains Engineering Corporation Pty. (1977) Manual
    for the Upper Nile Basin Model. Cooma, NSW, Australia.

World Meteorological Organization (WMO) (1975) Operational
    Hydrology Report No. 7. Intercomparison of Conceptual
    Models used in Operational Hydrological Forecasting.
    Report No. 429. Geneva.

HYSIM—A PHYSICALLY REALISTIC, GENERAL PURPOSE, HYDROLOGIC
MODEL

R.E. Manley

INTRODUCTION

Over the past 15-20 years many hydrologic simulation
models have been developed. Of these only a small proportion
have been much used other than for comparatively limited
research exercises.

This paper describes the HYdrologic SImulation Model
(HYSIM). It has been used for 3 years in the Severn-Trent
Water Authority, the second largest in England and responsible for providing the full range of water services to 8 million consumers. It has also recently been made available to
additional organizations including other water authorities,
research institutions, and consultants.

The paper starts by briefly describing the model itself
and then its development. The remainder, and major part, of
the paper describes the application of the model and the role
it has played in the functioning of the water authority.

HYSIM

The mathematical model is built around two FORTRAN subroutines, the first of which simulates the hydrology of a
catchment and the second of which simulates the hydraulics.

The hydrological component is based on seven reservoirs.
These are

(i) If the precipitation is in the form of snow it is
added to the *snow* reservoir. It is released by melting into
the interception storage reservoir.

(ii) *Interception storage* is represented by a finite
reservoir that is filled by rain or snowmelt. The first loss

179

from this reservoir is evapotranspiration. If there is any
moisture present in excess of the storage limit, part of it
is diverted direct to minor channel storage, to represent
impermeable areas, and the remainder passes to the upper
soil horizon.

(iii) The *upper soil horizon* reservoir represents the
"A horizon", or "top soil". The potential infiltration rate
is based on Philip's equation (Philip 1957). The variation
of effective permeability and capillary suction (and hence
downward percolation, interflow, and actual evapotranspiration) with moisture content is modeled using the work of
Brooks and Corey (1964). Any unsatisfied potential evapotranspiration is satisfied from this horizon if the capillary suction is less than 15 atmospheres.

(iv) The *lower soil horizon* reservoir represents the
remainder of the zone of rooting. It is based on equations
similar to those of the upper soil horizon for percolation,
interflow, and actual evapotranspiration; but it has its own
parameter set.

(v) The *nonsaturated zone*, i.e., the zone between the
soil horizons and the groundwater table, is represented by
a linear reservoir. Part of its discharge goes to minor
channel storage and the remainder to groundwater.

(vi) *Groundwater* is treated as a linear reservoir.

(vii) Runoff from reservoirs (iii) to (vi), together
with the runoff from the impermeable areas enters the *minor
channel storage*. This reservoir, as its name suggests, simulates the effects of channels, ranging from ephemeral riv-
ulets to larger streams, which are too small to be modeled
as individually identifiable reaches.

The hydraulics subroutine is based on a version of the
"kinematic method". It treats the input to each reach of
the river in each time increment as a kinematic wave and
calculates its time of arrival at the downstream end of the
reach. Since, in general, the waves do not arrive at a
time coincident with the time-steps of the model, the output of the reach is set equal to the average discharge in
each time increment.

The model is very flexible in its data requirements.
It can use five types of data. These are: precipitation,
potential evapotranspiration, potential snowmelt, the net
value of abstractions from rivers and discharges to them,
and abstractions from groundwater. The use of each type
of data is optional. The data can be of a monthly, daily,
or any shorter time-step. The time-steps of each type of
data need not be the same as those of any other type of
data, nor need they be the same as the time-step used either
for the hydrological or the hydraulic calculations.

The catchment can be divided into as many subcatchments as are necessary to represent its hydrologic or meteorological heterogeneity. Similarly the channels can be divided into any number of reaches. The channel reaches can be either open channels or reservoirs.

The computer requirements of the model can be adjusted to the complexity of the catchment and the frequency of the data but are typically about 10K words when using daily data and 14K words when using hourly data.

Two versions of the model have been produced. The first is the standard one and produces six different forms of output.

● Tabulated values of parameters, daily mean simulated and recorded flows, monthly summaries, and a statistical analysis

● Simulated daily mean flow in the standard format used for model data

● Flows for each channel reach or runoff from each subcatchment for each time increment

● Recorded flow and simulated daily mean flow for each reach

● Discharge from each reservoir, the transfers between each reservoir and actual evapotranspiration

● Moisture in each reservoir at the end of each day

The last three forms of output are in a format suitable for use with a graph plotting program.

The second version of the model is the optimizing one. Two modes of optimization can be used. The first is a Rosenbrock multiparameter one, for which a choice of three objective functions can be used. The second mode is a linear search, either to obtain the correct simulated mean flow or to obtain the correct mean flow at a particular time. The latter facility is used to make the model adaptive for real-time flood forecasting.

MODEL DEVELOPMENT

Development of the model started in 1972. It was decided to develop a new model as, after a literature search, there appeared to be no hydrologic model suitable for the proposed use. Development of the model was occasioned by a proposal to develop a telemetry system for flood forecasting and control of water resources. Since the only computer available for model development was a 16K word mini-computer,

and the telemetry scheme would have been controlled by a
mini-computer, it was a requirement that the model be able
to run on such a machine.

Two other important decisions were also taken at an
early stage. The first was that because the time taken to
develop any model would be considerable it would be better
to make the model as general as possible, rather than developing a range of models for different purposes. The second
decision was to make the model as physically realistic as
possible, principally to enable good starting values to be
obtained for the calibration process.

Among the factors that were not settled until much
later, however, was the exact method to be used for calibration, or even whether this should be a "trial-and-error" or
an "automatic" method.

During the first few months of the project a "model of
a model" was developed, to try out the relative influence
of different components. At this time a literature search
was also carried out into theories suitable for incorporation into the model. After a further 6 months the model
had been programmed and was running with a data set for one
catchment. Fitting was done on a trial-and-error basis.

At the end of 2 years the model and its application to
this one catchment were presented (Manley 1974). The model
was still of very restricted application, for example, it
could only use data of a given frequency in a particular
format. On the other hand, the basic concepts behind the
model, particularly with regard to the soil components and
the use of the kinematic method for routing, were established. During the next year, the model was tested on two
other catchments and the groundwater component was modified.

Future developments of the model went hand in hand
with its application. The first development was to enable
the model to handle daily, rather than hourly, precipitation
data and a number of small changes associated with this.
Because of the urgency with which the results were required
this was done with a minimum of change to the model.

The next modification was an almost complete rewriting
of the model. There were two principal reasons for this.
The first one was that earlier modifications of the model
had led to some inelegant, and therefore uneconomic, coding
of the model program. The second reason was that HYSIM
could demonstrably be calibrated semi-automatically (Anastassiou 1976). At the same time the routing component of
the model was modified. It was still based on the kinematic
method but a faster and more stable algorithm was developed.
A User Manual describing the model was produced.

The most recent change to the model has involved a
number of minor improvements including: a more complete

description of flood plain dimensions for the routing
component, a wider range of output from the model particularly at intermediate stages of the calculations, and an
increase in the available methods of model calibration.
The model in its current state is described in the latest
version of the User Manual (Manley 1978a).

USES OF THE MODEL

HYSIM was first used to produce an extended flow record
for the River Severn. A good record, which started in 1921,
is held by the Bewdley gaging site for the upper half of the
catchment (4,300 km^2). The record at the lower end of the
catchment, total area 9,900 km^2, was of only 3 years' duration and of dubious quality. The River Severn is used extensively for water supply, principally by river abstractions which are supported by releases from an impounding
reservoir in its headwaters. Its current yield is estimated
to be 500 Ml/d and the Authority proposes to extend its
yield by sinking boreholes in a groundwater subcatchment for
conjunctive use with the river. The existing prescribed
flow condition, fixed by an Act of Parliament, applied to
Bewdley, but it was not certain whether this gave adequate
protection to the whole length of the river. It was therefore decided to simulate the subcatchments of the Severn
downstream of Bewdley. The data available for the exercise
are shown in Table 1. The period for which simulations were
required was from 1930 to 1974.

The model was calibrated to the available flow records
for three gaged subcatchments using a trial-and-error approach. The simulation was then extended below each gaging
station to the Severn using the parameter values obtained
in the upper part of the subcatchment and the meteorological
data pertaining to the lower part. For the 4 years when
comparison was possible, including 1 year for which records
were not available at the time of calibration, the flows in
the lower part of the river were accurately simulated.
This exercise has been described more completely by Manley
(1978b).

Water resource simulation of the River Severn using
the flow record described above showed that while a prescribed flow condition at Bewdley provided adequate protection for the whole river, it needed modification to give it
greater flexibility in view of the travel time of releases
from the reservoir. The Authority is now seeking statutory
powers to make the modifications.

After checking the same simulated flow sequence against
long records of flood flows in two of the larger subcatchments, it was concluded that the simulated record was also
accurate at the higher range of the hydrological spectrum.
This record has therefore been used to provide the input
for a detailed mathematical hydraulic modeling exercise.

TABLE 1   Data available for simulation.

Application	Area modeled (km^2)	Number of rain gages		Number of climate sites		Explained variance (%)	
		Total	Inside catchment	Total	Inside catchment	Daily flow	Monthly flow
Lower River Severn	5,600	12	10	2	0	95.9	99.4
River Derwent	1,100	4	3	3	1	89.8	96.1
River Dove	900	4	1	1	0	76.0	92.0

The exercise is estimated to cost around £100,000 (this for running the hydraulic model and providing river survey information), whereas the original use of HYSIM had cost £5,000.

The other two main water resource rivers in the Authority's area are the adjacent Dove and Derwent. The combined yield of these rivers is 530 Ml/d and the Authority has recently been given powers to construct a pump filled reservoir which will increase the yield by a further 230 Ml/d.

For the modeling of the River Derwent the version of the model that used the Rosenbrock optimization algorithm was available. This reduced the total time required and the cost, relative to the Severn exercise. This exercise, with particular reference to the optimization procedure, has been described by Manley (1978c).

For the River Dove great care was taken in establishing the initial values of the model parameter before calibrating the model to the flow record within the catchment. This meant that initial runs of the model could be considered to be those that would have been obtained had the model been applied to an ungaged catchment. The accuracy of the fitting, particularly when measured in terms of the correlation coefficient rather than the explained variance, was good. Further fitting increased the explained variance, but had little influence on the correlation coefficient (Manley 1978d).

These data have been used to develop operating rules for the reservoirs in the catchment. One of these is pump filled and a considerable saving in electricity has already been achieved.

Figure 1 shows the location of the flow records that are used for water resources analysis in the Severn-Trent Water Authority. For this purpose the daily simulated flows are converted to pentad (i.e., five-daily) flows. As can be seen the simulated flow records obtained from using HYSIM have provided a significant proportion of these flows.

One advantage of using a hydrologic simulation model to produce flow data, rather than a stochastic method, is that the data are consistent with those available at gaged sites, a very important consideration when the conjunctive use of alternative resources is being considered.

A further major project for which the model is currently being used is a study of the groundwater catchment mentioned earlier in connection with the River Severn. The model is presently being developed for flow forecasting, and one of the changes to the model's optimizing procedure has been to make it suitable for an adaptive real-time mode of operation. Tests have shown that using hourly data the model can be updated and can produce its forecast for a number of intermediate points in a river system, in addition to a point at

186

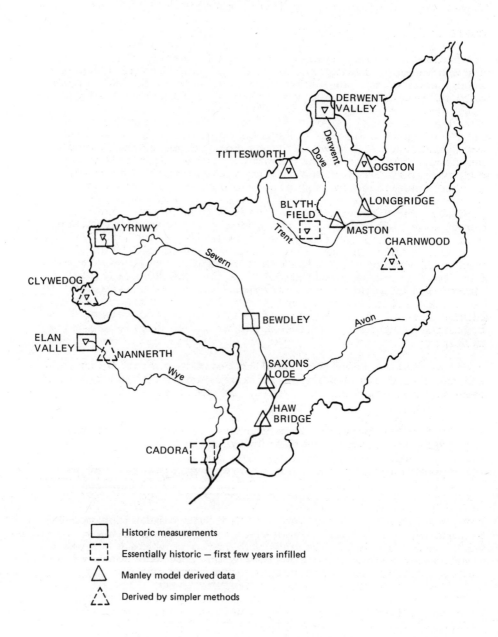

FIGURE 1   Severn-Trent Water Authority regional resources
data bank of pentad flows, 1932 to present.

which flow is measured, in around 1 minute on a mini-
computer costing less than £20,000.

COSTS AND DIFFICULTIES OF USING THE MODEL

Table 1 shows the data that were available for each of
the projects mentioned. Although the data are somewhat limited in quantity, they were all that were available for each
catchment since 1930. Much effort was required to get a
consistent data set. Two particular problems were encountered.

The first was that it is very rare for a rain gage to
remain in the same location and to catch a consistent amount
of rain, when checked by double mass plotting against a
group of nearby stations. Often this problem was made worse
by the fact that the records from nearby stations used over-
lapped. The data were all adjusted to produce linear double
mass plots.

The second problem concerned data for estimates of
potential evapotranspiration. The basic minimum requirement is for dry-bulb temperature, wet-bulb temperature,
run-of-wind, and hours-of-sunshine, on a monthly basis.
These were rarely available consistently and frequently a
compromise had to be adopted. For example, one record was
based on dry-bulb temperature and hours-of-sunshine measurements at the site chosen, wet-bulb temperatures at two other
sites for different periods, and run-of-wind based on subjective estimates of wind force (on the Beaufort scale) and
a linear correlation with similar estimates at a site 30 km
away which had an anemometer.

The approximate cost of the above exercises was about
£5,000 for the Severn exercise and £3,000 each for the other
two. The costs were about 40 percent staff time and 60 percent computer time at a commercial bureau.

One of the major components of the cost was that of
simulation runs, which proved abortive as a result of data
errors. Typical examples of data errors were flow data that
had not taken the effects of weeds in the summer into consideration and data on discharges to the river from sewage
works that disregarded substantial discharges from factories. An approximate breakdown of the costs is

Data preparation and checking	50%
Abortive simulation	30%
Useful simulation	20%

An example of how much of the difficulty is due to data
preparation can be gained from the fact that to produce
simulated flow records for two supplementary sites, using

climate and rainfall data already available, took 4 days'
staff time and cost £200 in computer time.

Aside from the difficulties with data the other major
difficulty encountered has been that of knowing when the
model is as accurately calibrated as the available data will
allow. There is always a feeling that a particular change
in the parameter set will result in further improvements,
when, in fact, it may do nothing or may only improve fitting
for a singular event, for example, a summer storm for which
daily data are inadequate anyway. While objective measures
of goodness of fit in the automatic calibration of the model
have been used, it has been found that graph plots are a
more powerful method of deciding the adequacy of a particular simulation.

A further problem found recently in transferring the
model to other types of computers has been that of the differences in FORTRAN "dialects". Most computer manufacturers
describe their compilers as providing "FORTRAN PLUS"; unfortunately, the "plus" parts are often incompatible with those
of other manufacturers. Were I to start again, I would certainly attempt to confine myself to a fairly strict ANSI
FORTRAN IV.

CONCLUSIONS

The above section highlighted the difficulties of using
the model, but it should be noticed that most of these difficulties are external to the model. The principal conclusions I would draw from my past and current work are

• Most of the costs associated with simulation are in
the data collection and verification, be they historical or
real-time data

• Even with sparse meteorological data of uneven quality, accurate flow simulation can be obtained

• The cost of providing a simulated flow record is
small ($< £10^4$) compared to the cost of the resources
($> £10^7$) which are better designed and better managed as
a result

• Much of the time and effort in the development of
a model are spent in making it flexible and easily usable
for other people

• A general purpose model which can be used for both
real-time and off-line simulation has the big advantage
that staff have only to be taught the essentials of one
model, rather than a different model for each purpose

That HYSIM has succeeded as a hydrologic model is largely a result of the way it started out and of the decisions which were taken, or imposed, at that time, i.e.,

- It should fit on a mini-computer, with the associated economies for whatever computer it is run on

- It should be general purpose

- It should be physically realistic

ACKNOWLEDGMENTS

The author wishes to thank the Chief Executive of the Severn-Trent Water Authority for permission to publish this paper. The views expressed in this paper are those of the author and do not necessarily represent those of the Authority.

REFERENCES

Anastassiou, X. (1976) Optimisation of Catchment Models. Master of Science Thesis. University of Birmingham, England.

Brooks, R.H., and A.T. Corey (1964) Hydraulic Properties of Porous Media. Hydrology Paper No. 3. Fort Collins, Colorado: Colorado State University.

Manley, R.E. (1974) Catchment Models for River Management. Master of Science Thesis. University of Birmingham, England.

Manley, R.E. (1978a) HYSIM—User Manual. Sheldon, Birmingham, England: Severn-Trent Water Authority.

Manley, R.E. (1978b) The use of a hydrological model in water resources planning. Proceedings of the Institution of Civil Engineers, Part 2, 65:223-235.

Manley, R.E. (1978c) Calibration of hydrological model using optimisation technique. American Society of Civil Engineers, Hydraulics Division Journal 104(HY2).

Manley, R.E. (1978d) Simulation of flow in ungaged basins. Bulletin des Sciences Hydrologiques 23(1).

Philip, J.R. (1957) The theory of infiltration, part 1. The infiltration equation and its solution. Soil Sciences 83:345-357.

LOGISTICS AND BENEFITS OF THE EUROPEAN HYDROLOGIC SYSTEM

M.B. Abbott, R. Clarke, and A. Preissmann

INTRODUCTION

During the last two decades, computer-based hydrologic mathematical models, like specific-hydraulic mathematical models, have been transformed from subjects of academic research into tools of engineering practice. As this transformation has progressed, the models have grown in complexity and cost to such an extent that it has become increasingly difficult to develop them within the constraints of a university environment. The seat of this development, therefore, has tended to shift to organizations that are more appropriately organized and financed. In the areas of hydraulic and coastal engineering especially, modeling work has developed rapidly within the environments of the larger laboratories and institutes (100-500 staff, US$5 x 10^6 - US$25 x 10^6 funds, annually). It has been possible to build up mathematical modeling research, development, and application groups that include individuals of different but complementary expertise. These groups liaise with other groups or sections on field studies and on matters concerning instrumentation, data processing, and design. During the last few years it has become clear that the mathematical modeling component has a central and even strategic importance in the activities of laboratories and institutes, as other components are modified to suit the requirements of the mathematical models in such a way as to increase dramatically the capabilities, cost-effectiveness, and, hence, competitiveness of operations. This increase in competitiveness in turn increases the money available for system research and development, further emphasizing the dominant position of these larger organizations.

Since these laboratories and institutes are mainly concerned with feasibility and other preliminary studies (which are "initiating operations"), their activities influence the job-acquisition possibilities of follow-up consulting engineers and contractors. However, this follow-up work is larger by some orders of magnitude than the work of the initiating organizations. In monetary terms, therefore, the influence of initiating organizations is very much greater than their direct incomes might suggest. Since the mathematical model influences the competitive capability of initiating organizations and since this capability in turn modifies the expectations of follow-up consultants and contractors, the cost-benefit relations of a mathematical model cannot be expressed simply in terms of its own immediate costs and generated incomes; it must be extended to account for other, indirect benefits provided to those groups and organizations that it serves. For example, since 1971 the System 21 (S21) of the Danish Hydraulic Institute has been used for 44 jobs in 13 countries. The income to Danish industry from one job alone has already exceeded US\$$20 \times 10^6$, and may well increase, while the total value of works for which the S21 has provided modeling studies exceeds US\$$10 \times 10^9$. It follows from this situation that there are strong national and community interests in developing competitive mathematical models in hydrology, just as in hydraulic and coastal engineering.

ORIGINS OF THE EUROPEAN HYDROLOGIC SYSTEM (SHE)

Throughout the early 1970s, European organizations had difficulty obtaining consulting work that involved hydrologic modeling, even though they were succeeding in the related areas of hydraulic and coastal engineering modeling. This situation came up for discussion at a meeting of the heads of European hydraulic software groups held in 1975, and it was decided to explore various possibilities for improving the situation in hydrology. The various groups separately evaluated existing models available in hydrology, paying particular attention to their reliability, data requirements, costs, and development potential. Analyses were also made of chosen and runner-up bids for various jobs with a view to identifying key requirements. Two further meetings were held in 1976 at which the results of these evaluations and analyses were reviewed. The following conclusions were reached:

● Existing hydrologic models are satisfactory only for limited components of the hydrologic cycle and/or over limited ranges of application. When used outside their calibrated ranges, as they often are, they can give very erroneous results.

● These models often make poor use of available data

● It is often difficult to introduce known physical properties of hydraulic components, such as constraints or controls, into these models because their energetic balances and overall thermodynamic consistency are often dubious

● Development potential of the models is limited

● Engineering applications would require a range of modeling that could only be satisfied with a great variety of systems if existing approaches were used

● Existing models of the complete land phase cannot provide a distributed description of hydrologic processes and cannot utilize space-dependency in measurements

● Their application to water quality problems is correspondingly restricted

● Similarly, the models are incapable of simulating changes in land use

● All in all, little overall competitive advantage would accrue from developing existing models

These conclusions led to the elaboration of a specification for a general modeling system with the following properties:

● It should have the greatest possible range of application with the capability of extrapolating outside its calibrated range

● It should, correspondingly, have a modeling system form like hydraulic systems of the S21 type (Abbott *et al*. 1973, Abbott 1976, Abbott 1978, and Abbott *et al*. 1978), which is described later in this paper. Such a system generates models when presented with the description of the prototype in a simple convenient form.

● It should introduce only mathematical operations that have definite physical interpretations or counterparts in order that parameters and coefficients are identified with physical properties and are so constrained. The elements themselves and their interrelations should, therefore, be thermodynamically reasonable.

● It should incorporate the advances made in the understanding and descriptions of specific parts of the hydrological cycle, such as in unsaturated flow mechanics, in studies of snowmelt mechanisms, and in plant hydrobiology

● It should incorporate the lessons learned from hydraulic and coastal engineering modeling practice, for example, it should use efficient frame codes (grid codes, Boolean filters, etc.), advanced numerical schemes (high accuracy, algorithmical appropriateness, unconditional stability, etc.), and efficient input and output and other service facilities. Moreover, it should be consistent with advanced, economical instrumentation, data collection, and data processing components.

● It should be capable of meeting the expected requirements of engineering practice throughout the 1980s and 1990s

These requirements led to the external specification for a distributed, deterministic modeling system capable of meeting the demands of practice or capable of penetrating the market. The next stage was to determine whether such a system was scientifically and economically feasible and, if it was feasible, to decide upon an internal specification. It was clear that the proposed system would be so exceedingly demanding of specialized staff and so expensive that no single organization could afford to research, design, develop, and market it. Three of the best endowed organizations in Europe therefore agreed to cooperate in the feasibility studies, market research, product research, design, construction, testing, and initial marketing of the system. In view of the strategic importance of the system for the European consulting and construction industries, the first part of the project (specifically, the exploratory study leading to the initial specification) received the support of the Commission of the European Economic Community. The system is called the "European Hydrologic System—Système Hydrologique Européen" (SHE); the association made up of the Danish Hydraulic Institute (Denmark), the Institute of Hydrology (UK), and SOGREAH (France) that is constructing SHE is the "Association for the European Hydrologic System—Association pour le Système Hydrologique Européen" (ASHE). Work on SHE is divided among the ASHE organizations, but SHE is the property of each of them. After initial marketing, the ASHE organizations will be free to apply SHE as they wish, subject, of course, to constraints on its availability to non-ASHE organizations.

DESCRIPTION OF SHE

The general layout of SHE-generated models is described in Figures 1 and 2. Any model can be distributed in the horizontal plane, whether in the full two dimensions or degenerating to one dimension or even to one single point. It is planned to use up to 2,000 descriptive points in the horizontal plane. These points are currently located at the nodes of a rectangular mesh. At each of these "horizontal points", the model is distributed in the vertical with one point at the ground surface (subsuming the vegetation levels), several points throughout the unsaturated zone, and one or more points throughout the saturated zone. Currently between 10 and 30 points are used in each vertical. The speed objective of the prototype is 200 horizontal points, or between 2,000 and 6,000 total points, per machine-second on an IBM 370/165. The SHE test case has given 2,120 total points per machine-second. However, the production system is intended for highly optimized operation on machines with the capacity of the IBM 370/3033. Exchanges between core storage and background storage were incorporated in the system at the beginning. These exchange facilities may not be necessary for the large machines available to ASHE organizations, but they will be necessary for certain contract installations. For flexibility in application, the official code of ASHE is FORTRAN. However, at

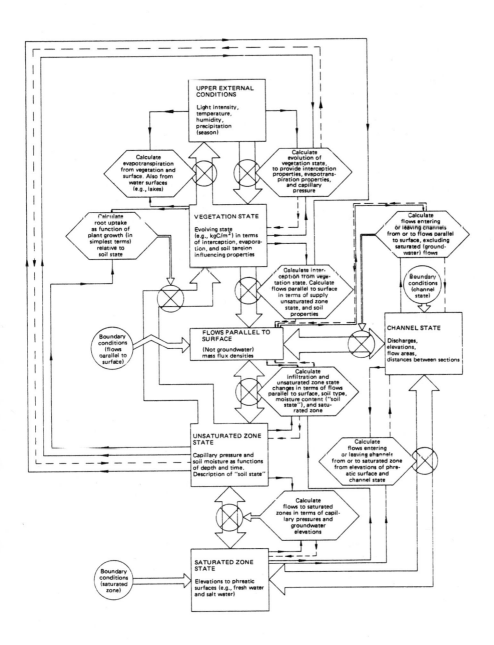

FIGURE 1   Structure of the European Hydrologic System (SHE)
            showing semantic information flows and correspond-
            ing water flows.

196

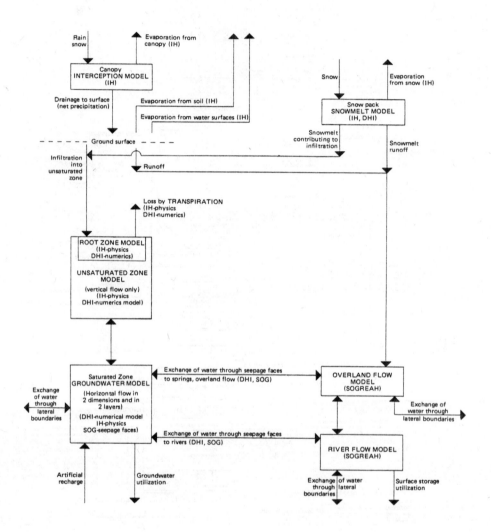

FIGURE 2   Mass flow through the European Hydrologic System
         (SHE).

least one ASHE organization also keeps a version prepared
in PL/1. The overall work schedule for SHE is shown in Figure 3.

SYSTEM INVESTMENT AND COST

A large part of the cost of any scientific software
system is the research. It is convenient to divide this
research into market research (elaborating the external specification) and product research (elaborating the internal
specification). Since the internal specification has to do
with the scientific and technical means for meeting the requirements of the external specification, these two lines of
research progress interactively.

The research costs of SHE amount to some 40 percent of
all costs incurred up to the time of production operation.
Although this is a typical proportion for scientific software, it is much higher than is usual in other high-technology
industries (Mahieux 1972). Mahieux has shown how the level
of uncertainty of the outcome of a project increases as its
research content increases, with the corollary of a higher
level of uncertainty of commercial viability. A considerable
effort then has to be made to assure the relevance of research, primarily by maintaining liaison between its market
and product components.

The market research so far carried out for SHE encom-
passes the following points:

● Identification of areas of application and of the
nature of application

● Capabilities required in order to succeed in these
applications

● Estimates of investments in each area of application

● Estimates of accessibility of the system to non-
national or noncommunity organizations

● Expected direct returns of SHE applications, by
application area and by geographical-political area

● Expected indirect returns accruing from SHE applications, by application area and by geographical-political area

● Determination of relations between the costs incurred
from developing a range of capabilities and the expected
direct and indirect benefits from these applications

SHE application areas were investigated in detail, both
for the nature of applications and their influence on the
external specification and for the associated investments in
engineering works. The application areas are described later
in this paper.

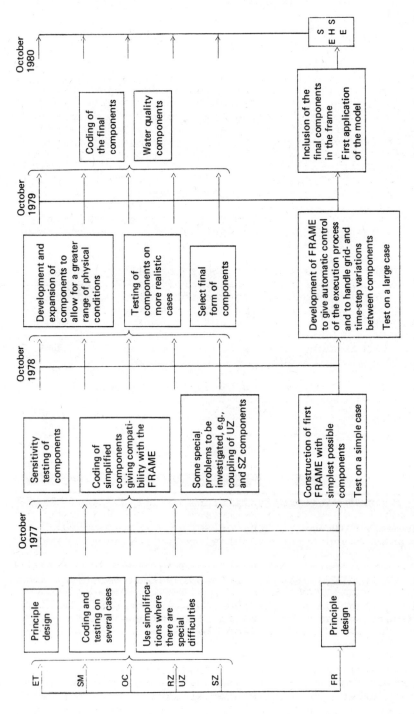

FIGURE 3 Timeplan for development of the European Hydrologic System (SHE). The abbreviations on the left-hand side stand for the following: ET—evapotranspiration, SM—snowmelt, OC—overland/channel, RZ/UZ—root zone/unsaturated zone, SZ—saturated zone, FR—frame.

Product research for SHE covers plant physiology to
hydrogeology, involving some 12 areas of specialization.
It also covers the whole of any one specialization, from the
word-descriptions of physical and biological processes,
through their possible continuum-mathematical descriptions
and their possible numerical or discrete-mathematical descriptions, to their description in algorithms, control
structures, and code. As SHE is designed as a modeling system, it is essential that its components should operate under
the widest possible range of conditions and this requirement
puts heavy demands on all components in all their interactions. Thus, for example, it is easy to make a numerical
solution for the unsaturated zone that will function well
for a very dry soil, and it is just as easy to make another
numerical solution that will work well for a nearly saturated
soil. However, it is difficult to make one numerical scheme
that will function equally well in both cases. One scheme
may well contain two numerical solutions as options, but the
transfer from one to the other, often within a single computation, is difficult to organize satisfactorily because such
a compound scheme can easily become too expensive to meet
the needs of the market. As a rule of thumb, it can be said
that development of any component costs about an order of
magnitude more than that of a one-off model or a model built
for one particular situation. Since, however, the system is
to be used very many times, so as to generate very many models, it is expected that this investment in a system form
will be repaid.

The design process develops from the research processes
as a matter of "freezing" particular component developments
at a stage at which they interact with other components in
order to satisfy the external specification. A critical part
of the design process is the design of the frame of the system. The frame is the "nervous system" of the modeling system, coordinating the operations of all components on the
basis of feedback from "sensors" placed at suitable points
within the system. In a SHE type system, the individual components have very different internal boundary requirements,
time-steps, accuracy-cost relations, and stability conditions;
however, these components may interact in very different ways
in different situations. Thus the design process is a demanding one in such a modeling system and absorbs considerable investments.

Total investment in research and design for SHE is estimated to be about US$540,000. The most expensive stages in
the elaboration of such a modeling system are those of construction, testing, and preproduction development. In the
construction stage the flow diagrams, algorithms, code-
fragments, and other design elements are translated into a
working code. This process itself involves extensive testing. The various components have already been tested against
analytical results, experimental results, and field results
during the design process; but following the construction,

it is possible to test the complete system, albeit initially only in simple, controllable situations.

Just as in other fields, the initially-constructed prototype functions as a test case. The test case of SHE became operational in October-November 1978 (Figure 2). It is being used to check all components *in situ*, to control mass balances, energy balances, error sensitivity, and stability sensitivity, and to investigate accuracy vs. machine time. The latter is, of course, critical to commercial viability. The test case should be developed into a prototype suitable for testing against real-world data during 1979. Already a program of field studies, literature studies, and data sensitivity analyses is under way to provide material for this stage of the development. It is expected that, throughout the development period, the components and frame will be subjected to many changes, so that the production version of SHE will be a reliable and economically viable instrument during 1980. However, it will require continuous development in order to suit it to the challenges of the 1980s and, perhaps, beyond.

The total cost for the construction, testing, and development of SHE up to the production stage is estimated to be about US$660,000. SHE will be owned and utilized by each of the ASHE organizations. Repayment of investments (historical costs) and the generation of new investments (maintenance costs and replacement costs) will accrue from a hire charge on SHE use. This hire charge will most probably take the form of a percentage of machine costs, varying between 50 percent and 200 percent of machine costs. The expected returns under various assumptions of exploitation and hire charges have been investigated as part of the market research, using the marketing results of the S21 over the period 1973-1978 as an analogy. The investigation indicated that SHE will be economically viable in the 1980s, while providing services with cost-benefit relations superior to those currently accepted.

DATA REQUIREMENTS OF SHE

The new requirements that a modeling system places upon data are well known from hydraulic and coastal engineering practice. It has been observed that much more intensive field studies made over shorter periods are required. However, the choice of instruments and their positions, operating range, and sensitivity can be determined by an iterative process with a mathematical model of the area. In effect, the model provides a first estimate of the best positions of instruments and instrument characteristics. The results flowing from these instruments, when introduced into the modeling study, indicate gaps and the means of filling these gaps, suitable times for installing further instruments, and so on. It is observed in hydraulics that data available on one component

of a model (e.g., salinity) can be used to provide coefficients for another component (e.g., turbulent mixing).

A similar situation is anticipated in the case of the
distributed, deterministic hydrologic system. On the one
hand, a model generated by such a system has to be supplied
with more coefficients than spatially-lumped or linear-system
models. On the other hand, intelligent first guesses can be
made for many of these coefficients since the deterministic
coupling between elements allows some calibration of one element to be made on the basis of observations made of another
element. Progress being made in satellite imagery may considerably aid in this area. The availability of SHE will,
no doubt, in turn contribute to the work being done on satellite imagery.

An important point here is that if field data are insufficient, a range of corresponding possible parameter values
can be used to provide a range of simulations. A range of
possible outcomes (works, policies, or operations) can then
be determined to indicate the level of uncertainty in projects designed and executed on the basis of such inadequate
data.

It should be explained that the use of large ensembles
of descriptive points distributed in the horizontal does not
imply the fitting of different coefficients at each and every
such point. The purpose of such ensembles is to permit an
acceptable resolution of continuous variations with finite
schemes. It is to be expected that coefficients will be
"blocked in" as constants or as varying quantities over most
of the domain of the solution. Degenerate one-dimensional
and zero-dimensional (single point) models of SHE will provide the same services as linear-system models and spatially-
lumped models and not necessarily at a higher cost. These
same degenerate forms can be extended to full two-dimensional
forms when there are sufficient data, or pseudo-data, to war-
rant such an extension. Thus, although SHE is seen as an instrument particularly suited to larger jobs backed by a suitable data base, its use for smaller jobs is by no means excluded.

Finally, advances in data collection in hydraulic and
coastal engineering have shown that once a viable system is
available, more relevant data are collected. The interaction
between modeling capability and data collection is such that
the modeling group cannot normally just wait for suitable
data for their models, but must take the initiative to make
models available that will justify the collection of suitable
data.

SYSTEM APPLICATION AND BENEFITS

The specific application areas and benefits of SHE are
given below.

Industrial Use of Water

EXPLOITATION OF ALTERNATIVE SOURCES OF WATER AND THE ALLOCATION OF
WATER FROM THESE SOURCES

Different natural sources of water with different unit
costs for treatment and distribution have different utilities
to different industries. How should these sources be exploited to minimize total treatment costs, while taking
proper account of the needs of other water users? This
problem is often posed simply as one of establishing that
conjunctive use of surface and subsurface resources that
maximizes total community benefits. It is usually further
constrained by the need for predictable, preferably controllable and even constant, discharges.

SHE can predict the behavior of the water sources, essentially stream waters and groundwaters, under alternative
evaporation demands and surface characteristics. The predicted behavior automatically takes into account exchanges
between surface waters and groundwaters (e.g., recharge of
groundwaters from surface waters), partial depletions of
various waters, drawing up of unsuitable (e.g., salt) waters,
water exchanges between aquifers and even between basins,
and similar coupling effects. By running SHE through a set
of competing exploitation strategies, the cost of each ele-
mental strategy of this set can be related to the industrial
benefits that it provides and the elements then aligned to
provide some minimal total costs. This optimization can be
made dependent upon historical conditions, being periodically
updated in accordance with the meteorological conditions experienced to date and the current and expected industrial
exploitations. One cannot cover all possible combinations
and permutations of works and exploitation strategies with
SHE, but rather a selected, economically attractive subset.
In fact, in this and several of the successful applications,
one can trace various stages in the evolution of a water resource project, starting at long-term planning and proceeding
through designing of works and their long-term operation to
the real-time operation of works. SHE is directly applicable
at the designing stage, and at the real-time operation stage
it can be combined with other techniques, such as dynamic
programming, to provide valuable information for the other
stages.

POLLUTION TREATMENT AND POLLUTION COSTING

Industrial effluents must often be subjected to expensive treatment before they can be reused directly or recycled. It is usual, and in a sense economical, to only partially treat these effluents and then to discharge them into
larger bodies of water where the pollutants are dispersed
and may be slowly degraded to less noxious forms by natural
processes. Water so introduced can later be extracted from
these larger water bodies at an acceptable level of purity.

The process of natural purification depends strongly upon the amount of water present to absorb the incoming effluents since this determines the degree of dilution of pollutants and the buildup of concentrations of degradation-inhibiting pollutants. The quality of recipient water bodies, usually rivers, lakes, ponds, and other freshwater bodies, depends strongly upon hydrological conditions. SHE makes possible the calculations of water balances in these water bodies that are distributed in space following the distribution in space of pollution. The influences of such pollution-intensifying conditions as low discharges in rivers, or of such pollution-spreading conditions as the charging of groundwater from surface water, can be followed in any required detail, using SHE in conjunction with an appropriate hydrologic measuring program.

On the basis of results so obtained and cost estimates from water treatment, the effective cost of pollution can be approximated, even for individual factories, mines, local industrial complexes, and other polluting entities. Although the first version of SHE does not incorporate coupled transport-dispersion and water quality stages, it was designed *ab initio* to carry these superstructures in later developments.

REUSE AND RECYCLING OF WATER

The costs of exploiting "natural" waters (originating directly from rainfall and snowmelt) may become so high that treatment and subsequent reuse of water become preferable. Thus the waters of the Rhine have already been used at least twice; in a sense, they have been "recycled" at least once. The cost of various water treatments varies widely. Often, raw, untreated water is simply discharged into watercourses, lakes, and ponds for treatment under natural conditions. Increasingly, however, wastewater is treated mechanically, biologically, and even chemically before discharge to a natural watercourse and is further treated before reuse. It is also often injected into groundwater to be filtered and to be subjected to slow anaerobic treatment before withdrawal. Most reuse and recycling processes involve some exposure of surrounding areas to contamination. In its later development, SHE will be capable of predicting the path of contaminated water both overland and through the soil. This will make possible a more rational planning of investments in water treatment works and will aid further in the determination of various side effects, including the long-term effects. The place of these determinations as an aid to legislation and litigation is discussed in a later subsection.

HYDROPOWER GENERATION

Hydropower generation depends upon the availability of nearly predictable and preferably controllable discharges,

with significant head differences. The predictability of
the discharge and the head requirement are usually realized
through the construction of a dam or barrage impounding a
reservoir of suitable capacity. The design, construction,
and operation of a hydropower station require accurate estimates of water quantities entering and leaving the reservoir,
including losses under and around the dam structure. These
estimates should be made taking alternative evaporative demands and surface characteristics into account. SHE will be
able to describe hydrologic processes occurring throughout
the region supplying water to the hydropower station. Thus
it will convert the meteorologic data into predictions of
water availability and thence into flows to be accommodated
during the construction period and into predictions of relations between reservoir levels and station water throughputs.
Moreover, it will do this for a variety of operational policies at the design and operation levels. Hydropower projects
may well be combined with pumped storage projects and even
with nuclear power generation; in these cases further constraints on predictability are introduced.

COOLING OF THERMAL POWER STATIONS

A considerable part of all industrial water use is at-
tributable to the cooling requirements of thermal power stations. In many ways this corresponds to a recycling application with heat as the pollutant. The applications of SHE
follow similar lines to those introduced in the subsection
on pollution treatment and costing.

DISPOSAL OF TOXIC WASTES

It is becoming increasingly common to dispose of toxic
wastes in coal and salt mines and similar workings that are
no longer in use, where they may subsequently diffuse through
groundwater and be brought back to the earth's surface
through the mechanics of the unsaturated zone and vegetal
root tensions. This process could be modeled by SHE, at
least in sufficient detail to provide some time scales for
the process. This application again is significant to legislation and litigation, as discussed later, particularly at
the international level.

Agricultural Use of Water

WATER BALANCE OF RAINFED AGRICULTURE

As in industry, a variety of sources of water are available for agricultural purposes. Each source has its own characteristics and unit costs. However, since agricultural water
use is so distributed, a large part of agricultural water is
provided directly by precipitation stored in the surface,
nonsaturated, and root zones. A related problem of rainfed

agriculture faced by several European countries is waterlogging.

In general, sound water-use practices, whether in rainfed or irrigated agriculture, involve the maintenance of optimum soil moisture with the removal of excess water and avoidance of damage from overland flows.

In practice an extremely complex series of relations exists among water, soil and crops. Often this creates a very delicate balance between suitable and unsuitable land and water management, especially in rainfed farming, which offers no opportunity for artificial compensation against the vagaries of precipitation and must therefore take advantage of all possible means to reduce risks of crop loss from a shortage, or sometimes even a surplus, of rainfall.

Such measures extend far beyond methods of preparing the land to receive and retain moisture, and efficiency of water use depends on the selection of appropriate crops with compatible water requirements and growing seasons; correct time of planting to coincide with probable rains both for growth and sometimes to establish ground cover before high intensity storms induce damaging run-off; proper density of stand to give optimum production and protection while making the best use of soil moisture; improvement of soil fertility; development of good soil structure; weed control; and other essential activities, the importance of which is dictated largely by conditions of rainfall and other climatic factors (Biswas 1978).

Since all of the above features vary in space, their description demands the use of a distributed model. Moreover, since changes introduced in the hydrologic behavior have to be entered into any model used to describe the process, it is best to introduce these changes into a deterministic model. Thus the SHE models will be very well suited to detailed hydrologic-agronomic studies of water balances in rainfed agricultures. In particular, the use of SHE can estimate the extent to which intensive development of agriculture (rainfed or irrigated) can be detrimental further along in the hydrological cycle.

WATER BALANCE OF IRRIGATED AGRICULTURE

The world's food production is decreasing, while the world's population is increasing. Irrigation is being promoted as a means of increasing food production. Already, some 15-20 percent of the world's cropland is under irrigation, producing 30-40 percent of total agricultural output,

despite a generally low level of efficiency in water use.
However, while potentially the most rewarding of combined
land and water uses, irrigated agriculture is also one of
the most complex, with vast and far reaching effects on water
quantity and quality. Problems arise of water supply to irrigation, choice of irrigation system (channel, surface inun-
dation, sprinkler, drip, etc.) relative to crop and weather
expectations, choice of corresponding drainage system, and
disposal of drainage water. These problems themselves encom-
pass problems of salting of soils, as salt is drawn up from
lower layers by root tensions and unsaturated zone (capillary) flows; corresponding soil leaching attempts; disease
transmission (principally malaria and bilharziasis); and
the overall reliability and viability of the irrigation-
drainage system in a given socioeconomic environment where
mistakes and abuses are unavoidable. Inadequate drainage
commonly gives rise to waterlogging in irrigated agriculture.

The solution of these irrigation and drainage problems
will require simulations of the soil and vegetation system
under alternative evaporative demands and surface characteristics, utilizing a very large part of the entire SHE capacity.

CHANGE OF LAND USE

The need for more food for still rapidly growing populations has led also to the cultivation of large areas that
were previously in a long established ecological equilibrium.
The areas concerned are often those with a highly developed
("high-information") ecosystem, that is correspondingly
highly sensitive to unprogrammed alterations of the type proposed. The results of unsuitable change will be the failure
of crops and the consequent failure of drainage systems, the
erosion of soil cover, large-scale formations of gullies,
slips and other extreme features, and the ultimate abandon-
ment of the land, that may well convert to desert conditions.

In studying changes of land use, SHE will be used to
simulate the existing situations and possible alternative
situations, using meteorologic records and, possibly, prog-
noses of meteorologic conditions consequent upon the proposed
land changes. To date, SHE appears to be the only instrument
capable of describing such changes in land use.

AQUACULTURE

The production of fish is highly dependent on the quantity and quality of a controlled water supply. It can be
related to irrigation and thermal wastes in a mutually benef-
icient manner, and in this respect represents a certain balancing of the agricultural-industrial ecosystem. SHE will
be capable of determining the water balances and thereby, in
its water quality development, the nutrient and contaminant
balances of the fished waters.

Domestic Use of Water

CHANGES IN SOURCES OF DOMESTIC WATER SUPPLY

The continuous and simultaneous processes of increased
urbanization, increased per capita use of water, and the pollution and overall depletion of traditional water sources,
necessitate an intensified exploitation of existing sources
and the exploitation of new sources of suitable quality.
Hydrologic problems then naturally arise. For example, the
extraction of groundwater may lead to a reduction in the
capacities of surrounding wells, spreading water shortages
for traditional crops, subsidence of urban and industrial
lands, and other such undesirable side effects. SHE will be
used to investigate the consequences of new and augmented
exploitations of water sources, providing predictions of
these consequences over the affected regions, by virtue of
its distributed nature, and taking account of physical features, by virtue of its deterministic nature. It will thus
provide the basis for designing an exploitation strategy with
the best balance of costs (investment and operational) and
losses of amenity.

CHANGES IN WASTEWATER DISPOSAL

Not only does the quantity of domestic wastewater increase continuously during the processes of urbanization and
industrialization, but the quality of effluents changes also.
The increasing resort to chemical processes that have no natural equivalents results in increasing quantities of wastes
that are not biodegradable or that interact in undesirable
ways with natural biological processes. Treatment of effluents is expensive, both at the investment stage and at the
operational stage, consuming ever larger amounts of ever more
expensive energy, so that in most cases only a partial treatment can be financed. Contaminated water passes into surface
waters, infiltrates groundwater, and thence spreads over increasing areas. Once again, SHE will provide, in its future
development, a means of following this process in its water
quality form, under physically realistic meteorologic conditions, to determine the reaction of the natural system to
pollution. These simulations then provide a basis for waste
disposal planning, for balancing treatment costs against
surrogate loss of amenity costs, and for interacting with
water supply planning in order to influence urban development.

In the common situation where the sewerage net conveys
rainfall or storm runoff, SHE can be used to determine, for
observed or "standard" precipitation events and various initial conditions, the form of the hydrographs introduced to
the sewerage net. These hydrographs are the basic data for
the dimensioning of the pipes and their gradients in the sewerage net.

SETTING TARGETS FOR COMMUNITY WATER SUPPLY AND WASTE DISPOSAL

The above applications of SHE will provide space- and time-distributed predictions of the consequences of various local and regional water policies. They will thus indicate what is possible for given levels of investment and energy consumption. By balancing the consequences against the allocation for water resource investment and energy consumption, it should be possible to arrive at rational targets for water quantity and quality for a particular locality or region.

ALLOCATION OF FUNDS FOR COMMUNITY WATER SUPPLY AND WASTE DISPOSAL

By comparing further the result of the exercise introduced in the previous subsection on setting targets for different localities or different regions, it is possible to determine advantages, in water resource terms, of one locality or region over another. These advantages may be changed by water transfers or they may be used as components in more general plans for urbanization and economic development. It will be possible to check the influences of water transfers and the water resource consequences of draft development plans by using the SHE models.

Flooding and Flood Management

FLOOD FORECASTING

Floods have always been a hazard to life and property, but their intensity has increased as the reclaiming through dike construction of floodplains has progressed and as the concentration of industry and urban settlements in these "protected" floodplains becomes greater. A large part of the determination of the effects of floods in the floodplain is a subject of hydraulics. It will be possible to use SHE to generate more reliable flow inputs to the hydraulic model compared to other types of models. These inputs correspond to the more detailed meteorologic condition that SHE will be able to process. This will result in a more reliable flood-warning capability, as well as a means of designing flood attenuation strategies for a wider and more realistic variety of meteorologic situations or scenarios. For example, with SHE it will be easy to determine the direction of propagation of rainstorms, which is complicated or even impossible with other hydrological forecasting methods. SHE will also provide valuable data on zoning in the floodplain relative to the cost of necessary protective measures, the socioeconomic utility of the zone, and flood relieving strategies.

RETENTION OF FLOODWATERS

One method of reducing flood waters in river basins is to construct flood-control reservoirs that are filled during the most flood-critical periods and then emptied, as soon as possible or as required, at a later date. The decision about what constitutes the most flood-critical period and essentially the prediction of the expectation of yet more damaging floods when the relieving capacity is already used up, can only be based on simulations of the effects of preflood evaporative demands and surface characteristics on stream discharges. SHE provides, again, a means of making these simulations for a wider and more realistic variety of meteorologic scenarios.

FLOOD DAMAGE ASSESSMENT

In several, mainly industrialized, countries it has become common to simulate various flood situations in order to assess the physical damage done by the floodwaters. The assessments are usually used for determining insurance claims and for associated litigation. Since SHE can account for more realistic meteorological conditions and provides space-distributed assessments directly, it should be much better suited to these applications compared with other hydrologic methods.

Drought and Drought Loss Management

ASSESSING WATER RESERVES AND PREPARING CONTINGENCY PLANS

The assessment of water reserves on the basis of observations (geo-electric surveys, pumping tests, etc.) is aided by a deterministic, distributed model, in which the transfer of water from one source to another under varying exploitation procedures is conveniently studied. These studies provide the starting point for evaluating various contingency plans, each plan comprising one or more strategies for exploiting water resources under drought conditions. Once again, the deterministic, distributed SHE constitutes a natural instrument in these evaluations.

DROUGHT AMELIORATION PROGRAMS

Evaluations of possible strategies to be adopted under drought conditions point to various possible means of reducing the socioeconomic impact of the drought conditions. These means may comprise such measures as the construction of reservoirs or the extension of the capacities of existing reservoirs to beyond those needed outside of drought conditions, the sinking of additional wells, the planting of drought-resistant species in critical areas, the determining of more efficacious water-allocation arrangements, and the establishment of various procedural and legal measures. The last two measures will usually involve regional and international agreements. For all of these purposes, simulations using SHE will provide information that is essential for obtaining sound investments and reasonable arrangements, and thus well-founded agreements.

CLIMATOLOGICAL CHANGES

Large-scale changes in land use, such as the turning over of forest and savannah lands to agriculture or the spread of desertification, may cause local climatological changes. The SHE models would interface easily with meteorological models, even deterministic and distributed meteorological models, so that they could be used to investigate the mutual influences of climatological and hydrological changes.

Inland Navigation and Other Water Uses

Inland navigation depends, on the one hand, on a sufficient depth of water being available along navigation channels and, on the other hand, on such low velocities that acceptable transport times can be attained. These requirements have led to the extensive development of river systems, extending even so far as the canalization of these rivers and the further construction of systems of canals, locks, and control structures linking river systems. These changes can lead to considerable losses of water from the overland flow system to the subsurface system. The deterministic, distributed SHE models will be able to simulate the interaction between surface and subsurface systems for various proposed changes introduced to promote navigation and for the various works intended to change water exchanges (e.g., canal linings). The SHE system also makes possible a valuable interaction with existing numerical hydraulic models that are almost invariably deterministic and distributed.

Legislation and Litigation

Since this area plays a role in all the areas mentioned, and since its consequences, in economic, social, and political terms, are so far reaching, extending even to acts of belligerency, it warrants separate consideration. The reasons for an excess of legislation and litigation concerning water resources are not difficult to find. Water is the source of innumerable conflicts. For example: extraction of water from a well in one place may cause other wells to dry up; discharge of wastes may pollute a neighboring source of water; factories in a city upstream pollute water downstream that is needed by another city or other factories; a new canal may be so constructed that it diverts groundwater from regions where it has long been exploited; industrial wastes may spoil fishing, bathing, and recreation in a river; a large metropolis may obtain its water supply from increasingly further distances and thus remove the resources of neighboring rural regions; changes in land use may cause more frequent flooding downstream; biological life of the sea may be threatened by pollution from rivers, ships, and coastal industries.

In all places and at all times, large or small
scale conflicts set neighbours or the members of
the same profession against one another and set
cities against rural areas, industrialists against
fishermen, agriculture against electrification and
upstream areas against downstream areas.

The role of the public powers is to settle such
conflicts. The usual means of settling conflicts
in human societies is to resort to the arbitration
of a wise man or the courts...

However, when conflicts become extremely numerous
and involve forces as powerful and necessary as
the development of agriculture, cities, industry
and recreation, flood protection or the development
of mountain areas and consequently require enormous
investments for their satisfactory solution, simple
arbitration is no longer sufficient (Biswas 1978).

Since so many conflicts over water resources are concerned with the distribution of these resources and/or involve physical changes in the hydrologic system, legislation
and judgments in processes of litigation must make use of
quantifications of changes in distributions and/or quantifications of the effects of physical changes. Since it is
precisely these quantifications that SHE provides, SHE becomes an important instrument in the area of legislation and
litigation.

Quantifications

On the basis of the marketing analysis, it has been
estimated that the total value of investments in water resource works in all areas in which SHE is applicable, excluding hydroelectric investments in CMEA countries and China,
will amount to some US$66 x 10^9 per year throughout the period
1980-1990. This value is, of course, strongly dependent on
energy prices, essentially oil prices, during this period.
The total value of works that will be accessible for EEC organizations is estimated to be between US$14 x 10^9 and US$30
x 10^9, per year. From these figures and on the basis of the
arguments advanced earlier, it is possible to quantify the
expected indirect benefits accruing from SHE.

CONCLUSIONS

The European Hydrologic System—Système Hydrologique
Européen, SHE, constitutes one of the most ambitious and
demanding projects undertaken in the area of hydrologic modeling. The expertise and financial resources apportioned to
this project appear to be commensurable with the tasks set.
The production system, when available, should be able to
generate models capable of covering a large part of the
demands of engineering practice. SHE is envisaged as an

instrument suited particularly to larger contracts and supported by a data base that is adequate and system-relevant.
It is expected that the use of SHE will, in time, influence
data collection programs, providing an incentive to new
approaches and especially encouraging methods of satellite
imagery. Although the development of SHE to its full capacity will be dependent to some extent on the development of
complementary data collection programs and instrumentation,
SHE has the full potential for such development.

REFERENCES

Abbott, M.B. (1976) The Application of Design Systems to
    Problems of Unsteady Flow in Open Channels. Presented
    at the International Symposium on Unsteady Flow in Open
    Channels, held by the British Hydromechanics Research
    Association—Fluid Engineering, April, Newcastle-upon-
    Tyne, UK.

Abbott, M.B. (1978) Scientific and commercial aspects of
    applied mathematical modelling, in Proceedings of the
    International Conference on Applied Mathematical Model-
    ling, Madrid. Guildford, UK: IPC Press.

Abbott, M.B., Aa. Damsgaard, and G.S. Rodenhuis (1973) System
    21, "Jupiter", a design system for two-dimensional
    nearly-horizontal flows. Journal of Hydraulic Research
    11:1-28.

Abbott, M.B., H. Petersen, and O. Skovgaard (1978) On the
    numerical modelling of short waves in shallow water.
    Journal of Hydraulics Research 16(3):123-205.

Biswas, A.K. (1978) Water Supply and Management, Proceedings
    of the UN Water Conference, Mar Del Plata, Argentina,
    March 1977, 4 Vols. Oxford: Pergamon.

Mahieux, F. (1972) Le Calcul de la Rentabilité de la Re-
    cherche, Sélection des Projects (Calculation of Research
    Profitability, Selection of Projects). Paris: Eyrolles
    (in French).

THE IMPLEMENTATION AND APPLICATION OF A SUITE FOR THE
SIMULATION OF COMPLEX WATER RESOURCE SYSTEMS IN EVALUATION
AND PLANNING STUDIES

D. Pearson and P.D. Walsh

INTRODUCTION

Water Supply Infrastructure

The North West Water Authority (NWWA) is one of 10 regional water authorities in England and Wales whose responsibilities cover the whole water cycle, including water resources and supply, sewerage, sewage disposal, and river
management. The Authority covers an area of almost 14,500 km^2
and serves some 7 million consumers. The supplies to the
main conurbations have been developed independently in the
past with Manchester deriving its main supplies from the
Lake District in the north of the region and Liverpool developing sources in North and Mid-Wales, which are outside
the Authority area. Figure 1 illustrates the major reservoirs and aqueducts that form the basis of a water grid
available to the Authority for supply flexibility.

Planning Studies

Appraisal of previous water resource studies (Water
Resources Board 1974) produced a short list of four alternative schemes capable of meeting anticipated deficits at the
turn of the century. These schemes (see Figure 2) are quite
different in character and in their environmental implications. The Morecambe Bay scheme involves the construction
of bunded reservoirs in a large estuary which is an important European breeding ground for many species of birds.
The enlargement of the existing Haweswater reservoir would
be within the Lake District National Park, an area very sensitive to new water resource development. The other two
alternatives require completely new reservoirs. Borrowbeck
is a moorland valley on a tributary high up in the River
Lune, whereas Hellifield is a lowland reservoir comprising
good agricultural land on the River Ribble.

213

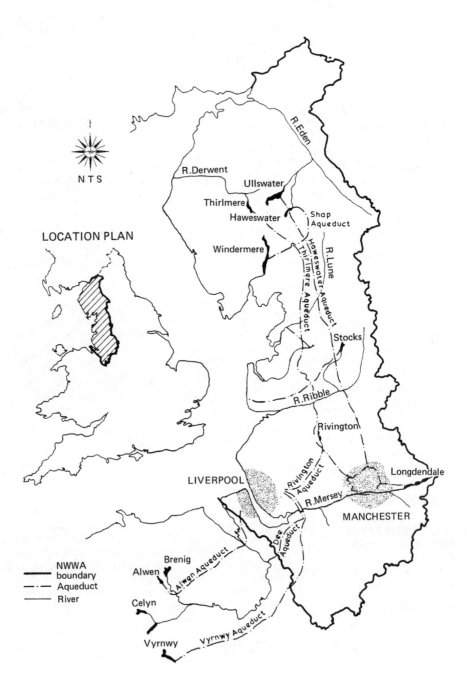

FIGURE 1   North West Water Authority's regional aqueduct
system.

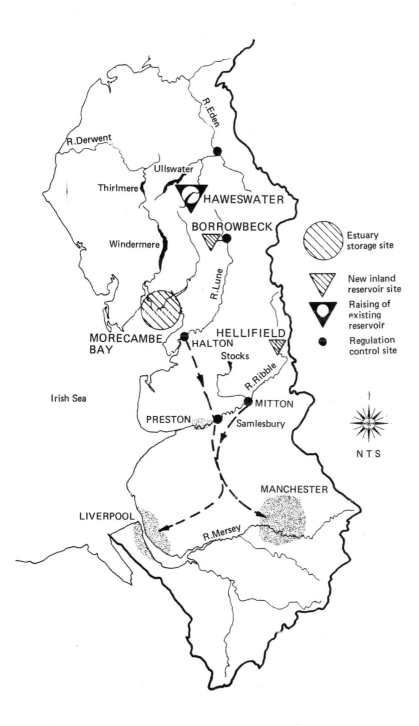

FIGURE 2 Alternative water resource developments.

The Authority decided that any further investigation of these alternatives must pay full regard to the environmental and social considerations at each site as well as to the engineering and economic factors. The study by the Land Use Consultants (1978) has therefore been carried out with the full participation of the Structure Planning Authorities through whom, in the final phase, consultations are taking place with all interested parties. It was important, therefore, that any information made available should be intelligible to specialists in other disciplines, to senior management, and to nonspecialists alike. Considerable use was therefore made of computer-produced graphical output when presenting the results from the models used.

Organizational Considerations

The water resource investigations are under the control of the Director of Resource Planning who has a small staff in Head Office covering all aspects of corporate and physical resource planning. Seconded staff from Divisions assist by working both at Head Office or in their own offices. The mobility of staff can create additional problems in specialized investigations because of the staff's unfamiliarity with computer applications in general and especially with a particular suite of programs.

Head Office and each of the Divisions (eight in all) are well served by a central computer facility through a system of communication links involving remote job entry terminals with local printing facilities and visual terminals. These provide for on-line editing and interactive or background job initiation. Potential difficulties due to the location of staff were, therefore, overcome by using these extensive computer links which also permit the use of the same programs and data base.

Water Resource Analysis

Long historical runoff sequences were not available at or near many of the sites that had to be considered for the Regional Resource Study. It could also not be assumed that the long runoff records that were available would include droughts of all durations, to the same severity. In order, therefore, to reduce the computer time involved and to weight the historical droughts to a common subjectively assessed severity, it was decided to use the technique of synthetic droughts (Twort *et al.* 1974, Stall and Neill 1963, Bannerman and Boulton 1964) for the yield analysis. Three-year sequences were prepared which contain within them droughts of every duration, from 1 to 36 months, to an equal severity. Thus the yield of a system can be assessed by the analysis of only a 3-year sequence with considerable logistical benefits compared with say, a 50-year sequence. No assumptions have to be made concerning the critical period of the reservoir or the relative severity of historic droughts of different durations and problems of data generation are also avoided.

Early in the studies it was realized that many variants of each alternative would have to be analyzed in terms of yield and average pumped quantities to ascertain approximate optimum developments for various pumped refill sites. It was also realized that new sites may have to be investigated. Therefore, a general simulation program was written that would allow new system configurations to be analyzed without recompilation. This program was written to be capable of representing both the main features of the existing major water resource system and the proposed developments, using a simple daily accounting process, so that the additional gain in supplies made available by any new development could be assessed. The need to fully take into account the interaction of new and existing developments added a considerable degree of complexity (see Figure 3). At the height of the studies, some 1,500 simulations were performed over a 6-month period.

The simulation program together with the probability programs used to analyze the runoff records formed the beginning of the computer suite for hydrologic analyses and from the start all the data were assembled in a consistent format and unit. The knowledge of the authors, who had not previously worked together, amounted to nearly a decade and a half of experience in water resource planning and modeling. This was pooled in the crystallization of ideas for the suite and many lessons learned from previous work were incorporated into the suite with full allowance for the organizational issues and for the nature and size of the anticipated workload.

RESOURCE PLANNING SUITE OF PROGRAMS

Data Requirements

The importance of adequate data on which to base the studies was recognized early in the life of the Authority. Data were assembled from all possible sources often in differing units and formats; therefore, several special programs were written to convert, validate, and write these data to disc in the common unit. Since this initial period, it has been possible to reduce the number of input options to:

● New data input via coding sheets and a standard validation program

● Input of paper tapes received direct from the Water Data Unit (WDU), which holds the national archive of river-flow data

● Direct transfer from the NWWA river-flow data processing suite and archive

218

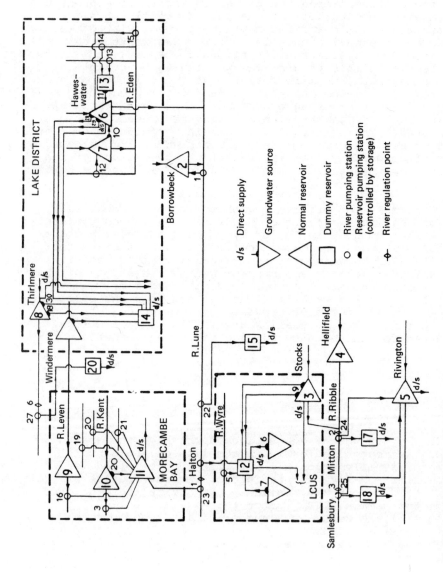

FIGURE 3 Schematic diagram of resource model.

If other computer-based sources are used, specific "one-off" programs are written to produce the data in a form acceptable to the main input program. This reduces the programming effort required, ensures consistent and thorough validation of all data, and simplifies the tasks of carrying out more thorough analyses. Some 750 station-years of daily flow data, 750 station-years of monthly flow data, and 600 station-years of rainfall data are held in the system at present and form the basic data to the suite. In addition some 1,000 station-years of predicted river flows and predicted reservoir storages from simulation runs of preferred variants are being retained at present for answering any queries that may arise.

Management of the Suite

To facilitate the control of the amount of flow data and derived data available to users, a file holding up-to-date information describing the data available, their time periods, lengths of records, and file names is held on the computer and can be accessed at any time. The same file is used to control security dumps of the data. This file is amended by a user whenever the files are changed or updated, or when new ones are formed.

To assist in the management and promotion of the use of the suite in a wider context, a User Group has been formed. This group consists of representatives of the principal users and also of the Computer Services Section. The main functions of the group are to discuss further applications of the suite, modifications to the existing programs, and difficulties with the suite. Any new program suggestion is circulated before a specification is agreed so that the final program will be flexible and appropriate to the needs of all hydrologic staff in the Authority.

A *User Guide* to the suite is maintained to explain the scope and use of each program and the necessary control data. Standard data sheets are prepared as these are a considerable help in minimizing errors and facilitating the use of programs by staff with limited experience of the suite.

General Structure of the Suite

The main programs of the suite are written to access the data files and when appropriate to write to files in the same format. They are written to be able to access any part of a record. In the case of programs that produce monthly or daily output, these data are not printed by each particular program; instead the data are written to a file in the standard format and then printed using the appropriate standard printout program or, if required, the graph plotting program. This reduces the programming effort for a new program and output is reduced. It also means that the data are

readily available to the other, or same, programs in the
suite. The programs have collectively been named the RP
(Resource Planning) suite and are referred to by the ini-
tials followed by a two digit number. The numbering system
has been chosen in groups to correspond to similar types of
programs. Table 1 lists the programs available at present
in the suite and Figure 4 illustrates their interrelation-
ships.

Two programs (RP66 and RP67) have been written so that
data can be transferred to and from on-line storage for use
by suites developed outside the Authority. At present this
facility has been used for data generation applying programs
developed at Birmingham University, based on the bivariate,
autoregressive model suggested by Hamlin and Kottegoda (1974),
and to link with the HYSIM model developed by R.E. Manley
(see the paper by R.E. Manley in this volume). The suite
has also been linked with the model used for the operational
study of the Lancashire Conjunctive Use Scheme, which is
being developed in the center of the region, based on the
Stocks reservoir, the Fylde aquifer, and the Rivers Lune
and Wyre.

General Simulation Model

To minimize the direct involvement of engineers in unnecessary computer programming and systems organization, it
was decided to generalize a previous daily water resource
simulation program. Originally this program had a general
input and printout section and utilized generalized subroutines to simulate particular elements of the resource systems
(reservoir, pumping station, and regulation control point).
However, the order in which they were simulated, the inter-
linking "natural" river system, and the points where information could be output were defined by specific programming in
the central logic of the program. Although such a program
is reasonably general and few changes are required if different resource systems are to be simulated, problems did arise
in responding quickly to changed systems, in the availability
of suitably experienced staff, and in keeping a record of the
program version used for a particular run. Such problems
prompted the further generalization of the program so that
the river system and the order of operation of the sources
(elements) could be specified by data. Similarly, the choice
of output is specified by data and can include the flow at
any point in the system, any reservoir storage, any pumped
transfer, or any regulation release up to a maximum of nine
items for a run. Thus the program can handle most circumstances from very simple configurations to very complex configurations without any program changes and has facilitated
the use of staff with no computer programming experience on
the studies that have used the suite. The program has been
readily and quickly applied to other resource studies including very simple water resource systems with ease and confidence.

The general simulation program may not be able to simulate the idiosyncrasies of a particular resource system precisely, but it is surprising how versatile the three elements have proved to be. By judicious use they have been used to simulate quite complex and unique circumstances with satisfactory results for investigational studies. It is not intended that the general program be used for the modeling of an existing system for operational studies since this would involve computing overheads due to system flexibility where this was unnecessary. In such cases specific models would be written (for example, for the Lancashire Conjunctive Use Scheme, the Lake District sources) so that the system configuration and operation can be modeled precisely and in far more detail. Where necessary, conceptual representation of the hydrologic processes would be incorporated in these more detailed models. The present exercise did not require a high degree of sophistication and the simplest adequate representations have been used.

Despite its flexibility, the simulation program is not excessive in its core requirement or use of mill time. The program requires 17K words of store and a run of a typical system of one direct supply reservoir, a regulation reservoir, plus bankside storage. The output of daily information takes 14 seconds per year of simulation.

TYPICAL APPLICATIONS

The control data required by most programs in the suite are, where possible, reduced to an absolute minimum and punching documents have been prepared for each program; these generally cover one side of an A4 sheet. These documents reduce the chance of data input errors and facilitate the utilization of punching staff rather than qualified technical staff. However, when urgent jobs are required the quantity of data is sufficiently small to be easily input via an interactive terminal. The running of the program is controlled by a comprehensive high-level program (macro) which allows various options such as erasure of the control data file, saving of line printer output in a file, interactive or background running, assigning of peripherals, loading of the program, error routines, disc file allocation, etc., so that only one short line of instruction is required to run a program. Jobs utilizing several programs, with data being produced by one and "handed" on to another, are assembled simply, by calling the relevant programs with the associated control data, in the correct sequence. Such jobs can be assembled either in background mode or interactively.

Reservoir Control Curves

A typical example of the assembling of a job is the production of control curves for a complex reservoir system involving regulation, direct supply, natural inflow, pumped inflow, and conjunctive use demands. Initial runs are carried

TABLE 1 Water resources and hydrologic analysis suite—programs available and core requirements.

No.	Brief description of use	Input files	Output files	Core (K words)
RP01	Input of daily data		Single daily	5
RP02	Aggregates several daily data files to form multistation file	Up to 9 single daily	Multistation daily	6
RP05	Input of monthly data		Monthly	5
RP06	Editing of daily data files	Single daily	Single daily	5
RP07	Merges two daily data files to form a single file of the arithmetic total	2 single daily	Single daily	5
RP08	Input of daily data from WDU		Single daily	6
RP09	Disaggregates multistation file into separate files	Multistation daily	Up to 9 single daily	7
RP11	Independent events analysis	Single daily/monthly		12
RP12	Seasonal events analysis	Single daily/monthly		16
RP14	Fixed starting (finishing) date analysis	Single daily/monthly		20

Code	Description			
RP21	General resource simulation	Single daily/multistation daily	Multistation daily	17
RP23	Tabulation of yield/storage for direct supply reservoir			6
RP24	Monthly simulation of direct supply reservoir with control policies	Monthly		12
RP25	Monthly conceptual model (rainfall-runoff)	Monthly	Monthly	
RP31	Printout of daily data file	Single daily/multistation daily		11
RP32	Printout of monthly data file	Monthly		7
RP33	Flow frequency analysis and plotting of daily data files	Single daily		22
RP34	Hydrograph plotting of data files	Single daily/monthly		13
RP35	Probability distribution plotting on line printer (under development)			13
RP41	Analysis of daily data for releases, abstraction, or residual flows	Single daily	Single daily	5
RP42	Net additions to storage	Single daily/monthly	Monthly	6
RP43	Reservoir back-routing	Single daily	Single daily	6
RP66	Transfers data from file to on-line storage	Single daily/monthly		7
RP67	Transfers data to file from on-line storage	Single daily/ monthly	Single daily/ monthly	7

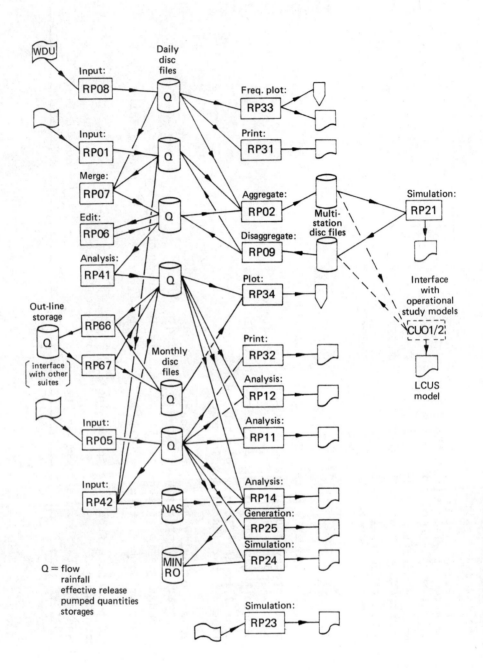

FIGURE 4   Water resources and hydrologic analysis suite, system arrangement.

out using the design droughts and with no control curves to
find the yield and preferred operational rules for the system. This is usually carried out interactively since the
work requires feedback from previous simulations. When the
yield and operating rules of the system are defined, an historical simulation is made to determine the demands on and
the maximum possible inputs to the reservoir subject to the
system constraints and parameters. From this simulation run
the demands and the inflows to the reservoir are written to
a multistation file that is then disaggregated into separate
temporary work files. These separate files are then combined,
together with the historic natural inflow and direct supply
demands by a program (RP42) to produce a single value of the
total "net additions to storage", for each month of the historic record available; whereupon these are written to a
monthly file. This file can be analyzed using the fixed
starting date analysis program (RP14) (which is capable of
working on runoff, effective releases, or net additions to
storage) to calculate the control curve (Walsh 1971), i.e.,
the storage required at the beginning of any month to with-
stand the worst historic event of any duration starting
that month.

The "job" described above, involving the running of several programs, can be assembled from a few coding sheets
easily completed, punched, and run. If required, the job
can be saved for subsequent runs of a similar system with
little or no alteration. Such a job loads and deletes the
programs in sequence so that the maximum core demand is that
required by the largest program of the job (see Table 1).

Simulation

After the manual adjustment of the control curve, a
normal run of the simulation model then gives the predicted
performance of the system over the historic period available
including maximum drawdown each year and annual pumped quantities and releases. The same run can be used to output
daily information of, say, reservoir storage, river flows,
and pumped quantities for further analysis. This may include
printing (RP31), hydrograph plots (RP34), and frequency analysis plots (RP33) of the whole period or of selected years.
Again this work can be assembled into a single job using very
little control data.

The amount of control data needed for the simulation
program is directly proportional to the complexity of the
system, requiring approximately 20 lines for a single reservoir system involving regulation and pumped refill. However,
it can be extensive for complex systems (120 lines for a system involving several reservoirs, river, lake and groundwater
abstractions, licences, conjunctive use, dual and multiple
regulation, and similar complexities). The control data are
normally held on file in on-line storage and often retained
for some time. Use can then be made of the comprehensive

on-line editor for changing parameters, such as pump capacity, direct supply, and regulation level, between runs; listings can be produced easily if extensive editing is required when the system is being changed.

The model can be run in an interactive mode in which case a reduced output giving a line of information for each reservoir is shown on the terminal for immediate assessment. This is particularly useful when yield/storage or similar curves are being produced and the results of one run determine the changes required in the parameters for the subsequent run. These changes can be assessed from the information shown; the parameter file is then edited and the model is rerun. Thus, a yield/storage curve can be produced rapidly and with the minimum of computer runs. A choice of whether to print the full results can be made after each run; often the first estimates are not worthy of retention. The main output of the model gives details of all the parameters and of the system configuration so that reference to the parameter file is not necessary and the run can be scrutinized at any time in the future.

Part of the study was designed to enable the Authority to assess the river management aspects of the various schemes. These aspects related to land drainage, fisheries, water quality, ecology, and amenity. Abstraction conditions for the various refill and abstraction sites were adopted based on previous experience with due regard for downstream water users, water quality, and fishery management.

The impact of the schemes of the rivers was assessed by using the simulation model to predict the flows that would have occurred over the past 18 years of historic record had the schemes been in operation. The flows at eight sites along three different rivers were produced and presented in the form of flow frequency curves, for various seasons of the year, as well as annual hydrographs. To show the flows both with and without the schemes, 150 flow frequency graphs and 100 hydrographs were produced. The impact of the schemes was assessed by the analysis of residual flows, the number of days of likely fish movements, and the change in flow regime. A selection of schemes was subsequently reassessed to show the sensitivity of the gain in available supplies to changes in abstraction conditions.

Similarly, results from the simulation model of predicted storage levels were used to provide drawdown information for consultation purposes and to help in the consideration of landscaping. A combination of both river-flow and storage predictions was analyzed in order to assess the relative proportion of different types of water in storage and in the releases so that the ecological implications of interbasin transfer could be assessed.

SUMMARY

The suite of programs and the standardized data base developed at NWWA to meet the needs of an extensive water resource investigation have provided a sound foundation for the analysis of many types of water resource problems. They have enabled staff to analyze complex systems using the computer but without having to be versed in the computing intricacies of the programs involved. Over a dozen staff have used the suite at various times and for varying periods over the last 3 years. They have used it either as part of their normal duties or because they have been called in as part of a special study in which case they have been able to move in and out of the studies with the minimum of time being lost due to familiarization problems.

It would have been impossible to run the study if it had been necessary to carry out program alterations between runs since staff may not have any programming experience. Therefore, the programs were designed, or have evolved, to be as flexible and general as realistically possible. This may increase the "overheads" in running a program that is more complex than is strictly necessary but reaps dividends in terms of more rapid response times and the utilization of engineering and other noncomputer staff on engineering and environmental problems rather than computing problems. There is also less chance of possible errors in that once a program has been fully tested it is likely to remain unchanged for some time. The general nature of the programs has enabled the user to respond rapidly to various requests from internal and external groups, and it has allowed the analysis of other water resource systems without additional and new computer programming and attendant problems beyond those in the formative days of the suite. This has allowed far more alternatives to be covered by the staff available than would have been the case if the programs had to be altered between runs.

The suite is in no way specifically applicable to the Regional Resource Studies. It provides a framework for the analysis of any water resource problem and has been applied to many other types and areas of study. These have included the operational problems during drought conditions, such as in 1976, and the prospects for the subsequent year, the study of the reliability of water resource systems under various emergency operating policies, the investigation of operating policies of existing schemes and schemes under construction, as well as the facilities of the suite being used for the presentation of information in printout or graphical form. New programs are being considered all the time, and it is expected that the number of programs in the suite will continue to grow.

The scope of the suite has allowed the investigation of the ecological impacts of water resource developments to be carried further forward than has been attempted in the past. It has been possible to provide information in a form that can be appreciated and assimilated readily by noncomputer orientated disciplines, and can be used for presentation purposes. Far more analyses have been possible than in previous studies, giving better design understanding and confidence in the choice of preferred variants, and the impact of a proposed scheme has been shown in terms of river management and ecological issues.

ACKNOWLEDGMENTS

The suite could not have been formed without the corporate efforts of many parts of the Authority. However, the views expressed here are those of the authors and not necessarily those of the North West Water Authority.

REFERENCES

Bannerman, P.B.W., and A.G. Boulton (1964) Hydrological Survey Work, Lancashire Rivers. London: Ministry of Housing and Local Government, Her Majesty's Stationery Office.

Hamlin, M.J., and N.T. Kottegoda (1974) The preparation of a data set for hydrologic system analysis. Volume 1, pages 305-320, Proceedings of Symposium on Design of Water Resources Projects with Inadequate Data, Madrid, June 1973. Paris: UNESCO-WMO-IAMS.

Land Use Consultants (1978) Environmental Appraisal of Four Alternative Water Resource Schemes. Warrington, UK: North West Water Authority.

Stall, J.B., and J.C. Neill (1963) Calculated risks of impounding reservoir yield. Proceedings of the American Society of Civil Engineers, Journal of the Hydraulics Division 88(HY1):23-34.

Twort, A.C., R.C. Hoather, and F.M. Law (1974) Water Supply. London: Edward Arnold.

Walsh, P.D. (1971) Designing control rule for the conjunctive use of impounding reservoirs. Journal of the Institute of Water Engineering 25(7):371.

Water Resources Board (1974) Water Resources in England and Wales. London: Her Majesty's Stationery Office.

EXPERIENCES OF THE HYDROLOGIC ENGINEERING CENTER IN
MAINTAINING WIDELY USED HYDROLOGIC AND WATER RESOURCE
COMPUTER MODELS

W.S. Eichert

INTRODUCTION TO THE HYDROLOGIC ENGINEERING CENTER

The Hydrologic Engineering Center (HEC) of the United
States Army Corps of Engineers, located in Davis, California,
was established in 1964 to serve all 52 offices of the Corps
of Engineers (Corps) in the area of hydrologic engineering.
Its mission was later expanded to include development and
implementation of analytical planning techniques. The Center's basic purpose is to assist practicing engineers
throughout the Corps in applying state-of-the-art technology
to current planning, design, and operation problems. This
basic purpose is accomplished by locating, evaluating and/or
developing new procedures and techniques (primarily mathematical models), by teaching these and other state-of-the-art
techniques in approximately 24 weeks of formal training
courses each year, by developing and maintaining a library
of some 12 major state-of-the-art computer programs, and by
assisting Corps offices in applying these techniques in current studies. The above missions are presently accomplished
through a staff of approximately 40 employees, including 25
engineers, 5 computer system analysts, and 10 technicians
and clerical support personnel. An annual budget of about
$1,850,000 includes about $500,000 reimbursable work for
assisting in project studies, $250,000 for training, $150,000
for program maintenance, and $950,000 for research and devel-
opment (including developing and improving computer models).

MAJOR HEC PROGRAMS

All major HEC programs (see Table 1) are written to be
useful on a fairly wide range of problems in a specific area
of hydrologic engineering or water resource planning. They
are also generalized so that they can be used in about 95
percent of the studies without any code changes. Input data
are used to describe site-specific data. The programs are

TABLE 1 Major HEC computer programs.

Program	Program size		No. of offices on list of source deck holders as of 15 November 1976			
	No. of statements	Core storage (words)[a]	Corps	Other govt., universities, foreign	Private	Total
HEC-1, flood hydrograph package	4,150	68K	28	141	231	400
HEC-2, water surface profiles	8,000	44K	42	228	362	632
HEC-3, reservoir system analysis for conservation	4,030	66K	20	64	41	125
HEC-4, monthly streamflow simulation	1,985	60K	15	76	45	136
HEC-5C, simulation of flood control and conservation systems	12,000	122K	11	42	17	70
HEC-6, scour and deposition in rivers and reservoirs	6,000	53K	18	33	15	66
Urban runoff: storage, treatment and overflow (STORM)	5,200	66K	19	109	113	241
Regional frequency computation	1,330	43K	19	44	34	97
Gradually varied unsteady flow profiles	4,300	55K	25	37	26	88
Water quality for river-reservoir systems (WQRRS)	7,800	71K	5	43	23	71
All others	—	—	122	423	269	814
TOTAL			324	1,240	1,176	2,740

[a] Core storage requirements are based on a CDC CYBER 175 located at Boeing Computer Company, Seattle, Washington, and are shown in words (base number).

written using FORTRAN statements which are acceptable on most computers; thus the programs are transportable to many different computer systems with little or no modification. Specific rules, which will be discussed later, followed in producing this code were derived by experience gained from converting the programs to many other systems over several years. The major HEC programs that are being supported by HEC in the production mode are shown in Table 1. Many smaller production programs are available and several other major programs are still in the research stage, such as our work in two-dimensional hydrodynamics.

HEC CYCLE OF PROGRAM SUPPORT

The HEC cycle for computer support includes the following important steps:

● *Research:* Program development and improvement

● *Documentation:* User manuals, programmer manuals, training documents, special application reports

● *Training:* Formal courses (1-2 weeks each), video tapes, individual training

● *User support:* Consulting, answering telephone calls, reviewing jobs mailed to HEC, correcting errors in program

● *Distribution:* Mailing publications, source decks, test data, and computer solutions

● *Feedback:* From user to HEC on input problems, program errors, desired program improvements

The methods used by HEC in each of the steps above are described as follows.

Research. Most HEC supported programs were developed by HEC, but a few of the programs such as the STORM and WQRRS programs were initially developed by others and have been adapted and improved by HEC or by contractors to HEC over the years. Improvements to the programs are important, for unless the programs are kept up-to-date, they will no longer be used and the results of the research will be terminated.

Documentation. Computer program documentation is generally accomplished with separate user and programmer manuals. The programmer manual provides useful information for implementing the program on the user's computer. The user manual explains what technical procedures are used in the program, how the program operates, how to code input for the program, and how to interpret output. Notification of program corrections and improvements is made periodically to all current source deck holders. Other HEC publications include training course notebooks, newsletters, professional papers, and computer program abstracts.

Training. Each year approximately 24 weeks of training are provided by HEC for Corps personnel in 1- to 2-week courses. Approximately 10 percent of the space in these courses is reserved for personnel from other U.S. federal, state, and university offices. Two special 4-week courses were given to foreign representatives in 1972 and 1974 as a U.S. contribution to the International Hydrological Decade. A number of U.S. and Canadian universities are using HEC-developed courses or are using HEC computer models in their courses.

Individual training is given by HEC to meet specific needs not met by the formal courses. Arrangements have been made by the U.S. State Department for foreign training by HEC. Fifteen of the HEC courses have been videotaped, and the 223 tapes are available for loan along with instructional material (lecture notes, visual aids, and references). These tapes are particularly useful when someone who has taken the course is available to answer questions after the tapes are viewed. Visitors to HEC desiring individual training on a certain computer model often use these videotapes before receiving individual help in solving a particular problem. Eleven visitors from Brazil recently received 4 weeks of training at HEC using this approach. In spite of the above, insufficient training is currently available to the non-Corps user.

User support. HEC provides support to the HEC programs by assigning each program to an engineer. The engineer answers calls on the program concerning program capabilities and limitations, input problems, and program aborts. Sometimes program executions are reviewed to help the user find input errors or to correct program errors.

Source deck distribution. As shown in Table 1, the HEC has distributed source decks to a variety of offices. Based on our November 1976 survey, over 2,700 source decks are still considered active by the using offices. Each year approximately 700 new source decks are requested. Assistance to program users is provided, to the extent possible, in implementing the models in their equipment, answering questions on use of models, and eliminating program malfunctions. These services are provided without charge; however, private firms are charged a $60 reproduction and handling fee for each source deck and set of documentation provided.

Feedback. Users of HEC programs have provided valuable feedback to HEC in terms of needed improvements in program capabilities, documentation deficiencies, program malfunctions, etc.

Each of the steps in the program support cycle is an important link. If one or more of these steps is missing or

neglected, it will eventually stop the cycle and prevent the
generalized code from being used effectively. The program
support cycle cannot be started until the models are in demand by various users.

WAYS TO ENCOURAGE USAGE OF THE MODELS

Technology can be transferred very effectively through
computer models. However, many very good computer models
have been developed which will never be effectively used because of model limitations, poor model documentation, or lack
of support for the model. The HEC has tried to observe the
following principles in order to make the models more attractive and useful to the user.

Use Commonly Accepted Techniques

In HEC models we have tried to provide several of the
best available methods so that a user's personal preference
can be satisfied. For instance, some six different flood-
routing methods and four different loss rate functions are
incorporated into our HEC-1 Flood Hydrograph Package.

Make Models Generalized and Flexible

A complex computer model that is designed for a specific
project may be very valuable for that project, but it is
probably not useful for the same type of project at another
site. At HEC we try to write major models so that a large
proportion of similar types of problems at other locations
can be solved without any program modification. The programs
are written in large packages so that most problems in a general field of interest can be solved with the same model.
All programs are written in FORTRAN IV in such a way that
they are easily transported to a wide range of computers.

Make Input Simple

Most models in use today are difficult to use because
not enough attention was given to making the input user-
oriented. The amount of use the program will receive by
others is heavily influenced by how easy the program is to
use.

Make Documentation Simple and Readable

Models that have extensive computational capabilities
in solving complex programs are easy to find. Models with
good documentation are very hard to find. Too much documentation will scare away a potential user, and too little will

leave a potential user frustrated and angry. The documentation should be written so that the beginner can easily use the model on a simple problem and the experienced user can use the model on a complex problem.

Support the Finished Model

In very few cases are knowledgeable personnel available to help users effectively use the models. All major HEC models are supported by one or more persons who help users by answering questions on the telephone and by tracking down user problems. A lack of model support by the developing office is perhaps the most important reason why some models are not effective in transferring technology. A good model sitting on the shelf without any backing is worthless. Model support can require a substantial amount of manpower and funds. Good documentation and simple input can greatly help reduce the required aid. While the increased use of the model increases the success of the technology transfer, the requirements for support of the model are also increased, sometimes beyond the office's capability to provide that support. The support required on the HEC-2 model with over 600 offices currently using it has reached the point where 2-3 people are spending almost half their time on the support activity.

The amount of support that is provided for a model should be dependent on how much the model is being used. If a program has few users, perhaps the support effort (mainly improvements) should be transferred to more successful models. Determining the extent of use of the models is very difficult when many different computers are being used. Results from surveys such as that shown in Table 2 are quite useful when based on questionnaires of known program users. Table 2 shows that much more use is being made of our HEC program in the private sector than in our own Corps offices. Other results show what additional program capabilities need to be added and where difficult input coding problems occur. Where programs are used by many offices on the same computers, routines like our SNOOPY program can be added to provide periodic information on program usage, options called, etc., as shown in Table 3.

COST AND MANPOWER FOR PROGRAM SUPPORT

The estimated costs and manpower requirements for supporting the generalized computer programs in the HEC library are shown in Table 4. The support efforts are a function of many factors, including the number of users, the extent of use by each user, the technical background of the user, the amount of training the user has in the subject area and subject program, and the amount of experience the user has in using a particular program. Two or three of our programs require about half of our total support efforts, while

TABLE 2   Release of November 1976 version of HEC-2.

Source deck distribution

Type of user	No.
Private (U.S.)	98
Corps	18
Other federal	11
State or local government	54
University (U.S.)	29
Private (foreign)	7
Foreign government	11
University (foreign)	3
TOTAL	231

Usage survey

Type of user	No. of offices responding	Program has been used during last 3 months	No. of people using HEC-2	Approx. no. of program executions per year
Private	137	101	921	84,161
Corps	24	21	243	34,010
Other federal	12	7	57	1,045
State or local government	52	35	284	12,665
University (U.S.)	25	13	216	2,488
Others	3	3	10	1,000
TOTAL	253	180	1,731	135,369

236

TABLE 3   Number of executions of HEC computer programs at
the Lawrence Berkeley Laboratory during a 10-month
period.

Month	HEC-1	HEC-2	HEC-5C	Frequency analysis	Unsteady flow
		No. of executions			
October 1976	374	1,307	82	80	86
November 1976	295	1,363	64	129	89
December 1976	270	1,462	100	164	79
January 1977		1,661	357	162	35
February 1977		1,712	954	176	123
March 1977		2,243	420	195	32
April 1977		899	363	199	28
May 1977		1,764	187	218	91
June 1977		2,807	284	176	66
July 1977		2,412	306	104	103
TOTAL	939	17,630	3,117	1,603	732
PROJECTED ANNUAL TOTAL[a]	3,756	21,156	3,740	1,924	878

(SNOOPY not operational for HEC-1, January–July 1977)

[a] The projected annual total is obtained by dividing "total" figures by number of months' figures where available and multiplying by 12.

TABLE 4 Cost and manpower for program support.

Item	Approx. no. of products per year	Annual cost of HEC programs ($)	Equivalent full-time employee
Training courses: development and presentation	22 weeks	250,000	4.0
Program: development/improvement	12	200,000[a]	3.5
User support	12 major programs	85,000	2.0
Documentation: development/improvement	15	30,000	0.5
Maintain programs on two 3-computer systems	3	20,000	0.5
Videotapes and support documents: distribute	500	5,000	0.5
Source decks: reproduce and distribute	700	40,000	0.3
Documentation: reproduce and distribute	4,000	15,000	0.2
Videotapes: development	100	15,000	0.1
TOTAL		660,000	11.6

[a]Estimated part of $950,000 annual research program used for 12 major programs currently supported by HEC.

several programs require very little support. Our development and improvement costs vary considerably from year to year and from program to program. Initial development costs of a typical large HEC program are $100,000. While the program is still in a production mode, additional improvements over a 5- to 10-year period may increase that total cost to about $500,000.

Total support costs (which exclude the development/improvement costs) of the 12 major programs in the HEC have not changed greatly in the last 2 years since the number of users has gradually leveled off.

COMPATIBILITY WITH OTHER COMPUTER SYSTEMS

Even though FORTRAN is a common computer language available in most scientific computing systems, care must be taken to prepare programs that can be executed on all systems. This is because most FORTRAN compilers made available by vendors contain variations or enhancements to the standard FORTRAN language that may not be available or at least implemented in the same way on other systems.

To produce the most usable code for all FORTRAN installations:

● Isolate file initialization statements at the beginning of the main program for easy adaptation to other systems

● Avoid BACKSPACE statements

● Use standard READ and WRITE statements for I/O operations

● Restrict alphanumeric input/output to four characters per word (A4)

● Use no more than three subscripts for arrays

● Prepare code in logical subroutine units that can be debugged independent of other routines and overlayed in smaller machines as necessary

● Avoid multiple entry points in a subprogram

● If variable dimensions are required, pass the dimension limit in the call statement, not in common areas

● Place DATA statements that preset labeled common areas in BLOCK DATA subprograms

● Use care where loss of precision may affect computer results, such as in differences of numbers of nearly equal magnitudes. It may require DOUBLE PRECISION in some machines to give the same result as single precision gives in others.

● Where special features of a system are germane to
the operation of a program, such as direct access I/O and
character manipulation, isolate them in a single subroutine
that may be easily adapted to other systems

IMPLEMENTING PROGRAMS ON OTHER SYSTEMS

The costs and manpower requirements to transport computer programs to other systems are difficult to estimate.
If programs are transported frequently and the difficulties
encountered are corrected, eventually the programs become
quite portable. This is the case with most HEC programs.
Recent HEC benchmark programs were converted to several different United States' computers in a few days' time. Typical
conversions for a single HEC program should require less than
1 man-day of work, given that the computer system is large
enough and that the programmer is skilled on his system.
Most difficulties for HEC programs have been encountered by
users who had IBM equipment because of lack of core memory,
symbol table storage deficiencies in the compiler, or problems with double precision (not knowing what variables have
to have double words). The most common problem for non-IDM
users has been a lack of core storage, but that problem is
very rare now except for one or two HEC programs.

The main problems in sending HEC source decks to foreign
countries are that many offices have the smaller IBM systems
and that the feedback from those countries to HEC is less
than adequate because of lengthy communication times and
security problems on both ends. In spite of a few problems,
success has been experienced in transporting HEC programs to
over 700 offices per year, including many in foreign countries.

CONCLUSIONS

The use of generalized models can be an effective tool
in accomplishing water resource studies if sufficient funds
and manpower are provided to support the necessary functions
described in this paper. Information on manpower and costs
provided in this report may be useful in estimating the necessary logistic support required for similar support centers
in other offices.

SUMMARY OF DISCUSSIONS

A.J. Askew, F. Greco, and J. Kindler

MODEL STRUCTURE AND VERIFICATION

The first questions considered by the Symposium participants were those relating to model structure and verification. The discussion was based on Professor J.C.I. Dooge's
report, which appears at the beginning of this volume.

It was not disputed that verification is very important, in fact essential. However, no clear-cut conclusions
were reached as to how it should be carried out. Well-
accepted methods, such as split-sample testing, were noted,
but the problems lie in the choice of verification criteria,
the presentation of results, and the amount of error that
might be considered acceptable. In view of the peculiarities
of each individual situation, based not only on the nature
of the model itself but also on its area of potential use,
it was suggested that decisions as to how models should be
verified would always have to be taken by the model builders
themselves. It is necessary that the model builder remain
completely objective in this regard. Ultimately, the most
important factors are the requirements, explicit or implicit,
of those who have to use the models' outputs and the extent
to which they are prepared to accept the verification results.

The stochastic nature of model inputs, and even model
parameters, presents many problems. These problems can be
overcome to a certain extent in real-time forecasting by the
use of procedures, such as Kalman filters, that use the most
recent data for continuous parameter optimization. However,
this stochastic element also greatly complicates attempts
to verify models, and it was suggested that if a model's
deterministic component could be examined on the basis of
cross-correlation between input and output, then the stochastic component might be studied with the aid of autocorrelation analysis of the residuals.

SIMULATION IN HYDROLOGY

One purpose for which hydrologic models are proving to be of great value is on-line simulation, particularly in conjunction with streamflow forecasting. The exact definition of the term *on line* was the subject of some debate. It was generally agreed that, in relation to the use of hydrologic models, on-line implies that the data are collected, transmitted, and fed to the model and the model's output is obtained and then used in one uninterrupted sequence of activities.

A vital element in this sequence, and one that is important when considering the use of models, is the role played by associated equipment, including computer hardware. Specific note was taken of the use of radar for obtaining real-time precipitation data. It was reported that radar had been used in conjunction with a catchment model as a basis for streamflow forecasting on the River Dee in the United Kingdom. The system had been developed as a research project but was no longer being used operationally. It was recognized that the size of catchment area and the potential time advantage to be gained, as well as available financial resources, are important factors in the choice of both data collection systems and hydrologic models. However, radar and other sophisticated systems are frequently operated on a routine basis for weather forecasting, and therefore it is sometimes possible to incorporate hydrologic uses at little or no extra cost. The need for reliability in data collection was also emphasized, particularly where the main purpose was to supply data under extreme conditions such as during major floods.

Computer hardware has a major role to play in most on-line systems, and it was noted that the relative cost of the hardware needed to solve a given problem has steadily decreased in recent years and that advanced mini-computers are now readily available. Nevertheless, the development and maintenance of necessary software is very time consuming and costly, especially in terms of trained manpower, a resource that is very scarce in developing countries.

During the discussion on equipment, emphasis was placed on the need to consider the relationship between equipment and the models used. Equipment should be obtained to suit the model or the model developed or chosen to suit the equipment or, preferably, the whole system should be designed to use the most efficient and economic combination of the two. At the same time due account should be taken of the need to maintain flexibility, especially in order to allow advantage to be taken of future developments in modeling or the availability of new instruments and better computers.

The type of model to be used for on-line simulation was a matter of major concern. It is not always necessary for streamflow forecasting to use complex simulation models based on large main-frame computers. Smaller, simpler models using mini-computers can often provide a better solution. It was pointed out that, for developing countries in particular, the costs and benefits of alternative levels of technology should always be considered. One important question was the degree to which the model can be updated on the basis of its past performance and the new data continuously being received. If the model cannot be easily updated and if it is operated over an extended period, forecasts based on its output may well prove to be of less value than those obtained by other, less sophisticated means.

Hydrologic models can also be used for non-real-time simulation, in particular for undertaking basic studies of the hydrologic regime, for deriving design data and criteria, and for filling in missing records of streamflow or other data. In theory, most simulation models, once developed, can be used either in a real-time or non-real-time mode of application. It was stressed that the introduction of complex models should not be attempted until simpler models are first tried and only then if sufficient additional accuracy is obtained to justify the added time and costs involved in their use. If a more complex model is considered, it may pay to investigate the possibility and value of operating it in both modes, thus making maximum use of the resources it will require for its development and maintenance. In practice, the variety of hydrologic processes requiring non-real-time simulation is wider than that associated with real-time simulation. In the former case, therefore, greater stress needs to be placed on the correct choice of model for the precise purpose intended including, in particular, consideration of the hydrological characteristic considered most important and the level of accuracy required.

SIMULATION OF WATER RESOURCE SYSTEMS

When considering the use of models in the simulation of water resource systems, it was noted that emphasis is frequently placed on the modeling result rather than on the model itself. This was seen as a sign of an approaching maturity of modeling science. The obsession with model construction, which still permeates the modeling literature, appears to be losing some of its momentum, and those who develop models are no longer ashamed to admit that the best theoretical model need not represent the best solution.

Real-world systems, whether water resource or hydrologic, are exceedingly, if not infinitely complex, and the modeler is forced to make many simplifying assumptions when developing his model. Some of the major reasons given for this are the limitations imposed by available computing facilities. In this sense logistics are seen as a limiting factor on model development and use. It was suggested that this constraint might have the effect of forcing the modeler to study his problem with greater care and could often lead to a more practical solution. However, it would appear that this limitation is no longer as severe as it once was, at least as far as model development is concerned; although it could pose major difficulties in model use, especially in developing countries. The relaxation of this constraint has now raised the possibility of what was referred to as the "tyranny of logistics", which in this context means the development of large and complex models simply because the computing facilities are adequate to the task, without sufficient thought being given to whether there is a real need for them. However, it is encouraging to see the growing recognition that, while models have been developed to make the handling of complex systems possible, it is important that they can also handle simple systems, that simple systems do in fact exist, and that there are often more-or-less autonomous subsystems that can provide satisfactory answers without invoking a global scale. It was hoped that this sign could be read as the beginning of the end of modeling "gigantomania".

One characteristic that commonly distinguishes a water resource model from a purely hydrologic model is the need to simulate the operation of the system. Operating rules are set or are themselves optimized as one use of the model, but here again, it is important to recognize the extent to which such rules are only abstractions of reality. Some of the models described are based on careful studies of the actual past behavior of operators, as opposed to the rules that should theoretically have been applied, and others are used with the assistance of the operators to investigate how and why the latter deviated from the set rules. It was noted that gaming-simulation was devised precisely for this type of study and offered the opportunity of incorporating the human factor directly into the modeling exercise.

The value of running the models in conjunction with individuals or groups of interested persons was also discussed with regard to the uses to which models might be put. No question was raised concerning the benefits to be gained from using models in the planning, design, and operation of water resource systems, provided the validity of the models could first be established. Problems arise when, usually due to a lack of adequate data, the models cannot be sufficiently tested. Are they then of any value? The answer was very much in the positive and a number of uses were proposed for such untestable models. It was the experience of many that attempts to develop and fit models to data proved, inadvertently, to be an excellent means of identifying errors in the input data and that the availability of a model could be used advantageously to raise the level of debate on the assumptions and data it required and to clarify the issues concerned. If it was possible to include in such a debate those not usually involved in technical considerations, then models had often proved to be excellent means of establishing meaningful dialog between them and the technologists. Major trends and uncertainties in the operation of systems can be studied and various scenarios tested.

This last point was considered very important because, no matter how completely the models are verified, the stochastic and uncertain nature of their inputs and environment make it impossible to present decision makers with single unambiguous solutions to the questions they pose. There was considerable debate and some disagreement concerning the extent to which nontechnical decision makers demand such solutions. It was agreed, however, that model operators should admit the limitations of their models. If appropriate, they should present a range of solutions reflecting the range of possible assumptions that might be made, plus associated accuracy estimates. If the range can be narrowed and, for example, various infeasible alternatives eliminated then this should be done; but, where all technical resources have been exhausted and no single preferable solution is identified, the decision maker must be presented with the facts and make a choice on the basis of his knowledge and experience. This is especially so where political questions are involved. It was readily recognized that a major difficulty is identifying the correct point of division of responsibility between the technologist and the politician. The higher the level of the decision maker, the greater the likelihood that he would demand a single solution. However, decision makers frequently have technical advisers, who are receptive to proposals shaped in uncertain terms and to alternative solutions. Model users would do well to consider presenting their findings in a form acceptable to technical advisers rather than the decision makers themselves.

In the same manner as models should be developed to simulate, as far as possible, the real nature of water resource systems, they should also be designed to take account of the real-world environment, both social and economic, in which these systems operate. This includes the political realities and requires recognition of the possibility that the model's output is being sought primarily as substantiation for a decision maker's preconceived ideas. Nevertheless, model developers and users must accept the responsibility of making the best use they can of the data and information available and of presenting their findings in an honest and usable form.

GENERALIZED MODELS AND SUITES OF PROGRAMS

The development of generalized models, suites of programs, and modeling systems is a natural response to the logistic problems of mathematical modeling such as those discussed at the Symposium. Therefore, special attention was paid to this question.

A shortage of trained manpower is one common problem to be faced and the use of program packages offers at least a partial solution. If program packages are available in a compatible modular form, they can be installed and operated on local computers with the minimum of external assistance.

In this connection it was reported that the World Meteorological Organization was currently considering the development
of a Hydrological Operational Multipurpose Subprogramme
(HOMS). This would be made up of a number of mutually compatible components each designed to accomplish a task in
operational hydrology, such as data collection, transmission,
processing, and analysis, and including as one aim, their
use in hydrologic simulation and flood forecasting. Some,
but not all of these components would be in the form of computer software.*

However, the development of standard program packages
raises its own problems. Among these is the need to make
the models general, in other words, suitable for solving
problems under a wide range of specific conditions. Experience has shown that this could add as much as 50 percent to
the time and cost of model development. A number of limitations were recognized in the use of general programs. However, far greater concern was expressed at the great proliferation of models. It was felt that much could be gained
from calling a moratorium on the development of new models
and offering an opportunity for the assessment of the worth
of those already available.

A greater degree of flexibility and generality is often
aimed for by the development of programming systems capable
of generating or assembling programs appropriate for the
solution of given tasks. This has proved, however, to be
an order of magnitude more difficult and costly than the
development of individual generalized programs.

A prerequisite for the application of models and programs by users other than those who developed them is that
they be transferable. An important distinction was drawn
between transferability and versatility. A model may be
well fitted by its developers to any number of systems, thus
demonstrating its versatility. The problem arises when it
is to be transferred and installed on a computer remote from
its developers and operated without the continuous support
of the developers. It was suggested that the important thing
is to transfer the approach used in the model, and that it
could often be easier for the recipients to develop their
own software based on this than to attempt to install someone else's programs. This view was challenged by those who
had experience with some of the more widely distributed
standard programs, such as those developed by the U.S. Corps
of Engineers. It was noted that even the most complex of
these had been installed in more than 40 centers remote from
their point of origin and that others were run by many hun-
dreds of different institutions throughout the world without

---

*HOMS was approved by the WMO Congress in May 1979 and
is being implemented on the basis of a detailed plan of action drawn up by the WMO Commission for Hydrology in Madrid
in April 1980.

encountering major problems. It was pointed out, however, that if the programs were to be transferable, that feature should be built into them from the start. If the preparation of adequate documentation and users' manuals is taken into account, this could mean a major increase in effect in their development. Increases of 100 percent were quoted by some participants, while others spoke of as little as 5 to 10 percent.

The problems and extra expense referred to above cannot be ignored, but at the same time the savings to be gained by recipients of standard programs can be very large. It is always right, therefore, to question the need to develop new software if such programs are available, especially if the costs involved for the recipient are low, as is often the case.

FUTURE DEVELOPMENTS

Mathematical models already play a major role in the study and analysis of hydrologic and water resource systems. This role can be expected to expand still further in the future, and care should be taken to ensure that efforts and resources expended on this work are used effectively. The development of new, frequently more complex models should be justified on the basis of the purpose they are to serve and the data base available to support them. There is certainly much still to be learned concerning the benefits and costs of using mathematical models, and those involved in model development and use should be encouraged to study this question and publish their findings.

The question of benefits and costs is particularly relevant to those responsible for taking decisions on whether models are to be used or not, and if models are to be used, those acting upon the results they yield must be concerned again with the benefits and costs. Models developed to study hydrologic or water resource systems as a scientific or technical exercise may not be appropriate for practical application. Unless the decision makers and planners can be involved in guiding model development, there is a real danger of inappropriate models being developed or selected for use. Account must also be taken of differing management philosophies and investment aims as well as the, often limited, resources of time and finances available to support any particular study involving the use of models.

It was proposed that national and international organizations take steps to bring together investment planners, model users, and model developers to exchange ideas and experience. It was suggested that, if these discussions could be held at a high level and be based on practical examples of the sort of problems to be faced, they could lead to a greater awareness on the part of decision makers of the many powerful techniques now available and, equally important, a

new understanding by model developers of the very practical
needs of potential users. Many mathematical models can be
of great value in describing hydrologic regimes or in studying the response of water resource systems. However, what
is needed most are models that can prove their worth as efficient and economic means of obtaining the data needed for the
design and operation of real projects.

APPENDIX A.   PROGRAM OF THE SYMPOSIUM

Tuesday, 24 October 1978

10:00—11:00   Opening Session

                  Chairman: R.E. Levien

                  Welcoming Remarks:

                  L. Lazzarino - Dean of the Faculty of Engi-
                     neering, University of Pisa
                  A.M. Galoppini - Municipality of Pisa
                  R.E. Levien - Director of IIASA
                  J. Nemec - Director of Hydrology and Water
                     Resources Department, WMO
                  A. di Seyssel - Director of Communications
                     and External Relations, IBM Italy

11:30—12:30   Session 1:   Model Structure and Classifica-
                     tion

                  Chairman: R. Marconi

                  General Rapporteur: J.C.I. Dooge

14:00—14:45   Session 1 continued

                  General Discussion on Session 1

14:45—15:30   Session 2:   On-Line Simulation in Hydrology

                  Chairman: J. Nemec

                  General Rapporteur: E. Bobiński

                  A.J. Hall, J.F. Elliott: Development of a
                     Computer-Based Flood Forecasting System
                     for Australia
                  V. Anselmo, L. Ubertini: Transfer Function-
                     Noise Model Applied to Flow Forecasting

                                249

A. Baniukiewicz: Computer Programme Arranging Optimization, Simulation and Computing of Forecasts

E. Bobiński, T. Piwecki, J. Żelaziński: Efficiency of the Real-Time Hydrological Forecasting Systems in Poland after System Operation in 1975 - 1977

S. Bergström: Operational Hydrological Forecasting by Conceptual Models in Sweden

J. Buchtele: Diffusion Equation as an Impulsive Response for the Flood Events Modelling

B. Wingard: The Use of Hydrological Models for Runoff Forecasts for Short-Time Optimization of the Norwegian Water Power System

A.O. Lambert: The River Dee Regulation Scheme: Operational Experience of On-Line Hydrological Simulation

A.J. Askew: Use of Catchment Models for Flood Forecasting in Central America

16:00—17:30   Session 2 continued

General Discussion on Session 2

Wednesday, 25 October 1978

08:30—10:00   Session 3: Simulation of Water Resource Systems

Chairman: R.H. Clark

General Rapporteur: V. Klemes

J.R. Sexton: The Thames Basin Water Resources Model

J.C. de Graan, F. Langeweg, B.H. Tangena: Simulation of the Water Movement and the Chloride Content in a Canal-Open Reservoir System

J. Kaczmarek, K. Malinowski, K.A. Salewicz: Long Term Resources Allocation for Control Purposes in a Water Management System

G.L. Wright: Developmental and Operational Aspects of Gaming-Simulations for Water Resource Systems

H.S. Nelson, P. Savasdibutr, R.K. Thomas: Logistics of Large-Scale Water Resources Modeling for Irrigation Planning in Northern Africa

G.W. Reid: Model for the Selection of Appropriate Technology for a Water Resources System

G. Ambrosino, G. Fronza, R. Soncini-Sessa: A Computer Simulation Model for the Management of Lake Maggiore Water System

O.T. Sigvaldason: Models to Aid the Planning and Management of Multipurpose Multi-
reservoir Systems

F. Fabi, G. Simonelli: Mathematical Models
of Water Resource Systems. Some Recent
Realizations at the Cassa per il Mezzogiorno

M.W. Liddament, D.B. Oakes, A.C. Skinner,
W.B. Wilkinson: The Use of a Groundwater
Model in the Design, Performance Assessment
and Operation of a River Regulation Scheme

J. Nemec, G.W. Kite: Mathematical Model of
the Upper Nile Basin

10:30—12:30   Session 3 continued

General Discussion on Session 3

14:30—18:00   Demonstration/Exhibition

Thursday, 26 October 1978

08:30—10:00   Session 4: Non-real Time Simulation in
Hydrology

Chairman: O.T. Sigvaldason

General Rapporteur: G.W. Kite

J.I. Matondo, S.V.K. Sarma: Multiple Regression Technique for Estimation of Sus-
pended Sediment Transport in Kizinga River
of Coastal Tanzania

R.E. Manley: HYSIM—A Physically Realistic,
General Purpose, Hydrologic Model

A. Tsuchiya, K. Ishizaki, K. Sasaki: Flood
Simulation Model

J. Ostrowski: Linear Mathematic Model Simulating Surface Outfall in a Mountain
Catchment Area

J. Jaworski: Mathematical Description of
Actual Evapotranspiration with Particular
Regard to Grass Cover

V.A. Rumiantsev: Optimal Development of
Hydrometeorological Network for Water
Resources Control

A.V. Romanov: An Experience of Indirect
Setting of the Basic Compound River Bed
Characteristics for Saint-Venant Equations
Numerical Integration

M. Sugawara: Automatic Calibration of the
Tank Model

G. Volpi, C. Chignoli: Stochastic Inter-
polation: A Package for the Automatic
Contour Mapping of Hydrological Data

G.G. Svanidze, Z.A. Piranashvili: On One
Non-Markovian Model of River Runoff

10:00—10:30	General Discussion on Session 4
11:00—12:00	Session 5: Suites of Programs

Chairman: C. Sinnot

General Rapporteur: M.B. Abbott

M.B. Abbott, R. Clarke, A. Preissmann: Some Logistic Aspects of the European Hydrologic System

D. Pearson, P.D. Walsh: The Implementation and Application of a Suite for the Simulation of Complex Water Resource Systems in Evaluation and Planning Studies

P. Handel, R.P. Spiegel, W. Stöhlin: Routing of Flood Events of Specified Probability in Reservoir Systems in the Prealpine Region

W.S. Eichert: Experiences of the Hydrologic Engineering Center in Maintaining Widely Used Hydrologic and Water Resource Computer Models

General Discussion on Session 5

12:30—13:30	Closing Session

Chairman: J.C.I. Dooge

APPENDIX B.   LIST OF PARTICIPANTS

M.B. Abbott
Danish Hydraulic Institute
Agern Allé 5
Horsholm, Denmark

G. Ambrosino
Center for Systems Theory
Milan Polytechnic
Via Ponzio 34/5
Milan, Italy

P. de Angelis
Institute of Mathematics
Via Mezzocannone 8
Naples, Italy

V. Anselmo
National Research Council of
   Italy (CNR)
Via Vassalli Eandi
Turin, Italy

A.J. Askew
World Meteorological
   Organization (WMO)
P.O. Box No. 5
Geneva, Switzerland

B. Bayoumi Attia
Master Plan — EXWAP
13 Giza Street
P.O. Box No. 33
Giza, Egypt

I. Becchi
University of Florence
Via di S. Marta 3
Florence, Italy

C. Berghins
ELC — Electroconsult
Via Chiabrera 8
Milan, Italy

S. Bergström
Swedish Meteorological and
   Hydrological Institute
Fack
Norrköping, Sweden

E. Bobiński
Institute of Meteorology and
   Water Management
Ul. Podlesna 61
Warsaw, Poland

J. Buchtele
Hydrometeorological Institute
Holečkova 8
Prague, Czechoslovakia

A. Buishand
Royal Netherlands
   Meteorological Institute
Wilhelminalaan 10
De Bilt, The Netherlands

254

A. Canfarini
Provveditorato alle Opere
  Pubbliche
Via dei Servi 15
Florence, Italy

C. Cao
Institute of Hydraulics
University of Cagliari
Piazza d'Arme
Cagliari, Italy

G. Capriz
Istituto di Elaborazione
  dell'Informazione
Via S. Maria 46
Pisa, Italy

S. Cavazza
Institute of Hydraulics
Via Caduti del Lavoro 34
Pisa, Italy

M. Cecchi
Istituto di Elaborazione
  dell'Informazione
Via S. Maria 46
Pisa, Italy

P. Celestre
Istituto di Idraulica Agraria
Via del Borghetto 80
Pisa, Italy

V. Chernyatin
International Institute for
  Applied Systems Analysis
  (IIASA)
Schloss Laxenburg
Laxenburg, Austria

C. Chignoli
IBM Scientific Center
Dorso Duro 3228
Venice, Italy

G. Cicioni
Istituto di Ricerca sulle Acque
Via Reno 1
Rome, Italy

T.A. Ciriani
IBM Italy
Via S. Maria 67
Pisa, Italy

R.H. Clark
Inland Waters Directorate
Department of Environment
Ottawa, Canada

J.C.I. Dooge
University College Dublin
Upper Merrion Street
Dublin, Republic of Ireland

W.S. Eichert
Hydrologic Engineering Center
United States Army Corps of
  Engineers
609 2nd Street
Davis, California,
United States of America

F. El-Shibini
Master Plan — EXWAP
13 Giza Street
P.O. Box No. 33
Giza, Egypt

F. Fabi
Cassa per il Mezzogiorno
Piazzale Kennedy 20
Rome, Italy

H. Feliciangeli
Centre Nacional de Computacion
Universidad de Asunción
Avenida Espana 1098
Asunción, Paraguay

M. Ferrario
Center for Systems Theory
Milan Polytechnic
Via Ponzio 34/5
Milan, Italy

F. Fiori
Cassa per il Mezzogiorno
Piazzale Kennedy 20
Rome, Italy

A. Gabos
C. Lotti and Associates
Via del Fiume 14
Rome, Italy

A.M. Galoppini
Comune di Pisa
Palazzo Gambacorti
Pisa, Italy

G. Giuliano
Water Research Institute
National Research Council of
  Italy (CNR)
Via Reno 1
Rome, Italy

F. Greco
IBM Scientific Center
Via S. Maria 67
Pisa, Italy

A.J. Hall
Bureau of Meteorology
150 Lonsdale Street
Melbourne, Victoria
Australia

P. Handel
Bayerisches Landesamt für
  Wasserwirtschaft
Lazarettstrasse 67
Munich
Federal Republic of Germany

P.G. Harhammer
IBM Austria
Obere Donaustrasse 95
Vienna, Austria

P. Hubert
Centre d'Information
  Géologique
Ecole des Mines de Paris
35 Rue Saint Honoré
Fontainebleu, France

K. Ishizaki
Public Works Research
  Institute
41-7 Shimo, Kita-ku
Tokyo, Japan

J. Kindler
International Institute for
  Applied Systems Analysis
  (IIASA)
Schloss Laxenburg
Laxenburg, Austria

G.W. Kite
Hydrometeorological Survey of
  Lake Victoria, Lake Kyoga,
  and Lake Mobutu Sese Seko
United Nations Development
  Programme (UNDP)
Box 30218
Nairobi, Kenya

V. Klemes
Hydrology Research Division
Department of Environment
Ottawa, Canada

A.O. Lambert
Welsh Water Authority
Shire Hall
Mold, Clwyd, Wales
United Kingdom

L. Lazzarino
Faculty of Engineering
University of Pisa
Via Diotisalvi 2
Pisa, Italy

R.E. Levien
International Institute for
  Applied Systems Analysis
  (IIASA)
Schloss Laxenburg
Laxenburg, Austria

H.J. Liebscher
Federal Institute of
  Hydrology
Kaiserin Augusta Anlagen 15
Koblenz
Federal Republic of Germany

L. Lippi
IBM Scientific Center
Dorso Duro 3228
Venice, Italy

G. la Loggia
Institute of Hydraulics
Viale delle Scienze
Palermo, Italy

D.P. Loucks
Cornell University
Hollister Hall
Ithaca, New York,
United States of America

U. Maione
Institute of Hydraulics
Milan Polytechnic
Piazza Leonardo da Vinci 32
Milan, Italy

R.E. Manley
Severn-Trent Water Authority
2297 Coventry Road
Birmingham, Warwickshire
United Kingdom

R. Marconi
IBM Scientific Center
Via S. Maria 67
Pisa, Italy

P. Mauersberger
Institute for Geography and
  Geoecology
Mueggelseedamm 260
Berlin
German Democratic Republic

A. McKerchar
Water and Soil Division
Ministry of Works and
  Development
P.O. Box No. 1479
Christchurch, New Zealand

A. Mendoza
CEFIGRE
B.P. 13
Sophia Antipolis
Valbonne, France

A. Meucci
Ufficio Idrografico
Lungarno Pacinotti 49
Pisa, Italy

M. Mulas
Ente Autonomo del Flumendosa
Via Mameli 88
Cagliari, Italy

J. Nemec
Hydrology and Water Resources
  Department
World Meteorological
  Organization (WMO)
P.O. Box No. 5
Geneva, Switzerland

N. Okada
International Institute for
  Applied Systems Analysis
  (IIASA)
Schloss Laxenburg
Laxenburg, Austria

L. Panattoni
IBM Scientific Center
Via S. Maria 67
Pisa, Italy

D. Pearson
North West Water Authority
Danson House
Great Sankey
Warrington, Lancashire
United Kingdom

M.A. Pirozzi
Institute of Mathematics
Via Mezzocannone 8
Naples, Italy

A. Preissmann
SOGREAH
6, Rue de Lorraine
Echirolles, France

U. Pulselli
ENEL — Servizio Idrologico
Corso del Popolo 245
Mestre, Italy

F. Putuhena
Directorate General of Water
  Resources Development
Jl. Patimura 20
Jakarta, Indonesia

G.W. Reid
College of Engineering
University of Oklahoma
202 West Boyd Street
Norman, Oklahoma
United States of America

S. Rinaldi
Center for Systems Theory
Milan Polytechnic
Via Ponzio 34/5
Milan, Italy

G. Rossi
ENEL — Servizio Idrologico
Corso del Popolo 245
Mestre, Italy

K.A. Salewicz
Institute of Meteorology and
  Water Management
Ul. Podlesna 61
Warsaw, Poland

J.R. Sexton
Thames Water Authority
Nugent House
Vastern Road
Reading, Berkshire
United Kingdom

A. di Seyssel
IBM Italy
Via dei Lucchesi 26
Rome, Italy

O.T. Sigvaldason
Acres. International Ltd.
5259 Dorchester Road
Niagara Falls, Canada

R. Silvano
Ente Autonomo del Flumendosa
Via Mameli 88
Cagliari, Italy

G. Simonelli
Cassa per il Mezzogiorno
Piazzale Kennedy 20
Rome, Italy

C. Sinnot
Thames Water Authority
Nugent House
Vastern Road
Reading, Berkshire
United Kingdom

R.P. Spiegel
Institut für Hydraulik und
  Gewässerkunde
Arcistrasse 21
Munich
Federal Republic of Germany

W. Sudharsono
Computer Center
Institute of Hydraulic
  Engineering
Jl. Ir.H. Djuanda 193
Bandung, Indonesia

M. Sugawara
6-13-30 Minami-Karasuyama
Setagaya-ku
Tokyo, Japan

B.H. Tangena
National Institute for Water
  Supply
Nieuwe Havenstraat 6
Voorburg
Leidschendam, The Netherlands

E. Todini
IBM Scientific Center
Via S. Maria 67
Pisa, Italy

A. Togna
Istituto di Idraulica
Università degli Studi
Monteluco
Aquila, Italy

M. Tomasino
ENEL — Servizio Idrologico
Corso del Popolo 245
Mestre, Italy

G. Torrigiani
Via della Libertà 27
Leghorn, Italy

B. Travaglini
Ministero Lavori Pubblici
Via Nomentana 2
Rome, Italy

L. Ubertini
Istituto di Idraulica Agraria
Borgo XX Giugno 74
Perugia, Italy

H.W. Underhill
Food and Agriculture
  Organization of the
  United Nations (FAO)
Via delle Terme di Caracalla
Rome, Italy

G. Volpi
IBM Scientific Center
Dorso Duro 3220
Venice, Italy

P.D. Walsh
North West Water Authority
Danson House
Great Sankey
Warrington, Lancashire
United Kingdom

W.B. Wilkinson
Water Research Centre
Medmenham
Marlow, Buckinghamshire
United Kingdom

A. Willen
Department of Physical Geography
P.O. Box No. 554
Uppsala, Sweden

G.L. Wright
Water Resources Commission
10 Wyee Street
Kogarah Bay, New South Wales
Australia